THE
PRESIDENTIAL
GAME

THE PRESIDENTIAL GAME

*The Origins of American
Presidential Politics*

Richard P. McCormick

New York   Oxford
OXFORD UNIVERSITY PRESS
1982

Copyright © 1982 by Oxford University Press, Inc.

Library of Congress Cataloging in Publication Data

McCormick, Richard Patrick, 1916–
The presidential game.

Includes index.
1. United States—Politics and government—
1783–1865.   2. Presidents—United States—Election
—History.   I. Title.
E310.M44   324.973   81-9619
ISBN 0-19-503015-X (cloth)   AACR2
ISBN 0-19-503455-4 (paper)

Printing (last digit):   9 8 7 6

Printed in the United States of America

*For
Richard Levis McCormick
with admiration
and affection.*

Acknowledgments

My largest debt is to the hundreds of scholars whose investigations of that most engrossing of topics, presidential politics, have illuminated my own studies. I remain grateful to my late mentor, Roy F. Nichols, whose influence will be evident but whose inspiration and encouragement transcend recognition. Three valued colleagues and friends—Gerald M. Pomper, John A. Munroe, and Richard L. McCormick—gave generously of their time and their learning in reading and commenting on my manuscript. I am especially obliged to Ms. Edith Saks, who not only volunteered to be my amanuensis but also cheered me throughout by actually seeming interested in what she typed. This book owes nothing to my wife, but I owe her a great deal.

Richard P. McCormick

Contents

I

Introduction and Overview

Shortly after the untimely death of William Henry Harrison, John Quincy Adams reflected on the manner of choosing the President of the United States. "This election of a chief magistrate for the whole Union will never be settled to the satisfaction of the people," he asserted. Lending greater emphasis to this somber judgment, he added that "never, never will any great people be satisfied with the result of their own election of an Executive head."[1] Adams's verdict was not entirely the product of his often pessimistic cast of mind. His sentiments were widely shared in his own time, and they have since been echoed by innumerable commentators. No feature of the American Constitutional system has been more subject to criticism, more unstable, more open to improvisation, or less regularized, than the method of selecting the chief executive.

Senator Mahlon Dickerson voiced a typical complaint when he stated in 1817 that scarcely any official was "elected or appointed by a rule so undefined, so vague, so subject to abuse, as that by which we elect the Chief Magistrate of the Union."[2] Congressman George McDuffie some years later was even more vehement, arguing that "we have no constitutional provision at all" to regulate the election of the President.[3] The Framers, of course, had contrived an elaborate method for choosing a President, but it had become apparent as early as 1789 that their scheme was so defective as to be unworkable. Consequently, rules were improvised—and changed —within the shifting context of the political scene. Thus, paradoxically, a nation that has made a fetish of constitutionalism has lacked a constitutionally sanctioned method for selecting its most important official. Efforts to remedy this deficiency, in the form of more than five hundred proposed amendments designed to produce a "Constitutional" selection process, have resulted only in frustration and failure, and the informal process has continued to reflect the ambiguities of the American political culture.

The subject of this study is the presidential selection process during its awkward and unpredictable infancy, starting with the efforts of the Framers to contrive a suitable method of election and ending more than half a century later with the very different rules that were to shape what can be termed "the party game." The improvised rules must be seen not as essential corollaries to the prescriptions of the Framers, not as a means of implementing the Constitutional process, but rather as providing informally devised alternatives to the plan embodied in the Constitution. We use the term "game" in its simplest sense as a contest conducted according to definable rules. The rules of a game are not necessarily immutable. Affected by various influences, they may be altered, just as they may be manipulated or transgressed. Our focus will be on identifying the rules of the presidential game and on explaining how and why they changed over time.

All inquiries must recognize some limits, and this one is no exception. It was not my intention to write another history of presidential elections, although it has been necessary to treat many contests in at least a cursory manner. Neither have I sought to deal intensively with the history of political parties, even though that engaging topic is inseparably related to my main line of inquiry. I have not attempted to evaluate the consequences of changes in the presidential game in terms of the qualities of the Presidents or the nature of the presidency, intriguing and important as those matters may be. My preoccupation has been with the process, rather than its outcomes. And candor obliges me to state at this point that I shall offer no specific prescription for yet another version of the presidential game.

For roughly half a century, embracing fourteen presidential elections, the rules of the presidential game were quite unstable and even discontinuous. That is, the rules did not "evolve" in an orderly or sequential fashion. Rather, there were four successive types of game, each with its own characteristic features.

The first four elections were conducted under extremely uncertain and even hazardous rules. The uncertainty derived chiefly from the variety and manipulability of the methods employed by the states for appointing electors. The hazards were occasioned by the fact that the electors were required to vote for two persons for President, creating the possibility that the individual intended to be the Vice President might, through inadvertence or intrigue receive more votes than the person who was recognized as the candidate for the presidency. This hazard, referred to by contemporaries as the "fatal defect" in the constitutional process of presidential selection, was eliminated in 1804 when the adoption of the Twelfth Amendment required electors to cast distinct ballots for President and for Vice President.

A second version of the game developed during Jefferson's administrations and continued through 1820. I have termed it "the Virginia game" because it was dominated by Virginians and their allies, who introduced new rules and exploited them successfully to control the presidency for twenty-four years. It was a one-sided game, pitting the small and ineffectual Federalist party against the Virginia-led Republicans, who were superior in numbers, strategy, and organization. Using the congressional caucus to confer the party's stamp of approval on the candidate for the presidency, and to endorse an innocuous vice-presidential candidate who would not intrude on the Virginia succession, and placing the heir apparent in the office of Secretary of State, the Virginians managed the game with consummate skill.

But one-sided games cannot be played indefinitely. The Virginia game ended abruptly after Monroe's all but unanimous re-election in 1820, and a very different kind of game was introduced. It was "the game of faction." Factions were formed to support the aspirations of rival candidates for the presidency. Almost all the rules of the old Virginia game were cast aside, and for nearly two decades the game was in flux, featuring an extraordinary number of innovations as well as profound disagreements about the fundamentals of the presidential selection process. Then, gradually, between 1832 and 1844 the game of faction was transformed into "the party game." The contest was now to be waged by two electoral parties that were national in scope, that employed conventions to nominate their candidates, and that engaged in remarkably theatrical campaigns to arouse the mass electorate.

By 1844 the party game, and the rules by which it was to be played, had become well established. Most of its major features were to persist for more than a century. Even significant realignments of political parties in the 1850s and again in the 1890s did not drastically alter the character of the game. It is for this reason that I terminated this account of the origins of the presidential game with Polk's victory over Clay, or, more properly, with the Democratic victory over the Whigs.

Certain themes recur in this study. One of these is the continuing tension between a republican ideal and political actuality. As Bernard Bailyn, Gordon Wood, Richard Buel, Lance Banning, and others have described it, a particular vision of a republican polity came into focus with the founding of the nation.[4] It not only conditioned the actions taken by the Framers at the Constitutional Convention but also persisted in the form of a set of attitudes and beliefs that later generations felt obliged to honor. Ours should be a government of laws, limited by a written constitution expressive of the sovereign will of the people. It should foster and protect individual liberty and respect the rights and interests of minorities. The might of the government should be checked by dispersing the exercise of its powers among several centers of authority, no one of which was to be omnipotent. Similarly, the stability of the government was not to be altered abruptly by the manifestation of the will of a popular majority; instead, as so brilliantly conceived by Madison, the formal institutions of government would be so contrived as to maintain a near-equilibrium among a host of competing interests.

Electoral politics would be carefully constrained with a view to placing in positions of authority men of talent, virtue, and property and insulating them against undue popular influences. Demagogic appeals were reprobated, as was any overt seeking of office. Intrigues, cabals, and factions were viewed as the worst of evils in a republic, all representing evidence of corruption. There could be no legitimate role for political parties, for they denied the concept of an organic unity of the republic, fostered contention, and debased the election process. The ideal candidate in a republic was a man who, through his dedicated and disinterested civic service, acquired a reputation for probity and integrity and accepted the call of his fellow citizen to successively higher offices. The will of the people, at least in federal politics, was to be expressed directly only in the biennial elections of the House of Representatives.

With respect to the presidency, an office for which precedents were all but lacking, the Framers experienced great difficulty in designing it to conform to their republican theory. As they regarded their completed handiwork, the office was to be independent of the legislative and judicial branches, endowed with considerable authority, yet subject to checks by the other branches. What they sought was an office that would contribute to the stability of the government and provide for the efficient execution of the laws. They were especially concerned that the process of selecting the chief executive would be immune to the actions of factions or parties, proof against intrigue or corruption, and even remote from popular influences. The office should be conferred only on men of the largest reputation and loftiest—but pure—ambition. Accordingly, they exercised their talent for contrivances to the utmost to produce a novel and complicated scheme that involved the use of electors.[5]

The republican ideal was not, perhaps could not be, realized. All of the Framers' contrivances could not withstand the forces against which they had been erected. From the first, intrigue and manipulation figured prominently in the election of the President and Vice President. The notion that electors should be independent of all influences was abandoned in the first election, and they became little more than automatons. By the third election there was the recognition that the contest had assumed a partisan cast. Dominant parties from state to state altered the method of choosing electors to favor their candidates, and where popular elections took place there was extensive campaign activity in behalf of the rival tickets.

Over the course of time, and most notably by the 1820s, it became impossible to avoid the conclusion that the process of presidential selection bore little resemblance to that which had been contemplated by the Framers. Overt efforts by candidates to win support, biased appeals on their behalf by overly zealous newspaper editors, and intense organizational activities by increasingly professionalized political managers were only the most obvious departures from the republican ideal. Jackson's insistence that the

President should represent the choice of "the people" was a timely confirmation of a growing reality. The uniform adoption of the general-ticket system—whereby electors were chosen by popular vote from a state at large—signaled the triumph of crassly partisan considerations, and the institution of the convention system of nominations enhanced the ability of newly formed electoral parties to transform the contest for the presidency into the party game by the 1840s.

These changes in the rules of the game, marking as they did wide departures from the republican ideal, were a source of tension and anxiety. The Framers, and their ideas, were held in reverence by succeeding generations. They represented standards of political purity, of disinterested patriotism, that could not be repudiated. Their example should be emulated. How then, to justify the very different political behavior of their successors? How to reconcile the precepts of the Founders with the actualities of the new politics? How to devise a theory of politics to rationalize the new order without committing the crime of patricide? How to defend what was now termed "democracy" without rejecting republicanism? These were awkward questions, posing terrible dilemmas. Needless to say, the dilemmas were not resolved. Old theories and new and divergent practices existed side by side. The consequence was that in their sober moments of reflection, statesmen, politicians, and thoughtful citizens were filled with anxiety as they assessed how far the course of politics—and especially presidential politics—had moved from the republican ideal of the Framers.

A second and related theme is that of the ambiguousness of thought about every aspect of the presidential selection process. There were two fairly obvious methods of selecting a chief executive. He could be chosen by the national legislature or he could be elected directly by the enfranchised citizens. The Framers adopted neither of these simple alternatives, opting instead for an indirect election through the use of electors. How the electors were to be appointed was left to the discretion of each state legislature, and for several decades practices varied widely. In some states the choice was made by the legislature, in others by popular vote on a district plan, and in others by popular vote in the state at large. The point is that the underlying theory of the process was quite unclear.

It was yet to be determined what role, if any, the people were to have in the selection of the chief executive, and whether, if they were to be involved, the election would be by the people of each state as a political unit (general ticket) or by the people in electoral subdivisions (districts). By 1836 the general-ticket mode came to prevail, although its acceptance was based less on considerations of political theory than on the exigencies of practical politics, and especially of party politics. In effect, it had been determined that the President would be elected not by the people of the United States but by the people of the several states, a process that was justified on the basis of what was now termed the "federative principle."

There was initially much ambiguity about the question of whether the election would be decided by the electors or by the House of Representatives. Many of the Framers assumed that in most instances no candidate would receive a majority of the electoral votes, in which cases there would be a "contingent election" by the House. But the sentiment quickly developed that a contingent election was fraught with perils and was to be avoided at almost any cost. Indeed, the desire to avoid a contingent election came to be one of the most powerful arguments for conducting the election within the context of a two-party system, for such a contest would virtually assure one set of candidates the requisite majority. Indeed, as interminable congressional debates on the issue disclosed, there seemed to be no acceptable means, other than the two-party system, to avert the dreaded recourse to a contingent election. But, again, practice lacked the sanction either of theory or of formal constitutional acceptance.

The most glaring ambiguity, at least down to 1844, had to do with the relation of political parties to the selection process. The Framers had been unambiguous in their determination to make it impossible for factions or parties to influence the choice of the President. Nevertheless, the elections became politicized; they were managed by parties. This circumstance was generally deplored. Even the leaders of the dominant Republican party sounded the theme that when the menace of Federalist subversion was eliminated, partisan distinctions would end and elections would cease to be conducted as party contests. Later, when the Jacksonians mobilized as a party to elect Martin Van Buren as the Old Hero's successor, the opposition railed against the evils of partisanship with considerable effect. In time, the common rhetoric held that parties based on principles were acceptable, but that party-as-organization —mere electoral parties concerned with gaining office—were reprehensible. Because the fact was inescapable that the Democrats and the Whigs were, indeed, primarily electoral parties, attitudes toward them continued to be ambivalent. They had but a qualified acceptance as appropriate elements in the presidential selection process, even though they seemed to be indispensable.

There were also other ambiguities to cloud the process. What was the proper conduct for a candidate? Should he remain utterly aloof from the campaign; should he declare his views on relevant issues; should he actively solicit support? Should the election itself focus on a choice between personalities; should it represent a contest between parties; or should it give the electorate an opportunity to choose between courses of public policy? Should the President be viewed as representing uniquely all the people of the nation; should he be seen as the head of a party; or was he to be remote from both constituency and party, set apart as an independent figure whose authority derived solely from the formal attributes of his office? There could be no clear-cut answers to any of these vital questions. Rigorous deductions from the republican ideal of the Framers would imply one set of conclusions, but the shifting rules of the presidential game left all the issues in doubt.

For half a century, then, the presidential selection process was characterized by instability, tension, and ambiguity. A succinct explanation of these attributes would be that the Framers' theory of politics, especially as reflected in the rules that they laid down for electing the chief executive, was flawed and unrealistic and therefore new rules were improvised in response to immediate circumstances. By 1844 those rules had become reasonably stable and uniform; one could now predict with some assuredness how the presidential game would be played from election to election. But at the level of theory, or ideology, tensions and ambiguities remained, for the accepted rules lacked a clearly stated rationale. The rules established a process, but the assumptions on which that process rested defied simple elucidation. To explain why the rules ultimately assumed the form that they did—the rules of the party game—requires some explanation of the reciprocal relationship between the presidential selection process and political parties.

Once it became apparent that the process could be politicized, that it could be manipulated through political management, the importance and attractiveness of the presidency provided the basis for contests between rival aspirants. The Constitutional requirement that the victor must secure an absolute majority of the electoral vote, or risk a contingent election by the House, operated powerfully to restrict the contest to two major candidates, each of whom must seek to create a coalition of supporters that had the potential of producing the requisite majority. The logic of this basic rule of the game, therefore, fostered the creation of a two-party system. The ratification of the Twelfth Amendment (1804) facilitated and, in effect, confirmed this bimodal competition. There were to be departures from the pattern, but they were not so common as to invalidate the generalization. To put the matter somewhat differently, the most important single factor responsible for the characteristic two-party system in the United States is the constitutionally determined rule that the victor in the presidential contest must obtain a majority of the electoral vote.

The tendency of the Constitutional provisions to engender two-party competition for the presidency was clearly evident by 1796 in the confrontation of Adams and Jefferson, and the pattern persisted in subsequent elections. It was temporarily disrupted between 1824 and 1836, but was re-established in 1840 as the second American party system took shape. Although the parties of the Jeffersonian era differed in many important respects from those of the 1840s, the essential consideration is that political parties were to be critical elements in the presidential selection process. Indeed, they were extremely influential in shaping the process.

Partisan motives, for example, dictated that electors must be pledged in advance to vote for specific candidates, that the choices presented to voters be restricted to candidates nominated by some party agency, and that the President and Vice President run together on a single party ticket. Of even greater consequence, the exigencies of two-party competition in time led to the uniform adoption of the general-ticket system of choosing electors, perhaps the most extraordinary feature of the election game. Parties provided the connection between presidential politics and the patronage system, with the result that the election engaged the interest of thousands of office-holders and office-seekers; it pitted the ins against the outs. Parties reduced the importance of the stature of the candidates, as voters responded to partisan cues and to fervent appeals to their loyalty. Finally, parties vastly simplified the decisions to be made by the electorate. The choice was to be between A and B, and for the vast majority of the voters, that decision was largely predetermined by their partisan identity. Not all the rules of the presidential game are explainable in terms of parties, but the proportion is large.

Parties were partially responsible for two of the most striking features of the presidential game, the involvement of a mass electorate and the dramatic quality of the campaigns. Prior to 1824, during the period of the first party system, only a small minority of the eligible voters participated in presidential elections, both because electors were chosen by the legislature in many states and because in most states after 1800 there was little semblance of a contest. For similar reasons, and because of the prevailing inhibitions against demagogic appeals and overt activity by the candidates, campaigns were relatively sedate affairs. The beginning of a new era can be observed in 1828, when voter participation rose markedly and campaign techniques exhibited many innovations. The trend continued, until by 1840 about four-fifths of the electorate went to the polls following a campaign of unprecedented theatricality. The presidential game had now become a kind of mass folk festival, incorporating as well the enthusiasms of religious revivalism and the passions of a bloodless internal war.

To a detached observer, the phenomenon defied explanation in purely political terms. Neither the charisma of the candidates nor the quality of the issues at stake could seemingly account for such an extraordinary expenditure of emotional fervor or organizational energy. The presidential office itself had come to represent with Jackson and Van Buren essentially a negative influence, and the Whigs, denouncing what they termed "executive tyranny," were committed to curtailing the scope of presidential authority. It is not at all apparent that in the popular view the presidency was looked upon as a source of strong leadership in the government, except, perhaps, in the instance of Clay's supporters in 1844. Why, then, did the contest for the presidency come to be the great focal point of American politics, far transcending in intensity of concern congressional elections or, in most states, gubernatorial or legislative contests?

The answer to this question may well involve aspects of American culture that go beyond, or stand apart from, narrowly political concerns. For a people of diverse origins, of numerous but weakly institutionalized religious denominations, of parochial orientations, and with sparse symbols of national unity; for a people whose opportunities for cultural expression, for satisfying identities, or for cathartic release were starkly limited, the presidential game exerted a singular appeal by the 1840s. It offered them identities as partisans in a contest with the entire nation as the arena. It enabled them to immerse themselves in an elaborate ritual with millions of their fellow citizens, to march in processions, chant slogans, sing songs, join clubs, exalt heroes, and confront the enemy. It provided hosts of them with glorious roles as chieftains and lieutenants, marshalling their troops for the fray. It released them from the humdrum routine of their ordinary lives, much as their descendants were to seek such escape at the movies, or viewing television, or as enthusiastic fans of their favorite teams. In short, the form that the contest for the presidency assumed by the 1840s met a cultural need; it was something more than a political event.

As a political event, the presidential game cannot be understood as merely a means of selecting the nation's chief executive. Although the system contrived by the Framers was intended to focus exclusively on that single function, other considerations soon became inextricably involved in the process. The presidential election assumed a complex, three-dimensional character. With the early formation of political parties, those who participated in the election were conscious of making a choice not only between individuals but also between parties. The adherents of Jefferson and of Adams in 1800, for example, saw the contest as one between Republicans and Federalists, as well as between rival aspirants for the presidency. The significance of this dimension of the game lessened as the Federalists ceased to offer effective opposition and all but disappeared in the Monroe era, but partisanship acquired transcendent importance in the 1830s with the establishment of the second American party system. The issue of which party was to control the executive branch became of even greater moment than the identity of the candidates.

The election also served as a crude kind of referendum on national policies. Particularly when the parties in their conventions adopted formal platforms, expressive of their positions on leading issues, and when candidates set forth their views in public statements, the elections came to be regarded as reflecting the popular will with respect to policy questions. Thus Jackson, following the election of 1832, could claim a popular mandate for his destruction of the Bank of the United States, and Polk in 1844 could interpret his election as a mandate for expansionism.

Whether the presidential game as it had evolved by the 1840s was equally well suited to performing all three functions is yet another question more easily raised than answered. Given the notoriously loose organization and discipline of American political parties and the diffuse structure of the federal government, the presidential contest could not, in fact, determine which party would govern the nation; the system was not congenial to party government. Similarly, the capacity of the process for producing a clear mandate on policy issues was severely limited because of the multiplicity of factors that impinged on the electoral decision. Nevertheless, the understanding that the election had these three aspects— the choice of a President, of a party, and of a set of policies—was generally shared by political leaders and the electorate, thereby enhancing the momentousness of the contest.

When we review the remarkable course of developments over half a century, the contrasts between the plan set forth in Article II of the Constitution and the presidential game as it actually came to be conducted are striking. The Framers had been confident that their design would not merely control but eliminate the influence of factions in the selection of the President, but the process had succumbed immediately to politicization. They had envisioned an independent chief executive who owed his election only to his manifest talents and his conspicuous public service; instead, he was to be the creature of a party. The President, in their model, was to be remote from all popular influences. Now, his election was to draw forth the enthusiastic participation of the mass electorate and involve not only a choice among individuals but also among competing parties and policies. Their President was to be an aloof, even awesome figure, bound by a republican code of conduct that barred any semblance of electioneering. In the new order, he must garb himself in an image appealing to the common man, become Old Hickory or Old Tip, and even venture to advance his own candidacy. Delegate conventions, electoral parties, and spectacular popular campaigns, rather than artfully insulated electors, were to determine the event. Contingent elections by the House of Representatives, an accepted feature of the Constitutional scheme, were soon regarded as abhorrent and avoidable through the mechanism of the two-party system. Although the republican ideal of the Framers remained firmly embodied in the formal provisions of the Constitution, it was mocked by the practices of a political community that drifted awkwardly toward an inchoate version of popular democracy.

II

Rules for a Game Not Played

The Constitutional Convention was remarkable for its creativity. As the delegates assembled in Philadelphia in May 1787 not even the most astute observer of the American political scene could have envisioned what was eventually to emerge after four months of intensive deliberation, negotiation, and innovation. It was to be expected that the delegates would endeavor to strengthen and broaden national authority, for that had long been an avowed objective of those who were most active in promoting the calling of the Convention. It might also have been foreseen that some restraints would be imposed on the state governments. But it is hardly an exaggeration to assert that no one could have predicted the novel structure that would be contrived for the new government. Least imaginable, perhaps, was the design of the executive branch and the extraordinary method devised for selecting its head—the President of the United States.[1]

Early in the discussions within the Convention it became apparent that many delegates were disposed to favor a strong executive in order to provide the new government with the "energy" that had been lacking under the Articles of Confederation. Whether the executive would be subordinate to, or independent of, the legislature, as well as the extent of executive authority were objects of controversy. So also were the issues of whether the executive should have a plural or single head, what the term of office should be, and whether re-election would be permissible. Not until late in August, after weeks of diffuse and often heated discussions, did the general outline of the executive branch begin to assume some degree of clarity. There would be a single executive, who would be called the "President of the United States." He would execute the laws, have a qualified veto, recommend measures for the consideration of the legislators, convene the Congress on extraordinary occasions, exercise limited powers of appointment, act as commander in chief of the armed forces, receive ambassadors, grant pardons, and be subject to impeachment. Yet to be determined were his full powers in the area of foreign affairs and his relation to the heads of the executive departments. And there still remained in doubt the method of his election.

The concept of the executive as it seemed to be emerging from the Convention's deliberations was surely novel. Quite obviously it was not derived from the British model, for the President was to be neither king nor prime minister. The office was not patterned after that of the governors of the states, most of whom were little more than figureheads, although there is evidence that the governorship of New York—and to a lesser degree, Massachusetts—suggested some features of the presidential role. What happened was that in the course of the searching debates, the delegates groped toward the definition of a republican executive; one who could provide the desired energy in the system, manage executive affairs in a way that had been impossible for the Continental Congress, and constitute a check on the possible excesses of the legislature. But before the full character of the office could be delineated, crucial decisions had to be made about the mode of choosing the person who was to serve as President.

No problem caused more perplexity for the delegates than that of determining how the President should be elected. The subject was frequently on the Convention's agenda. On seven different occasions a decision was reached, only to be reconsidered or altered at a subsequent session. Not until the last days of the Convention, after virtually all other matters had been disposed of, was an acceptable plan contrived. Although it would be tedious to trace in full detail the tortuous process by which the Convention ultimately arrived at its decision, at least a cursory review is essential to an understanding of what shaped the final product.[2]

The mode of election initially favored by the majority of delegates was choice by the national legislature. This method had been proposed in the Virginia Plan, submitted to the Convention by Edmund Randolph. By early June, after discussions in the Committee of the Whole, there was substantial agreement that the executive would consist of a single person who would be chosen by the national legislature for a term of seven years and be ineligible for re-election. After further debate, and the defeat of several proposed amendments, this decision was confirmed by the Convention on July 17 and July 18.

In the meantime, however, several other proposals had been put forth, and on July 19 and July 20 the Convention suddenly embraced a plan devised by Oliver Ellsworth of Connecticut. Under this scheme, the executive would be chosen by electors appointed by the state legislatures, with the states having one, two, or three electoral votes, depending on their population. A few days later, the Ellsworth plan was reconsidered and abandoned, and the delegates reinstated their earlier resolution to have the choice made by the national legislature. There the matter rested until August 24, when—after attempts to win support for election by the people at large or by electors met with defeat—the Convention reaffirmed that the executive would be chosen by the national legislature. However, in a move that was to have a significant effect on the attitude of the smaller states, the election would be by the joint ballot of the two houses, rather than by a concurrent vote.[3]

Although the method of having the executive chosen by the national legislature seemed to command the most favor, there was strenuous opposition from such leading "nationalists" as James Wilson and Gouverneur Morris of Pennsylvania, who were soon joined by James Madison of Virginia, Alexander Hamilton of New York, and others. They cited formidable, and ultimately convincing, objections to this mode of election. To give the choice to the national legislature, they contended, would impair the independence of the executive, a point on which they had strong feelings. Moreover, such a method would open the way to cabal, intrigue, corruption, and the exertion of influence by foreign powers. Here they would cite as notorious examples the instances of Poland and Germany. Even the proponents of choice by the national legislature recognized these dangers, and it was for that reason that they were agreed that the executive should not serve more than one term; otherwise he would engage in intrigues for his re-election. But, argued the opponents, to limit re-eligibility would be to stifle justifiable and worthy ambition; the incumbent would thus lack the incentive to put forth his finest efforts.

In his characteristic manner, Madison on July 25 ably summarized the objections to an election by the national legislature:

> Besides the general influence of that mode on the independence of the Executive, 1. the election of the Chief Magistrate would agitate and divide the legislature so much that the public interest would materially suffer by it. Public bodies are always apt to be thrown into contentions, but into more violent ones by such occasions than by others. 2. the candidate would intrigue with the Legislature, would derive his appointment from the predominant faction, and be apt to render his administration subservient to its views. 3. the ministers of foreign powers would have and make use of, the opportunity to mix their intrigues and influence with the Election. Limited as the powers of the Executive are, it will be an object of great moment with the great rival powers of Europe who have American possessions, to have at the head of our Government, a man attached to their respective politics and interests. No pains, nor perhaps expense, will be spared, to gain from the Legislature an appointment favorable to their wishes. Germany and Poland are witnesses of this danger. In the former, the election of the Head of the Empire, till it became in a manner hereditary, interested all of Europe, and was much influenced by foreign interference. In the latter, although the elective Magistrate has very little real power, his election has at all times produced the most eager interference of foreign princes, and has in fact at length slid entirely into foreign hands.[4]

It was with such considerations as these in mind that several delegates sought some method other than an election by the legislature.

Two general alternatives were proposed early in the debates: election directly by the people at large and an indirect choice by electors, chosen expressly for the purpose either by state legislatures or popular vote. Again, however, there seemed to be severe disadvantages with both methods. Critics of a popular election insisted that the mass of the electorate lacked the information essential to a wise choice. George Mason of Virginia thought it would "be as unnatural to refer the choice of a proper character for a chief Magistrate to the people, as it would to refer a trial of colors to a blind man."[5] Elbridge Gerry of Massachusetts branded a popular election as "radically vicious" and predicted that it would be controlled by the secret Society of Cincinnati.[6] Others objected that a popular election would give preponderant weight to the most populous states, while Madison adverted to the peculiar disadvantage it would impose on the southern states, with their restrictive suffrage requirements and their non-voting Negroes. Although Wilson and Morris sought to counter these arguments, they made little headway.

To a choice by electors, who would presumably meet at the seat of government to cast their ballots, there were also objections. Voiced most frequently was the contention that capable and respectable men would not deign to accept such a limited assignment. Some delegates deplored the inconvenience and expense of bringing the electors together from distant parts of the union. Others thought that any plan involving electors was too complex. There was also the fear that if the electors assembled in one place they would be subject to improper influences; they might succumb to corruption or foreign intrigue.

Each discussion of the mode of election produced novel, not to say farfetched, proposals. John Rutledge of South Carolina urged that the choice should be made by the upper house of the national legislature. The eccentric Gerry would entrust the task to the state governors. John Dickinson of Delaware suggested that the people of each state might name their favorite sons, from among whom a choice would be made by the national legislature as an electoral college. James Wilson, the leading champion of popular election, experienced such frustration that he advanced the notion that the choice might be made by fifteen electors selected by lot from the national legislature, with the voting to take place immediately. Several delegates, including Wilson and Hamilton, proposed that electors should be popularly chosen in districts.

What seemed like the oddest idea of all, but which was to figure importantly in the final solution of the problem, was put forward by Hugh Williamson of North Carolina. He favored a popular election, but each voter was to vote for *three* candidates. His reasoning was that by this method men from the smaller states would have a chance to get into the race. Gouverneur Morris seized on this proposal but suggested that a vote for two persons—one of whom should not be from the voter's state—would be preferable.[7] Wilson, ever a fruitful source of proposals, originated the concept of a contingent election when he suggested that if a popular vote failed to produce a majority for any candidate, a final choice could be made by the national legislature.[8]

A careful perusal of the debates on this vexed issue makes it apparent that while the Convention ostensibly had settled on having the executive chosen by the national legislature, there were many misgivings about this mode. As late as August 24, the delegates were still groping for a proposal that would ensure the independence of the executive and be immune to any imaginable form of intrigue or corruption. It was at this point that the Convention's few remaining matters of postponed or unfinished business—including the election of the executive—were turned over to a special committee of one delegate from each state, chaired by David Brearley of New Jersey.

The plan presented to the Convention by Brearley on September 4 was amazing for its boldness, intricacy, and sensitivity to political exigencies.[9] It combined a number of proposals that had been put forth in the course of the debates with some completely novel features. Each state would appoint, in such a manner as its legislature might direct, a number of electors equal to its whole number of Senators and Representatives. The electors would meet in their respective states and vote by ballot for two persons, of whom at least one should be from another state. A list of the votes would be sealed and transmitted to the seat of government, there to be counted by the President of the Senate. The person having the greatest number of votes, if such number was a majority of the whole, was to be President. If no person had a majority, then the Senate was to choose one from the five highest. After the choice of the President, the person having the next highest number of electoral votes was to be the Vice President.

A number of considerations shaped this plan, but two were of over-riding importance. The first was to devise a method that would replace choice by the national legislature. The second was to ensure that the larger states would not completely dominate the election. The scheme of using electors, proposed initially by Wilson on June 2 and later refined by Ellsworth and others, addressed the first consideration. The second involved very complex contrivances.

Throughout the debates on the mode of choosing the President, the small states had been extremely sensitive about their roles in the process. They were generally averse to a popular election, for they saw that this would enable a few large states to control the choice. Similar objections were raised to the employment of electors assigned in proportion to population. The method that would be most advantageous to the small states would be an election by the *concurrent* vote of the two houses of the national legislature, for then the equal representation of the states in the Senate would, in effect, counterbalance the population advantage of the large states in the House. But on August 24 the Convention had voted that the election in the national legislature should be determined by the *joint* ballot of the two houses. At this point the small-state delegates lost all enthusiasm for vesting the choice of the executive in the legislature and devoted their energies to devising an alternative plan, utilizing electors, that would safeguard their interests. The plan concocted by Brearley's committee contained four important features designed to appease the small states.

First of all, there was the curious provision that each elector should vote for two persons for President, one of whom should not be from the elector's state. Suggested initially by Hugh Williamson and Gouverneur Morris on July 25, this was a device to enhance the possibility that small-state candidates would obtain electoral votes. But the objection had been raised that this "second vote" might be thrown away on insignificant or even unworthy characters. It was to mitigate this possibility that Brearley's committee invented the position of Vice President, an office that had never been mentioned previously in the Convention. It was hoped that with the prospect in view that the person with the second largest number of electoral votes would become Vice President, electors would give serious consideration to both of the persons for whom they were required to vote. As Williamson later observed, "such an officer as vice-President was not wanted. He was introduced only for the sake of a valuable mode of election which required two to be chosen at the same time."[10]

The second concession to the small states was the stipulation that if no candidate received a majority of the electoral votes, the Senate should choose from among the *five* highest. Here again, the assumption was that a small-state candidate might qualify for the contingent election. When it was proposed in the course of debate that this number should be reduced to three, Roger Sherman of Connecticut, who was especially ardent in defending the interests of the small states, protested vehemently and stated that he would prefer to see the number set at seven or thirteen.

The third and fourth devices were closely related; they were the contingent election and the vesting of that election in the Senate. The notion of a contingent election, in the event that no candidate received a majority, originated with James Wilson. The requirement of a majority would prevent one or two large states from combining to win the election with simply a plurality of votes, but it necessitated some provision for a run-off election. The solution put forth by Brearley's committee was to have the Senate elect from among the five highest, thus the small states would have an equal weight with the large in the final determination.

To its designers, and to the delegates generally, this plan was viewed as a compromise between the large and the small states, a fact that was adverted to frequently in the Convention, during the course of ratification, and subsequently. The understanding was commonly expressed that the large states would have the advantage in "nominating" candidates, through their control of large blocs of electors, but that the small states would be influential in the final choice by virtue of their equal representation in the Senate. To some, at least, this arrangement was thoroughly consistent with the federal principle, if not with the principle of majority rule.

The Brearley committee's plan did not gain immediate acceptance. The strongest opposition was directed against giving the Senate the responsibility for the contingent election. Numerous delegates, especially from the large states, professed alarm at such an important addition to the already great powers of that branch of Congress. Wilson spoke for many when he saw here "a dangerous tendency to aristocracy."[11] After nearly three days of wrangling, Sherman and Williamson collaborated on an alternative that met with prompt and overwhelming approval:[12] the contingent election would go to the House of Representatives, with each state delegation having one vote. In other actions the delegates specified that the electors should all meet and vote on the same day in their respective state capitals and that when it was necessary to have a contingent election, the House would vote "immediately" after the electoral count had been reported. Both emendations were intended to lessen the opportunity for intrigue. After other minor changes, the delegates, with an obvious sense of relief, referred their handiwork to the Committee on Style for a final polishing.

Surely these arrangements for choosing the President represented an exceedingly complex, and even delicate, contrivance. The objectives of the Framers are readily identified. They wanted to ensure, in a large degree, the independence of the executive from the legislature, in part because of their concern with "corruption" and in part because they saw the executive as a check on the legislature. They wanted a method that would be impervious to faction, intrigue, or any unwholesome form of manipulation; a method that would defy politicization.[13] It was also essential that the plan strike an acceptable balance between the interests of the large and the small states. What would appear to be equally evident is that the Framers were not especially concerned with providing the President with a constituency, or ensuring extensive popular participation in his election, or guaranteeing that he would represent the choice of a majority of his countrymen. Least of all, of course, did they intend to design a system that would facilitate the activities of political parties.

Although it involves some speculation, it is important to try to assess the expectations of the Framers as to how their plan of election would actually operate. From their statements in the Convention, during the debates over ratification, and—with reservations —later expressions of their views, we can derive some insights into this matter. Unfortunately, for our purposes, they did not leave a record of their opinions on all possible contingencies, but on a few key questions there is enough evidence to provide a reasonable basis for some conclusions.

On the matter of how the electors would be chosen, the general assumption was that they would be popularly elected. The fullest exposition of this expectation was set forth by Hamilton in *Federalist* No. 68, where he made several references to the choice of electors by the people. John Jay was equally explicit in *Federalist* No. 64. Similar statements were made in ratifying conventions by Edmund Randolph, James Madison, William R. Davie, Charles C. Pinckney, and James Wilson. The possibility that state legislatures might choose the electors was raised in the North Carolina convention by Governor Samuel Johnston, but James Iredell "was of opinion it could not be done with propriety by the state legislatures, because as they were to direct the manner of appointing, a law would look very awkward which should say, 'They gave the power of such appointments to themselves.' "[14] On the other hand, Madison, in *Federalist* No. 45, where he was seeking to counter the argument that the Constitution would seriously impair the authority of the states, introduced a note of ambiguity by remarking: "Without the intervention of the state legislatures, the President of the United States cannot be elected at all. They must in all cases have a great share in his appointment, and will, perhaps, in most cases, of themselves determine it." In the Virginia ratifying convention, however, Madison had said flatly that "the people choose the electors," and much later—in 1823—it was his recollection that the choice of electors by popular vote within districts "was mostly, if not exclusively, in view when the constitution was framed and adopted . . . ."[15]

Another common assumption was that in many, if not most, cases, a contingent election would be required. This belief explains the lengthy debate over the Brearley committee's proposal that the contingent election be conducted by the Senate. During that controversy George Mason estimated that a contingent election would be required "nineteen times in twenty," and only Gouverneur Morris was prepared to argue that it was probable that the electors would produce a majority for one of the candidates. Madison foresaw that with the provision for a choice among the five candidates highest in electoral votes, candidacies would be multiplied and thus the probability of a contingent election was enhanced. Like others, he often used the term "eventual election" when referring to a choice by the House.[16]

It is also apparent that the delegates expected that their plan of election would be proof against faction, intrigue, and corruption. Charles C. Pinckney explained to the South Carolina ratifying convention that because of the safeguards built into the plan "the dangers of intrigue and corruption are avoided" and—in particular —it was "almost impossible for any foreign power to influence thirteen different sets of electors . . . ."[17] William R. Davie was equally emphatic. "It is impossible," he told the North Carolina convention, "for human ingenuity to devise any mode of election better calculated to exclude undue influence . . . He is elected on the same day in every state so that there can be no possible combination between the electors."[18] In like vein, James Wilson extolled the electoral plan: "By it we avoid corruption; and we are little exposed to the lesser evils of party intrigue . . . ."[19] Hamilton, in *Federalist* No. 68, agreed that "every practicable obstacle should be opposed to cabal, intrigue, and corruption," and insisted that "the Convention had guarded against all danger of this sort with the most provident and judicious attention." One possible hazard pointed out by several critics was the President's eligibility for re-election; once in office, it was feared, he would find means of exerting his potent influence to secure another term.

The Framers' plan of election prompted little adverse reaction. In the ratifying debates, and in the other contemporary discussions, slight attention was focused on this section of the Constitution. The one major exception was the issue of re-eligibility. Several critics, most notably Thomas Jefferson and George Mason, foresaw that once elected, the President would hold office for life. "Experience concurs with reason in concluding that the first magistrate will always be re-elected if the constitution permits it," wrote Jefferson. "He is then an officer for life. This once observed it becomes of so much consequence to have a friend or a foe at the head of our affairs, that . . . [foreign powers] will interfere with money and with arms."[20] But on the other side, Washington, Madison, Franklin, Hamilton, and others argued that re-eligibility was essential and that there were adequate safeguards against undue influences.

Luther Martin continued to complain that the system placed the smaller states at a disadvantage, but the answer to this charge was that the plan was a compromise, which dealt equitably with both the large and the small states. Only Governor George Clinton of New York in his *Cato* letters went to the heart of the matter in arguing that it was "a maxim in republics that the representatives of the people should be of their immediate choice; but by the manner in which the president is chosen he arrives to this office of the fourth or fifth hand . . . ."[21] Notwithstanding these caveats the mode of electing the President was probably the least controversial feature of the Constitution.[22]

Now the time was at hand to place the new system in operation. On July 2, 1788, the Continental Congress received official notification that New Hampshire had become the ninth state to ratify the Constitution, and it appointed a committee to prepare an election ordinance to prescribe when the new federal officials should be chosen. Action was delayed, at first to await the verdict on ratification by New York—which came on July 26—and then by a prolonged dispute over where the officers of the new government should convene. Ultimately it was agreed that the site should be New York City, and on September 13 the election ordinance was finally adopted. With respect to the presidential elections, it specified that in the several states that had ratified the Constitution electors should be appointed on the first Wednesday in January, that these electors should assemble in their state capitals and vote on the first Wednesday in February, and that the first Wednesday in March should be the day for "commencing Proceedings under the said Constitution."[23]

This rigid timetable, coupled with the ambiguities and complexities of the related provisions of the Constitution on the election of the President, created awkward problems for the states. State elections were held at various times between March and November; none, of course, were scheduled in January. State legislatures, too, met at different times; some would have to hold special sessions to conform with the new requirements. Many states, particularly those from New Jersey southward, had no experience with conducting state-wide elections. Others, such as those in New England, encountered peculiar difficulties because of their requirement that any successful candidate for elective office must receive not merely a plurality but a majority of the total vote cast. Further complications arose from the fact that in several states bitter political animosities survived from the controversies over ratification, causing opposing factions to differ on specific means of appointing electors. The first presidential election, then, was to combine novelty, confusion, and intrigue in such a way as to reduce the carefully contrived plan of the Framers to a shambles. A close look at the experience of a few key states will serve to illustrate the problems that developed.

Because its legislature happened to be in session when the election ordinance was adopted, Pennsylvania became the first state to prescribe how electors would be chosen.[24] By an act of November 4, twelve electors were to be elected on a general ticket by the voters of the state at large on the first Wednesday in January; ten Representatives would be elected from the state at large on the last Wednesday in November. Evidently some consideration was given to having the choice of electors made by the legislature, but this alternative met with little favor, among other reasons because it would involve the considerable expense of a special session. The major controversy was over whether electors and Representatives should be elected from districts or from the state at large. The latter mode was adopted because of the manifest awkwardness of creating ten districts for the congressional election and twelve for the presidential election. The legislature was nearing the end of its session, and it was feared that if it tackled the problem of carving such districts, it would become bogged down in the effort. The political consideration involved in the decision to have a general ticket was that the dominant faction in the state—which numbered among its leaders James Wilson and Robert Morris—staunchly supported the Constitution and expected to carry a full slate of electors.

Massachusetts faced special difficulties in arranging for the choice of electors.[25] Even before the General Court assembled on October 29, a controversy had surfaced between those who favored choice by the legislature and those who insisted that the people must be permitted to vote. For more than two weeks, the legislature struggled with the issue. Those favoring choice by the legislature argued that there was insufficient time for a popular election, especially because it was unlikely any electors would receive a clear majority of the vote, in which case a second election would be required. The proponents of popular choice conceded this difficulty, but insisted that some means must be found to permit the people to participate. Ultimately, on November 20, a joint resolution was adopted providing for the election of Representatives and electors by districts on December 18. Specifically, the voters in each district were to vote for two persons as electors and transmit a list of the votes to the General Court, which would assemble on the first Wednesday in January. That body would examine the returns, and from the two highest in each district choose one by joint ballot to serve as electors. The General Court also appointed two electors at large. As had been anticipated, in six of the eight districts no elector received a majority. The General Court, in its discretion, named as electors for four of the districts men who had ranked second in the popular vote. Although in form the electors were chosen by popular vote, in actuality they were appointed by the legislature.

New Hampshire faced problems similar to those of Massachusetts.[26] There, after the proponents of an election by the legislature had met with defeat, it was determined that both Representatives and electors should be popularly elected from the state at large. When, as had been anticipated, no elector received a majority of the total vote, the legislature had the duty of choosing five electors from among the ten with the highest votes. But a dispute developed over whether that choice should be made by a joint or concurrent vote. A deadlock ensued until, on the evening of the day before the election must take place, the House yielded to the Senate's insistence on a concurrent choice, only in order that the state might not be deprived of its vote in the presidential election.[27]

In New York, an irreconcilable disagreement between the two houses of the legislature resulted in the loss of that state's electoral vote. Governor Clinton did not call the legislature into special session until December 11, by which date there was scarcely time to arrange for a popular election of electors. Essentially because the Senate was under Federalist control, while Antifederalists predominated in the Assembly, the houses could not agree on whether electors should be chosen by joint or concurrent ballot, with the result that none were chosen.[28]

It was a quite different story in South Carolina.[29] Although the legislature wrangled over the method of electing the state's five Representatives, opting at last for election by districts, it showed little interest in the matter of choosing electors. With minimal debate, it was agreed that those members of the legislature who happened to appear at Charleston on the first Wednesday in January should make the choice. On the appointed day, with less than a quorum of the Senators on hand, and about one-third of the House, the members assembled together, chose a chairman, and appointed the requisite seven electors. Thus the choice was made not by the legislature, strictly speaking, but by such members as were present.

New Jersey was equally diffident. Its legislature authorized the governor and his Privy Council—a handful of members of the upper house—to appoint the state's electors, no doubt because it wished to save the expense of either an election or a special session of the legislature.[30] Connecticut and Georgia both provided for electors to be chosen by the legislature. Maryland used the general-ticket plan, although five electors were alloted to the Western Shore and three to the Eastern Shore. Delaware employed a slight variation of the general ticket.[31] In Virginia, where there was the prospect of a close contest between Federalists and Antifederalists, neither side was confident of victory in a state-wide election. Consequently both Representatives and electors were to be chosen from districts. Ten districts were created for congressional candidates and twelve for presidential electors.[32] North Carolina and Rhode Island, which had yet to ratify the Constitution, were, of course, excluded from participating in this first federal election.

It will be apparent that the states employed a great variety of methods of choosing electors; indeed, no two states followed precisely the same mode. It is doubtful whether the Framers foresaw such diversity, although the Constitutional provision that each state should appoint electors "in such manner as the Legislature thereof might direct" certainly implied that they had no uniform method in mind. This key phrase, so critical in its consequences, was never the subject of reported discussions within the Convention, which suggests that it did not receive much consideration at the time. We can only assume that it was intended to provide for more latitude than was the case with Representatives, who were to be elected by those qualified to vote for the more numerous branch of the state legislature.[33]

With most of the Framers who expressed themselves on the matter having stated their belief that electors would be chosen "by the people," why did so many states place the choice with the legislature? The most important consideration was undoubtedly the time factor. According to the Constitution: "The Congress may determine the Time of choosing the Electors, and the Day on which they shall give their Votes; which day shall be the same throughout the United States." There was no requirement that the electors should all be *chosen* on the same day. Nevertheless, the Continental Congress in its election ordinance specified that all the electors must be chosen on the first Wednesday in January. Thus the states were permitted no latitude in scheduling the appointment of electors. Because of the difficulties cited previously, some opted for choice by the legislature, their decisions being influenced in part by when their legislatures were scheduled to meet. Another factor that may have operated was the general assumption that Washington faced no serious competition for the first office and that therefore it was not worth the bother and expense of providing for a popular election. Where the issue was debated, as in Pennsylvania, Massachusetts, and New Hampshire, strong feelings were expressed in support of the popular election, even though the latter two states had to leave the final choice to the legislature. On the other hand, states like Connecticut, New Jersey, South Carolina, and Georgia were not objects of condemnation because they adopted the legislative mode.

Having discovered in this first election that various methods could be employed for appointing electors, it was to be but a short step to the realization that variations in the mode could affect the outcome of the election. While the Massachusetts legislature was debating the method of election, Theodore Sedgwick advised Hamilton, "Should the Electors be chosen by the legislature, Mr. [John] Adams will probably combine all the votes of Massachusetts [for Vice President]."[34] With comparable astuteness, Tench Coxe informed Madison that the use of a general ticket would be "safe in Pennsylvania" but he was concerned that it would "give a precedent to the other states, where the majority are unfavorable, such as New York, etc., which may require the early attention of our friends in those places."[35] It did not take long to learn how variations in the rules could affect the game. As factional and party strife grew in scope and intensity, calculating politicians in every state would seek the adoption of the mode that would most favor their candidates.

The greatest virtue of the Framers' plan for the election of the President was supposed to be its invulnerability to intrigue. Politics, especially in the sordid sense of that term, were to play no part. Meeting at the same time in their respective states, the electors were to vote by secret ballot for two men for President, one of whom was not to be a resident of their home state. The presumption was that each elector would exercise his individual discretion in voting for two "exalted characters" and that there would be no opportunity for them to "conspire" with electors in other states or to be subjected to improper influences. The first election demonstrated the illusory nature of those expectations.[36]

The Federalists—the name adopted by those who had been ardent in support of ratification—quickly perceived the need to apply the arts of management to the election. They were determined that Washington should be President, but the revered general made it plain that he would not accept the office if he met with any competition. He was greatly concerned late in 1788 that the Antifederalists—those who had opposed ratification and who were seeking to call a second Convention to propose amendments—would rally behind an opposing candidate, with consequences that he might find embarrassing. Thus every effort must be exerted to secure an overwhelming, if not unanimous, vote for Washington. A second consideration was to secure a reliable person as Vice President, preferably from a northern state.[37] Finally, as the subtleties of the dual-vote requirement became apparent, the danger that the man intended for the second place might receive an equal or greater vote than Washington had to be addressed.

On their side the Antifederalists, who had demonstrated impressive strength in such key states as Massachusetts, New York, and Virginia, recognized the futility of opposing Washington but saw the possibility of securing the vice presidency. A "federal republican committee" in New York, after corresponding for several months with Antifederalist leaders in Virginia, sent a circular letter to the states in mid-November 1788 urging that Governor Clinton be supported for Vice President.[38] How grave this threat might be was difficult for the Federalist leaders to estimate, but there is considerable evidence that they took it seriously and responded accordingly.

The critical figure in the management of the Federalist campaign was Alexander Hamilton, with some assistance from Madison, Wilson, and other intimates.[39] It was Hamilton who first broached to Washington the delicate subject of his candidacy and who sought to assure him that he would have no competitors. It was Hamilton who, with obvious reluctance, finally concluded early in November that Adams was the inescapable choice for Vice President and announced, "My measures will be taken accordingly." And it was Hamilton, writing late in January to James Wilson, who observed, "Everybody is aware of that defect in the constitution which renders it possible that the man intended for Vice President may in fact turn up President. Everybody sees that unanimity in Adams as Vice President and a few votes insidiously withheld from Washington might substitute the former for the latter."[40]

So it was that, surprisingly, Federalist strategy came to focus on the vice presidency. Both Hamilton and Madison had serious misgivings about Adams, who reportedly was unfriendly toward Washington. But after weighing other possibilities—John Jay, General James Knox, General Benjamin Lincoln, and John Hancock—and receiving appropriate assurances that Adams would support Washington, the choice settled on the dour statesman from Massachusetts. But Hamilton, believing that "it would be disagreeable even to have a man treading close upon the heels of a person we wish as President," and motivated as well by some animus toward Adams, schemed to reduce his electoral vote to the minimum.[41]

He outlined a horrendous scenario to James Wilson. Suppose all of New England and the Middle States voted for Adams? Then suppose that southern Antifederalists, seeing the hopelessness of

Clinton's candidacy, threw their votes to Adams? "Here then is a *chance* of unanimity in Adams." And, finally, suppose that from personal caprice, or other motives, a few votes were withheld from Washington? Hamilton went on to explain that even if Adams received no votes from the South, he would still get forty-one votes, which was more than a majority, in the North. "Hence I conclude it will be prudent to throw away a few votes, say 7 or 8; giving these votes to no persons not otherwise thought of. Under this impression I have proposed to friends in Connecticut to throw away 2, to others in Jersey to throw away an equal number and I submit to you whether it will not be well to lose three or four in Pennsylvania . . . ." Was such manifest intrigue justifiable? "For God's sake," Hamilton exclaimed, "let not our zeal for a secondary object defeat or endanger a first . . . ." A few days later, Hamilton was cooly assuring Theodore Sedgwick, Adams's chief supporter in Massachusetts, that Adams would probably get all the votes of New Jersey, Pennsylvania, Delaware, and Maryland, as well as some from the South.[42]

Even Washington, who sought to remain completely aloof from the heated political scene, became involved in the intrigues over the vice presidency. He was genuinely concerned about the threat posed by the Antifederalists. In October he wrote General Lincoln expressing a thinly veiled endorsement of Adams, and late in January he reported to Lincoln that Adams would have "a considerable number of the votes of the Electors" in Maryland and Virginia. "Some of those gentlemen," he explained, "will have been advised that this measure would be entirely agreeable to me, and that I considered it to be the only certain way to prevent the election of an Antifederalist."[43]

Hamilton's machinations were effective. The New Jersey electors dutifully threw away five of their votes on John Jay, giving only one to Adams. In response to an urgent appeal from Hamilton's emissary, Samuel B. Webb, the Connecticut electors cast five votes for Adams and two for Samuel Huntington. In Pennsylvania, Wilson exerted his influence, with the result that two votes went to John Hancock; Adams received eight.[44] Evidently Washington's influence was less weighty, for the Maryland electors gave all their second votes to a local favorite, Robert H. Harrison, and in Virginia two Federalist votes were thrown away on Hancock and Jay.

While these maneuvers were taking place behind the scenes, the Federalists were active in mounting campaigns in those states where electors were to be chosen by popular vote. Discarding any pretense that the electors would exercise their own judgments, they sought openly to elect men who were pledged to cast their votes for Federalist candidates. In the process, they experimented with techniques of political organization—especially in connection with nominations—that were to forecast the pattern of later developments.

In Pennsylvania, for example, where electors were to be chosen by general ticket in a state-wide election, some means had to be found to concentrate party strength behind a single slate of electors. Dispersion of the vote among a host of candidates might lead to an Antifederalist victory. Accordingly, Federalist delegates from eighteen counties and the city of Philadelphia met in Lancaster on November 3 and agreed on an electoral ticket, as well as congressional nominees. These tickets were widely publicized by friendly newspapers. Meanwhile the Antifederalists had held a secret convention at Harrisburg for similar purposes, and their tickets, together with a lengthy address, were also published. After suffering defeat in the congressional election late in November, the Antifederalists put forth little effort in the January presidential election, but the Federalist presses, warning that the opposition was planning to make Patrick Henry the President, with George Clinton as the Vice President, exhorted the faithful to rally to the challenge. The result was an almost uncontested victory for the Federalist slate.[45]

A close contest was anticipated in Maryland, where both Representatives and electors were to be elected in January in a statewide vote. Through informal means, both Federalist and Antifederalist leaders prepared and published slates of approved candidates. In a brief but frenzied campaign, which featured public meetings, the use of militia companies to get out the vote, parades, barbecues, and strong ethnic appeals to those of German descent, the Federalists triumphed by two-to-one.[46]

In Virginia, where both presidential and congressional elections were conducted on the district plan, a different scheme of organization was required. Prior to the adjournment of the legislature in December 1788, a meeting of the Antifederalists agreed on electoral and congressional candidates to be supported in each district and publicized the slates. The Federalists seem to have used traditional, less formal, means within each district to achieve unified backing for their candidates. Although all the electors voted for Washington, nine had been elected as Federalists and three as Antifederalists.[47] In Massachusetts and New Hampshire, where there were popular elections also, organizational efforts were modest and not very effectual, as evidenced by the multiplicity of candidates and the attendant inability of most to obtain a majority.

Except in Maryland, where party competition was relatively intense and where congressional and presidential voting took place at the same time, voter participation was at a low level. In Pennsylvania, the turnout for the presidential election was less than half that for the congressional election which had been held in November and was far below the rate of participation in state elections. In both Massachusetts and New Hampshire voting was light, and many fewer votes were cast for electors than for Representatives.[48] The surviving Virginia returns are too fragmentary to permit any conclusions regarding the rate of participation, but, again, it would appear that more interest was aroused by the congressional than by the presidential election. No doubt the lack of any serious opposition to Washington dulled popular interest in the election, along with the awkward timing of the canvass and its novelty

The choice of electors having been made on the first Wednesday in January, speculation next centered on how the electors would cast their votes a month later, and, in particular, how they would distribute their second votes. It was during this interval that Hamilton and his co-conspirators pursued their plan to hold Adams's vote to the minimum. In the southern states this posed no problem, for the New Englander enjoyed little popularity in that region. The results of the manipulations in Pennsylvania, New Jersey, and Connecticut have already been described.

According to the prescribed schedule, the new Congress would meet in New York on the first Wednesday in March, and the electoral vote would be counted by the president of the Senate in the presence of both houses. But on the designated day neither house had a quorum; not until April 6 were sufficient members on hand to enable the count to proceed. Well before that date, however, the votes of the electors had been disclosed, and Adams was aware of the mortifying results.[49]

The total electoral vote of the ten states that participated in the election was seventy-three. However, two electors each in Virginia and Maryland failed to attend the meetings of the electors, with the result that only sixty-nine voted. Washington received a vote from every elector. But only thirty-four, less than a majority, also voted for John Adams. In the South, he received five votes; the rest were thrown away on such local figures as Harrison in Maryland, John Rutledge in South Carolina, and John Milton in Georgia. Only Massachusetts and New Hampshire were solidly for Adams; he was deprived of two votes in Connecticut, five in New Jersey, and two in Pennsylvania. George Clinton proved to be a hollow threat; his only votes came from the three Virginia Antifederalist electors. Not only had the Federalist leaders failed to work in Adams's behalf, they had worked against him in certain states, for mixed—if not dubious—reasons. Adams felt betrayed and insulted. After a year in the vice presidency he still complained bitterly that he had been "introduced into it in a manner that made it a disgrace." When he learned of Hamilton's responsibility for his humiliation, his enmity was terrible and lasting, with ominous consequences for the Federalist party in the future.[50]

This first attempt at conducting a presidential election demonstrated that the rules contrived by the Framers did not operate as anticipated. The rules had been shaped to make the executive largely independent of the legislature, to minimize the possibility that such undue influences as cabal, intrigue, or corruption would operate in the election, and to balance the political weights of large and small states. The President, as the rules implied, was not to be a *political* figure, deriving his power from a recognizable constituency; rather, he was to be an "exalted character" whose reputation, talents, and prior services would recommend him to his fellow countrymen and whose authority would be derived from the formal powers assigned to him by the Constitution.[51] The rules, in brief, reflected the Framers' conception of the presidency and of the legitimate means of access to that office.

On a narrowly technical level, the experience of the first election revealed many difficulties. The timing of the election was very awkward, in terms of the schedule of elections and meetings of legislatures in the states. Leaving decisions on the method of choosing electors to the state legislatures produced a bewildering variety of practices and opened the way to manipulation. The New York incident, almost repeated in New Hampshire, showed how a legislative deadlock could deprive a state of its electoral vote. The one-month interval between the choosing of the electors and the casting of their votes afforded opportunities for intrigue that were only dimly foreseen by the Framers. Similarly, the immediate announcement in several states of the results of the electors' votes, in spite of the injunction that they were to be sealed and transmitted to the seat of government, was probably not anticipated.

Far more serious was the "defect in the Constitution," as Hamilton characterized it, inherent in the dual-vote requirement. The expectation had been that each elector would cast two votes *for President*. To prevent the second vote from being thrown away on insignificant candidates, the Framers had created the office of Vice President, which ordinarily would be filled by the person who came in second in the voting. But it did not work that way. Immediately, the second vote was regarded as a vote for Vice President. The realization quickly dawned that if all the so-called second votes went to the same individual, and there was not unanimity on the first vote, then, as Hamilton phrased it, "the man intended for Vice President may in fact turn up President." Of course, if the Framers' intention that the electors should vote with the presidency exclusively in mind and that no cabals or intrigues should intrude in the process had maintained, there would have been no problem. But there were cabals and intrigues; consequently there was a very considerable problem.

It was ironic that the vice presidency, an office created with little consideration and only to enhance the efficacy of the dual-vote system so much desired by the small-state champions, assumed at once such vast political importance. Because there seemed to be the prospect late in 1788 of severe contests in many states between Federalists and Antifederalists and because Federalist leaders were alarmed by the possibility that someone hostile both to Washington and to the Constitution might be elected, they saw the desirability of giving some attention to the choice of a proper Vice President. But, aware of the "defect," and being concerned for various reasons that no candidate tread too closely on Washington, they schemed to elect Adams and yet place him in an inferior position.

What the first election demonstrated, above all, was that the process of choosing a President could be manipulated, that it provided latitude for intrigue, that it could be politicized. There was the potential for a contest. In this sense, the presidential game began to acquire new rules, rules quite different from those set down by the Framers.

As the game was now to be played, leaders of factions or parties must first, through informal or formal means, secure agreement on candidates. The candidates would include the Vice President as well as the President, and they should be from different regions of the country. The leaders must have reliable coworkers in the states who would seek to have the legislature adopt a method of choosing electors that would be most to the advantage of their candidates. Where electors were chosen by popular vote, arrangements would be made for the nomination of electors and for the ensuing campaign. Where the choice was made by the legislature, it was only necessary to secure the appointment of reliable men. In order to guard against the "defect" inherent in the dual vote, some electors would have to be instructed to throw away their second votes. Throughout, there would be the assumption that the electors were not independent agents but, rather, were pledged to vote for specific candidates. Finally, there was at least the intimation, suggested by the desirability of coupling Washington with a northern candidate for Vice President and by the obvious reluctance of southern electors to support Adams, that the large- *versus* small-state alignment that preoccupied the Framers was largely irrelevant to political calculations; the really important interests to be considered were regional.

The first presidential election was an important learning experience for American politicians, and it is apparent that they were apt pupils. They discovered the flaws, and the loopholes, in the formal rules, and they began to experiment with new rules. Fortunately, the risks were minimized because of the availability of Washington, whose presence ensured that there would be no serious division over the presidency. Had there not been a figure of such commanding stature, and if a bitter contest had taken place among lesser rivals, the defects in the election plan contrived by the Framers might well have proved disastrous.

III

Uncertain Rules
for a Hazardous Game

In a tract written in 1787 extolling the new Constitution, Noah Webster expressed a common judgment. "The president of the United States is elective," he explained, "and what is a capital improvement on the best governments, the mode of choosing him excludes the danger of faction and corruption." Later he was to note ruefully in the margin of his own copy of the pamphlet: "This proves how little dependence can be placed on theory. Twelve years experience, or four elections, demonstrates the contrary."[1]

Faction, more commonly referred to as "the spirit of party," came to dominate the presidential game. Evident in a new form by 1792, it produced a clear confrontation over the first office in 1796, and a virulent party battle in 1800. The nature of the contest, and the rules by which it was to be conducted, were shaped by the emerging parties. But two close approaches to catastrophe demonstrated that certain of the rules made it an extremely hazardous game, one that encouraged dangerous intrigues and seemingly frustrated the most careful calculations.[2]

Without exploring fully all the circumstances associated with their origins, we can observe that by the summer of 1792, two parties had formed within the higher echelons of the federal government. These are best described as "parties of notables." They involved relatively small numbers of prominent men and their connections, who held opposing views on public policy and on specific governmental measures. As yet they lacked formal organizations or well-defined constituencies, but each party viewed with passionate dread the course of the other, and both were conscious

41

of being engaged in a fateful rivalry to shape the destiny of the new republic.

The first overt sign of the new partisanship was the establishment of the *National Gazette* in Philadelphia in October 1791. Under the patronage of Secretary of State Thomas Jefferson, with essential assistance from James Madison, then a leading member of the House of Representatives, the new journal was edited by Philip Freneau. It was frankly intended to provide a national vehicle for republican doctrine and to serve as a counterpoise to John Fenno's *Gazette of the United States*, which was friendly to the measures of the administration. So effective was the paper in alerting its subscribers to the evils of Hamilton's policies that the Secretary of the Treasury, under various pseudonyms, was stimulated to bring both its editor and its sponsors under biting attacks. The controversies aired in the public press left no doubt that there was a sharp schism within the highest circles of the government. By September, Madison was presenting "A Candid State of Parties" in the *National Gazette*, in which he contrasted the republican views of which he approved with the insidious designs of those who aimed at a government "approximated to the hereditary form."[3]

The bases for the partisan clash were enumerated by Jefferson for Washington in May 1792. Pouring out his venom on Hamilton, Jefferson denounced his policies as Secretary of the Treasury on the grounds that they corrupted the Congress, unduly extended the scope of the federal government, and exacerbated differences between the North and the South. Worst of all, their ultimate objective was "to prepare the way for a change, from the present republican form of government, to that of a monarchy, of which the English constitution is to be the model."[4] At about the same time Hamilton was writing to a confidant "on the present state of political parties and views." His thesis was: "That Mr. Madison cooperating with Mr. Jefferson is at the head of a faction decidedly hostile to me and my administration, and actuated by views in my judgment subversive of the principles of good government and dangerous to the union, peace and happiness of the Country." After reciting numerous instances of opposition raised by his tormentors, Hamilton concluded, " 'Tis evident beyond a question, from every movement, that Mr. Jefferson aims with ardent desire at the Presidential chair."[5]

As the breach between the rival chieftains widened, each sought to enlist supporters and forge alliances. Through appeals in their highly partisan presses, through networks of correspondents, through intimate conversations in the boarding houses and taverns of Philadelphia, through alignments on politically charged matters in Congress, and through the judicious use of patronage, they built cadres of faithful adherents in the capital and in the states. By October, Jefferson was reporting: "Party animosities here [Philadelphia] have raised a wall of separation between those who differ in political sentiments."[6]

In the midst of this storm of divisive contention, President Washington had to decide whether he should retire from public life at the end of his term. He was pathetically eager to leave the presidency and spend his declining years as a private citizen at his beloved Mount Vernon. When he disclosed this intention to his intimates in May 1792, they all urged upon him the absolute necessity of his agreeing to serve a second term. After detailing the dire threats to the safety of the republic from "the monarchical and paper interest" and noting that the major divisions on public policy arrayed the North against the South in a manner that imperiled the Union, Jefferson made the plea: "North and South will hang together if they have you to hang on . . . ."[7] Edmund Randolph, the Attorney General, struck an even more ominous note. "Should a civil war arise, you cannot stay at home. And how much easier it will be, to disperse the factions which are rushing to this catastrophe, than to subdue them, after they shall appear in arms?"[8] Hamilton and Madison were equally importunate. Washington reserved judgment. He would serve again only if it was his conviction that his withdrawal "would involve the country in serious disputes respecting the chief Magistrate, and the disagreeable consequences which might result therefrom in the floating and divided opinions which seem to prevail at present . . ." Although Hamilton at the end of July thought that he detected some disposition on Washington's part to consent to another term, Jefferson, after a confidential talk with the President late in September reported him to be still "quite undecided."[9]

While he agonized over his decision, Washington tried to compose, or at least moderate, the disruptive clash within his

Cabinet. After receiving from both Hamilton and Jefferson lengthy disquisitions setting forth their differences, he deplored the "internal dissensions . . . harrowing and tearing our vitals" and threatening the very existence of the Union. He urged "liberal allowances, mutual forbearances, and temporizing yieldings on *all sides*." "My earnest wish," he told Hamilton, "is that balsom [balm] may be poured into *all* the wounds which have been given, to prevent them from gangrening . . . ."[10] His efforts were quite fruitless; the partisan wrangling continued.

Along with the emergence of partisan strife, the impending election was to feature an experiment with a new election calendar. The Constitution had given Congress the power to determine the time when electors should be chosen and the day on which they should vote and, in addition, to designate what officer should act as President in the event of the removal, death, resignation, or disability of both the President and Vice President. These matters were addressed at the second session of the First Congress, but action bogged down on the issue of whether the Secretary of State or the president *pro tempore* of the Senate should succeed to the vacant presidential office. The subject was revived in the Second Congress, where it consumed many days of debate over the course of nearly four months.[11]

There was little difficulty in agreeing that electors should not all be *chosen* on the same day, as had been the case in 1789, because of the varying times at which state legislatures were in session. But there was controversy over the length of the period during which electors might be elected prior to the first Wednesday in December, when they were all to cast their ballots. Some Congressmen favored as long a period as eight weeks, while others would have narrowed the interval to fourteen days or less. Thedore Sedgwick of Massachusetts, in arguing against any limitation, insisted that every measure must be taken to reduce the possibility that an election would have to be determined by the House, where evils would results from a "collision of parties." What he had in mind was that, given adequate time, the electors would exchange views and then produce a majority for one candidate. Alexander White of Virginia, at the opposite extreme, wished that the electors could meet and vote on the very day that they were chosen, to lessen the opportunity for intrigue. There was an effort by some Congressmen to raise the issue of prescribing the *manner* in which electors should be appointed, with a view to requiring popular elections, but the opinion prevailed that this matter must be left to the discretion of the state legislatures.

The eventual decision was to require that electors be chosen within thirty-four days of the first Wednesday in December, a law that remained in force until 1845, when the first Tuesday after the first Monday in November became the uniform date for presidential elections. In effect, states could choose electors at any time between the first week in November and the first week in December. This latitude was to have interesting consequences. By the time the last states voted, for example, either the results of the presidential election might already have been determined or—as in 1800—the whole election might hinge on the vote of the final state. Needless to add, the thirty-four-day period also prolonged the excitement of the election contest and provided adequate time to influence the eventual decisions of the electors.

In addition to setting the election schedule, the Act of 1792 prescribed in detail how the electoral votes of the states were to be transmitted to the president of the Senate and how the numbers of electors assigned to each state were to be determined after each decennial reapportionment. On the heated issue of presidential succession, the House by a narrow margin voted to place the Secretary of State next in line but was forced to accede to the Senate's insistence that its president *pro tempore* should be the designated officer. Behind this struggle, of course, was a clash between the supporters and opponents of Jefferson, and Hamilton acknowledged that he had used his influence to frustrate the effort of the House to make it possible for the Secretary of State to succeed to the presidency.[12]

Despite the signs of rising contention, the election of 1792 aroused less general interest and evoked less activity on the part of would-be political managers than had the first election. The new parties lacked as yet the clarity of the Federalist-Antifederalist alignment, especially at the constituency level, and, except to the small but zealous leadership groups, the stakes to be contended for were of lesser significance than had seemed to be the case in 1789. Nevertheless, for the relatively small group of insiders who became involved in the contest there were further opportunities to learn how presidential politics could be practiced.

There was a general assumption that Washington would accept a second term and that he would not encounter any opposition. The Federalists—by which we mean the party of notables identified with Hamilton—assumed that John Adams would be supported for re-election by most of the electors favorable to their cause. There was no apparent dissension within the Federalist ranks over his candidacy, nor were there to be the kinds of dubious maneuvers undertaken in 1789 to curtail his electoral vote.

The Republicans—and here we use the label appropriated to themselves by the adherents of Jefferson and Madison—sought to make a contest over the vice presidency for the purpose, as Jefferson put it, of "expressing the public sense on the doctrines of the mono-crats." If they could mobilize a respectable vote in opposition to Adams, it would be indicative of dissent from Federalist doctrines and measures and demonstrate the strength of the Republican cause. They encountered problems, however, in settling on an appropriate candidate.[13]

Jefferson might have been the logical choice, but in addition to his disinclination to be considered, he came from the same state as Washington and therefore could not expect to receive its large electoral vote. By June 1792, opinion seemed to have fixed on Governor George Clinton. His candidacy would appeal to the erst-while Antifederalists, with whom he had been identified. He was a northern man from an important state that had just re-elected him over a prominent Federalist, John Jay. And he and his associates had influential friends in Virginia, with whom they had sought to build a political relationship in 1789. There was, however, a serious drawback. Clinton's election as governor in April 1792 had been tainted with fraud. Jefferson thought Clinton's victory was so questionable that he should have declined to accept it. "I really apprehend that the course of republicanism will suffer and its votaries be thrown into schism by embarking it in support of this man . . . ," he wrote Madison. James Monroe acknowledged that Clinton was "no model for imitation" but argued that he was the best that New York had to offer, and on that shaky ground he had no hesitation in supporting him.[14] Thus, with no real enthusiasm, the Republican interest seemed to rest uncomfortably on an alliance between New York Clintonians and the Virginians.

Then what seemed like a bad situation suddenly worsened. In mid-September there were reports, first circulated by informed New York Federalists, that Aaron Burr, United States Senator from New York, would replace Clinton as the Republican candidate for Vice President. Hamilton, who to this point had displayed little interest in the election, was abruptly aroused to action. He immediately sent off to leading Federalists a stream of letters denouncing Burr as "unprincipled both as a public and private man." "I have hither to scrupulously refrained from interference in elections," he wrote. "But the occasion is in my opinion of sufficient importance to warrant in this instance a departure from that rule." For the ensuing several weeks, the Federalists remained in doubt whether Burr or Clinton would oppose Adams. Hamilton perceived an even more dreadful possibility. "'Tis suspected by some that the plan is only to divide the votes of the N[orth] and Middle States to let in Mr. Jefferson by the votes of the South," he warned a South Carolina correspondent. He described Jefferson as a man of "sublimated and paradoxical imagination"; Adams was "a firm honest independent politician."[15] Obviously, such uncertainties made calculations difficult.

Burr's possible candidacy produced consternation in the ranks of the Virginia Republican leaders when they learned of it early in October. Melancthon Smith and Marinus Willetts, influential New York Republicans, had sent a letter by special messenger to Madison and Monroe proposing the substitution, together with another communication indicating that Pennsylvania Republicans were prepared to back Burr. If the Virginians were unenthusiastic about Clinton, they were quite appalled by the prospect of endorsing Burr. He was, in the opinion of Monroe, "too young, if not in point of age, yet upon the public theatre"; some person "of more advanced life and longer standing in public trust" was required.[16]

After consulting together, Madison and Monroe wrote a diplomatic response to the New Yorkers, with whom they wished to maintain an alliance, expressing their reservations about Burr because of his modest public stature and signifying their preference for Clinton.

The delicate matter was finally settled at a conference in Philadelphia on October 16, with representatives in attendance from New York, Pennsylvania, Virginia, and South Carolina. The Virginia view prevailed; Clinton would be the Republican candidate. Melancthon Smith told the conferees that New York would give the bulk of its votes to Clinton and that he would personally undertake to solicit support in Vermont and Rhode Island. He urged that Monroe should persuade Patrick Henry to exert his influence in North Carolina. In this remarkably simple, informal manner, a roomful of Republican managers determined their vice-presidential candidate and plotted their campaign strategy less than three weeks before the states would begin to choose their electors.[17]

Given the rudimentary state of the parties, the ability of small cadres of notables to exert tremendous influence, and the method used in most of the states for appointing electors, little management was required. The number of states had increased to fifteen, and as a consequence of the congressional reapportionment that was made in 1792, there was to be a total of 135 electors. Virginia had the greatest weight, with twenty-one electors, followed by Massachusetts (16), Pennsylvania (15), New York (12), North Carolina (12), and Maryland (10). In only three states—Vermont, New Hampshire, and Pennsylvania—were electors to be chosen by popular vote on a general ticket. Massachusetts, Virginia, and Kentucky used variants of the district method. In nine states the choice would be made exclusively by the legislature. In these states, because the political complexion of the legislatures was known, it was possible to predict with some confidence their eventual electoral vote, although such forecasts might be upset by pressures exerted on the electors. Such popular interest as there was in the election, and it was negligible, was in those states where electors would be chosen by popular vote.

Even in Pennsylvania, where some excitement might have been anticipated because of the vigorously partisan press in Philadelphia and the commitment of certain leading politicians to work with associates in New York and Virginia in behalf of Clinton, the election aroused little interest. Tickets were arranged by cliques, but organizational efforts were minimal. Only about four thousand votes were cast, whereas 35,000 had voted a month earlier in the congressional election. Elsewhere there was comparable apathy and lack of party organization. Involvement in the contest over the vice presidency was confined to the parties of notables; it did not extend to the potential electorate.

With their low-keyed, behind-the-scenes activity the Republicans came close to upsetting Adams. Although Washington was again the unanimous choice of 132 electors—two electors from Maryland and one from Vermont did not vote—Adams had only seventy-seven votes. Clinton, with all the votes of Virginia, New York, North Carolina, and Georgia and a single vote from Pennsylvania, had a total of fifty. Kentucky cast four votes for Jefferson, and South Carolina produced one vote for Burr. Had Pennsylvania swung to Clinton, he would have defeated Adams.

The election of 1792 could be passed over as quite unremarkable in the development of the presidential game, except for two features. It reflected a Federalist-Republican alignment of political leaders that was to persist and broaden by 1796. Also, it forecast an alliance of anti-administration political figures in Virginia, New York, and Pennsylvania that was later to shape the strategy of the Republican party. Whether the alliance was even discussed in the course of Madison and Jefferson's "botanizing expedition" through New York State in the summer of 1791 is unlikely. But the strength of the Clintonian party in New York, its anti-Federalist orientation, and its victory—however tainted—in the state election in April 1792, made that party a desirable ally of the Virginians. Future Republican leaders in Pennsylvania, among them John Beckley and Albert Gallatin, were also perceptive enough to see the potentialities of a coordinated effort.[18] Despite notable vicissitudes, the political relationships among these three states was to be of critical importance to the Republican party in presidential politics and to the later Jacksonian–Democratic party.

The election assured that Washington would continue for another four years to give the impressive sanction of his authority both to the new government and to the party of notables—headed by

Hamilton—that dominated the administration. But there was to be no cessation of party strife. On the contrary, Madison and his increasingly cohesive associates in Congress mounted continuing attacks on the policies that they insisted were driving the nation toward monarchy, and into the embrace of Great Britain. Republican newspapers, the most strident of which was Benjamin Franklin Bache's Philadelphia *Aurora*, were unsparing in their assaults on the administration, even making the President a target of their vituperation. The retirement of Jefferson to Monticello at the end of 1794 and Hamilton's departure from the Cabinet a year later did not quiet the storm; there were other objects of controversy.

The political scene was enlivened by a series of clashes between opposing parties. First came the furious debate over the Giles resolutions censuring the Secretary of the Treasury and calling into question his financial practices. Then there was the furor over Citizen Genêt, evoking both praise and condemnation for the French Revolution. This was succeeded by differing appraisals of Washington's Neutrality Proclamation. The outbreak of the Whiskey Rebellion in Pennsylvania late in 1794, and associated with it the President's stinging condemnation of the Democratic Societies, contributed to the excitement. Most bitter and divisive of all was the long controversy over Jay's Treaty, extending from early 1795 into the spring of 1796.

These political battles served to clarify and harden divisions within Congress and to induce leading political figures to identify with one side or the other. This is not to say that even among the political elite, partisanship was firmly established. Such conspicuous figures as Edward Rutledge of South Carolina, Jonathan Dayton of New Jersey, Governor Thomas Mifflin of Pennsylvania, and Elbridge Gerry of Massachusetts—to cite but a few examples—defied partisan classification, but neutrality was becoming increasingly difficult to maintain. Neither did the heightening of partisanship extend deeply into the electorate or result in the creation of formal party organization. This was still the era of parties of notables; national politics was a game of the few rather than the many.

With the election of 1796 in prospect, speculation centered at first on Washington's intentions. Although there was a general assumption that he would decline to serve a third term, he had made no public statement and, with talk of the possibility of war with France in the aftermath of Jay's Treaty, some Federalist leaders clung to the hope that he could be induced to serve again. But by mid-May he had reached his decision, and he sought Hamilton's advice on the timing of his announcement, which he wished to delay until it should "become indispensably necessary for the information of the Electors . . . ." Late in June he regretted that he had not published his "valedictory address" earlier. "It would have been announcing *publicly*, what seems to be very well understood, and is industriously propagated *privately*," was his rueful reflection. He included among the reasons for his decision to retire "a disinclination to be longer buffeted in the public prints by a set of infamous scribblers."[19] Finally, on September 16, only about six weeks before electors were to be chosen, his Farewell Address was published. It was now certain that there must be a new President.

As a result of his decision, Washington in time was credited with having given his impressive sanction to one of the longest-standing rules of the presidential game: namely, that the President should be limited to two terms. Some of the Framers—and Thomas Jefferson—had been fearful that once elected, Presidents would use their awesome powers to remain in office for life, thus approaching the status of elective monarchs. Washington's renunciation of a third term lessened this concern, and the practice of his successors from Virginia in serving only two terms seemed to confirm the rule. Although the rule was to be tested on several occasions, it was not to be violated until 1940.[20]

Preparations for the first real contest over the presidency had been inhibited by the indecision over Washington's intentions, but they were not neglected. Early in 1795 Madison had raised the question of Jefferson's candidacy with him and had received a negative reply. "The question is forever closed with me," declared the Monticello farmer. But seeing no alternative, Madison and his associates agreed that even without his formal consent, Jefferson must be the Republican candidate. Throughout the ensuing campaign, Jefferson remained completely aloof, seemingly oblivious to the efforts being made on his behalf.[21]

The Republicans were surprisingly indifferent on the matter of a vice-presidential candidate. Burr was more than willing to fill the role, but a party conference in Philadelphia in mid-May produced no firm agreement. The Virginians remained cool to the New Yorker. Moreover, New York was now under Federalist control; it did not present the prospect of a profitable alliance. Although Burr was to campaign assiduously in his own behalf in several states, he was not generally supported by the Republican managers, except in Pennsylvania. For a variety of reasons, the Republican leaders decided to focus all their efforts on Jefferson and not attempt to marshall the second votes of their electors for a single candidate.

The Federalists' strategy was more complex, and far more hazardous. John Adams had every reason to anticipate their support. He was a senior statesman and as Vice President he was, in the eyes of many, the legitimate successor. Without making the slightest effort to advance himself, Adams felt he was now entitled to the first office. He was, however, not a favorite of the Hamiltonian circle, and he was distinctly unpopular in the South. He could not be thrust aside, but another Federalist might, through the "defect" in the electoral system, be brought in ahead of him, especially if by such means Jefferson could be kept out of the presidency. It was with these thoughts in mind that Hamilton and his friends laid their plans.

The first critical step was to identify a candidate to be coupled with Adams, preferably a southerner. Early in May, at Hamilton's instigation, John Marshall and Henry Lee sounded out Patrick Henry, whose party affiliation was still obscure but whose name carried great weight in the South. Henry was not willing to run.[22] Attention was then directed to Thomas Pinckney. His Spanish treaty had just been received with wide acclaim, he was a South Carolinian, and, because of his important Republican connections, he might undermine Jefferson's support in the South. Pinckney was still abroad—he did not return to the United States until December —but he was being regarded with favor by Federalist leaders in May, and by September, when Washington made his announcement, there was a general understanding that the Federalist ticket would be Adams and Pinckney—or Pinckney and Adams.

Despite the clear-cut contest for the presidency between the two parties, the first stage of the election process—choosing the electors—provided little excitement in most states. In eight states the choice was made by the legislatures and in five states by some form of the district system. Only in New Hampshire, Pennsylvania, and Georgia was there a popular election on a general ticket. Where the electors were appointed by the legislature, there was hardly a semblance of campaign activity. In the states that used the district method, there was scant inducement for the rival parties to develop state-wide organizations. Nominations were arranged by informal means within the districts, and although in such states as Maryland and Virginia there were some vigorous contests, with electors pledging to vote for specified presidential candidates, there was no overall co-ordination. In New Hampshire and Georgia, sentiment was so over-whelming for Adams and for Jefferson, respectively, that no great effort in behalf of their candidacies was required. That left Pennsylvania as the major battleground.

In that state Federalist and Republican legislators held caucuses—to which some non-legislators were admitted—in April 1796 and arranged their electoral tickets. In addition the Republicans had a state committee, on which the zealous John Beckley played the most active role. After Washington announced his retirement, both parties launched lively campaigns in the press, through correspondence, and by personal solicitation. Strong personal attacks on the candidates filled columns in the rival newspapers. As yet, local party organization was non-existent. The most exciting incident of the campaign was the deliberate attempt of the French Minister, Pierre Adet, to aid the Republican cause by issuing a statement on the eve of the election intended to arouse pro-French sympathies. The total vote was, again, much lower than it had been in the preceding congressional election, but it was almost equally divided between the rival tickets, with the highest Republican elector receiving 12,306 votes and the highest Federalist 12,217. Because returns from three counties were delayed, Governor Mifflin waited three weeks before certifying the election of fourteen Republicans and one Federalist elector.[23]

The most intense period of political activity in 1796 occurred *after* all the electors had been chosen. Early calculations had indicated that Adams could count on thirty-nine electoral votes from New England, plus twenty-two from New York, New Jersey, and Delaware, for a total of sixty-one. Seventy votes were needed. Some votes were expected from Maryland, but not enough to provide a majority. Early in November, when preliminary returns indicated a Republican victory in Pennsylvania, national Federalist leaders became alarmed. Adams's prospects seemed dim. "The Federal Ticket is lost here," Oliver Wolcott, Jr., reported to Hamilton from Philadelphia. "There are still hopes that Mr. Adams will be elected, but nothing more. I hope Mr. P[inckney] will be supported as the next best thing which can be done. Pray write to our Eastern friends."[24]

Hamilton understood the signal. He had been advised by Robert G. Harper of South Carolina that Pinckney would get all the electoral votes of Georgia, South Carolina, and North Carolina, and some from Virginia as well. If he were to be supported equally with Adams in New England and the Middle States, he could become President. But there was the possibility that Pinckney would be dissuaded from being a candidate when he returned to America. Writing to a confidant in South Carolina, Harper urged him to prevail on Pinckney to remain in the race, ". . . Major Pinckney may be assured, I speak from the most certain knowledge," he insisted, "that the intention of bringing him forward was to make him President."[25]

As soon as he received the reports from Wolcott and Harper, Hamilton went into action. He dispatched letters to his "Eastern friends" urging that no votes be withheld from Pinckney. "It will be to take one only instead of two chances against Mr. Jefferson," he explained, "and, well weighed, there can be no doubt that the exclusion of Mr. Jefferson is far more important than any difference between Mr. Adams and Mr. Pinckney."[26] Anxiety heightened when doubts were raised about the validity of the Vermont election, which, if invalidated, would deprive Adams of three votes. Fisher Ames, an all-out supporter of Adams, posed yet another problem. Perhaps some southern Jeffersonian electors, he reasoned, foreseeing the defeat of their candidate, would throw some votes to Pinckney. "Accident, whim, intrigue, not to say corruption, may change or prevent a vote or two," he speculated. "Perhaps some may be illegal, and excluded. What a question this would be, if made when the two houses convened! How could it be adjusted? *A la* Pologne?"[27]

There were plots within plots. In mid-November Hamilton was startled to receive from Theodore Sedgwick copies of letters that the Massachusetts Federalist had received from Jonathan Dayton. Dayton, now in the Federalist camp, presented a pessimistic analysis of Adams's prospects and proposed that, as the best means of stopping Jefferson, the Federalist electors should unite behind Aaron Burr! "I assure you that I think it possible for you and me with a little aid from a few others to effect this," Dayton had confided to Sedgwick. Knowing of Dayton's close relationship with Burr, Sedgwick was not taken in by the ploy. Neither was Hamilton, whose aversion to Burr was already notorious.[28]

As the first Wednesday in December approached, the day when the electors were to cast their ballots, Federalist managers engaged in frantic calculations. In the face of Hamilton's insistence that Pinckney must be supported equally with Adams, New England Federalists balked. They still retained the hope that Adams could be elected, but they saw that unless they deprived Pinckney of some votes, the South Carolinian would move ahead of Adams. But if Adams failed, and they cut Pinckney too severely, their actions might result in the election of Jefferson. Either course involved great hazard.

When the Massachusetts electors convened, Stephen Higginson showed them a letter from Hamilton urging a full vote for Pinckney. But amidst great indecision, they decided to give all their first votes to Adams and throw away three of their second votes. New Hampshire and Rhode Island gave no votes to Pinckney. In Connecticut the electors delayed their vote until late in the evening, waiting for the most up-to-date information before deciding what support they would give to Pinckney. "We stood upon very conjectural grounds," Oliver Wolcott, Sr., reported, "but upon such information as we had, and after a perplexing consideration, I was of opinion, and the majority of the electors adopted the same, that we ought to run very considerable risk, rather than not secure, if possible, the election of Mr. Adams, and that it would be expedient to lessen Mr. Pinckney's vote to the amount of four or five."[29] Accordingly, the electors gave four of their second votes to Pinckney and five to John Jay. Only in Vermont did the electors vote solidly for Adams and Pinckney.

More than two anxious weeks went by while reports of the electoral votes of the states trickled into Philadelphia. Jefferson, who had followed the results closely, thought it possible in mid-December that he and Adams would be tied in electoral votes and that there might be an equal division of states in the House of Representatives. "This is a difficulty from which the Constitution has provided no issue," he pointed out to Madison. If such a contingency should arise, he authorized Madison to state that he would yield to Adams. "He has always been my senior, from the commencement of my public life, and the expression of the public will being equal, this circumstance ought to give him the preference."[30]

When at last the full electoral count was known, it revealed the extent of the cross currents that had been brought to operate on the electors. Adams was to be President with seventy-one votes, one more than a bare majority. In second place with sixty-eight votes was Jefferson, now to be the Vice President. Pinckney, deprived of eighteen Federalist votes in New England, was in third place with fifty-nine votes. Burr was a distant fourth with but thirty votes, thirteen of them from Pennsylvania and only one from Virginia. Four states—Vermont, New York, New Jersey, and Delaware—cast all their votes for Adams and Pinckney; Kentucky and Tennessee did the same for Jefferson and Burr. Seemingly the most anomalous verdict was given by South Carolina, which cast eight votes each for Jefferson and Pinckney. But the results are explainable in part by the southern aversion to Adams and even more by the potent influence of Governor Edward Rutledge, who was Pinckney's father-in-law as well as a friend and admirer of Jefferson. In the final analysis, Adams might be said to have owed his narrow victory to the single electoral votes he picked up in Pennsylvania, North Carolina, and Virginia. But this would be to miss the main point, which is that the electoral vote is best viewed as a product of accident, intrigue, miscalculation, and poor management.

The election of 1796 displayed the worst features of what one zealous participant termed "the preposterous mode of election."[31] Beyond the acts of duplicity and the schemes to manipulate the votes of the electors, there were other disquieting features. In three states—Vermont, Pennsylvania, and Georgia—irregularities assocoated with the elections might well have offered grounds for challenges to their validity. One Pennsylvania elector, and presumably another one in Maryland, voted contrary to their pledges.[32] The possibility that the election would have to be decided by the House of Representatives was viewed with dread by several observers. The treatment of Burr by the Republicans and of Adams by the Hamiltonians produced resentments that were soon to have interesting consequences within both parties.

Curiously enough, the fact that the President and the Vice President were of different parties occasioned little comment or dismay. The Federalists were generally relieved that Jefferson had been kept out of the highest office, and the Republicans were heartened by their strong showing. Jefferson, who had expressed the wish that he might come in second or third in the voting, was more than pleased to accept the vice presidency and professed to be surprised by the rumors that he would decline the office. Through intermediaries he assured Adams of his good will, while Madison cherished the hope that Jefferson's closeness to Adams would moderate some of the latter's objectionable tendencies.

In the Federalist camp, postmortems on the election revealed some uneasiness. The Hamiltonians continued to justify their strategy on the grounds that their overriding objective had been to defeat Jefferson. "As the event of the election was all important and extremely critical, we judged it the soundest policy to take a double chance," explained Robert Troup of New York to Rufus King; "the contrary policy put everything at hazard, and we have made a hairbreadth escape." He was greatly concerned, however, that the Republicans were "fraternizing" with Adams and insinuating that Hamilton had engaged in treachery.[33] Partisans of Adams were irate at what they viewed as a dastardly attempt by the

Hamiltonians to win the presidency for Pinckney. Adams, himself, concluded that the Hamiltonians meant no treachery, "and they were frightened into a belief that I should fail, and they, in their agony, thought it better to bring in Pinckney than Jefferson, and some, I believe, preferred bringing in Pinckney President rather than Jefferson should be Vice President." But he did confess that "to see such an unknown being as Pinckney, brought over my head, and trampling on the bellies of hundreds of other men infinitely his superiors in talents, services, and reputation filled me with apprehension for the safety of us all."[34]

The election of 1796 was the first one in which there was a genuine contest over the presidency, and it was the last to be waged by narrowly based parties of notables. It was also distinctive in that the most intense political activity took place after the electors had been chosen. It revealed both the options and the hazards involved in playing the dual-vote game, with the Republicans choosing to disregard the second vote and the Federalists seeking to use it to gain a double chance at the presidency. As in 1792, the election was still very much an insiders' game; it was intensely interesting only to a small political elite. The mass of the electorate had yet to become aroused by the importance of the contest, and in most of the states they had no opportunity for direct participation in it. Few lessons were learned from the bizarre election, but one was of crucial importance; it was that parties could not risk the hazard of wasting any electoral votes. The application of that lesson in 1800, however, was to produce a new kind of crisis.

When Adams and Jefferson assumed their respective offices on March 4, 1797, there seemed to be at least the possibility that the strife between the parties of notables that had wracked Washington's second administration might end. Jefferson was genuinely disposed to restore his former cordial relations with the new President, and Adams, never a violent partisan, reciprocated his sentiments. Both shared with their contemporaries the belief that parties were an evil in a republic; neither of them was consumed by a burning zeal to be a party leader. Had the rapprochement succeeded, the election of 1800 might have been a tame affair, with Jefferson moving to the highest office and Adams retiring, full of honors, to his native Braintree. But such was not to be the scenario. Instead, party development proceeded at an unimagined rate after 1797, with the result that the election of 1800 was markedly different from previous contests for the presidency.

Adams's disposition to continue the policies of the Washington administration, and even to retain in his Cabinet conspicuous friends of Hamilton, quickly rekindled old suspicions and animosities. Soon Jefferson was communicating his concerns to congressional Republicans, now led by Albert Gallatin of Pennsylvania, and to other confidants. Party warfare was resumed. New issues inflamed opinion and provided rallying points. The failure to halt the deterioration of relations with France brought the disclosure in April 1798 of the "XYZ Affair," which was popularly interpreted as an intolerable insult to the United States. The Republicans were mortified, and the Federalist administration set about making preparations for a possible war. Washington was called from retirement to head an enlarged Provisional Army, with Hamilton as second in command. Funds were appropriated for an expanded navy, a direct tax was imposed to finance the defense efforts, and an undeclared naval war broke out. Then came the Alien and Sedition Acts, viewed by the Republicans as a vicious attempt to suppress political dissent.

For a brief period the Federalists appeared to have a complete ascendancy over their opponents. Congressional elections in 1798 and 1799 even brought them substantial gains in southern states. The Republicans launched their counterattack at the end of the year with the Virginia and Kentucky Resolutions, which had little immediate effect. By late 1799, however, popular sentiment for war had diminished. President Adams, to the dismay of the Hamiltonian wing of the Federalist party, dispatched a three-man mission to France to adjust the differences between the two nations. With the onus of being the "pro French" party lessened, and with discontent mounting over extreme Federalist measures, Republican prospects improved.

The rending controversies over foreign and domestic policies contributed to the extension of partisanship and to the creation of new devices of party management. Now functioning as a party leader, Jefferson was in direct contact with colleagues in Philadelphia and, through discreetly handled correspondence, with Republican leaders elsewhere, shaping strategy, guiding propaganda, and advising on tactics. In the Congress, party lines hardened; by 1799 virtually every member was identifiable as a Federalist or a Republican. Most were now elected under partisan labels. In many states even candidates for the legislature avowed their party affiliations, and within the electorate voters assumed the identity of Republican or Federalist.

Along with this intensification of partisanship, there was a rapid development of party organization. By 1800 the legislative caucus —or mixed caucus—was being used in such states as Massachusetts, New York, and Virginia to make nominations for state-wide offices, and New Jersey and Delaware were experimenting with state conventions made up of delegates from county organizations. Elsewhere, as in Pennsylvania and Maryland, local party committees were knit together through correspondence committees to achieve party unity. Whatever devices were employed, the rival parties in most states had mechanisms to secure agreement on nominations and to wage campaigns. The extent and the efficiency of the organizations should not be exaggerated, and in such states as Georgia or Tennessee organization was negligible, but a remarkable transformation had taken place in the conduct of politics since 1796. These were not merely parties of notables but broadly based structures competing for offices at several levels of government, and they altered the context within which the presidential contest of 1800 was to be fought out.

Among the factors that had stimulated party organization in the states was the recognition of the crucial role to be played by state legislatures in the presidential game. The legislatures determined how electors would be chosen, and they might vest that choice in themselves. Consequently, it became an important objective of party strategy—especially among Republicans—to win control of legislatures in the year preceding the presidential election. Held at various times between April and November, these elections could actually determine which party would win the presidency.

The strategic importance of the legislatures is well illustrated by looking at the changes that were made in the mode of choosing electors. Prior to the election of 1800, six states altered their laws in order to give the maximum advantage to the dominant party.

In four of those states—New Hampshire, Massachusetts, Pennsylvania, and Georgia—a shift was made from a popular election to choice by the legislature, with the result that in 1800 electors were chosen by popular vote in only five states.[35] Legislative choice was favored by party managers because it ensured that the majority party would name all of the state's electors and because the electors so appointed would be fully amenable to party control.[36]

In Massachusetts, where previously electors had been chosen from districts, the Federalists were alarmed by the growth of Republican strength, as evidenced by the 1800 gubernatorial election. At the urging of the state's congressional delegation, the legislature assumed to itself the privilege of appointing electors in order to guarantee a solid vote for Adams and Pinckney. Similar considerations applied in New Hampshire. Virginia Republicans consulted Jefferson on the wisdom of changing from district elections to a general ticket. He pointed out that with the majority of the states using either the legislative choice or the general ticket it would be "folly" for Virginia to risk a split in its electoral vote. Accordingly the Republicans put through a general-ticket law in January 1800. Maryland Federalists sought to change from the district system to choice by the legislature, but their efforts were frustrated by the governor's refusal to call a special session of the legislature for that purpose. A deadlock between the two houses of the Pennsylvania legislature over the issue of how electors should be chosen remained unresolved almost to the eve of the election, raising the possibility that this large state—like New York in 1789 —would have no part in the election.[37]

Attempts to manipulate the electoral process were of critical importance in New York. That state, still under Federalist control early in 1800, had previously vested the choice of electors in the legislature. The Republicans in the legislature, prodded by Aaron Burr, tried unsuccessfully to have the district system adopted. But with their surprising victory in the state election in April, they determined to retain the legislative mode. Hamilton, appreciating the great importance of New York's electoral vote to the Federalist cause, tried to prevail on Governor Jay to convene a special session of the lame-duck Federalist legislature for the purpose of enacting a law providing for district elections, but the high-minded governor declined to be an accomplice in such an outrageously partisan move.[38]

Calculated attempts to manipulate the rules of the game were not confined to the states; they occupied the attention of congressional partisans as well. The specific issue was that of how disputes over the validity of a state's electoral vote should be handled. Knowing that a controversy might arise out of the very volatile situation in Pennsylvania, Senator James Ross of that state, with the encouragement of a Federalist caucus, introduced a bill in January 1800 that would address the problem. His measure proposed that when the legality of an electoral vote was challenged, the matter should be referred to a special committee of six Senators and six Representatives with a chairman nominated by the Senate and elected by the House. This committee, which under existing circumstances would be controlled by Federalists, would have final authority to decide the case.

The Republicans were understandably alarmed by this bill. The leading spokesman for their side in the Senate debate was Charles Pinckney of South Carolina, who had been a member of the Constitutional Convention. Arguing strenuously against any congressional interference with the election of the President, especially at a time "when it is out of the question not to suppose that each party will use every means to secure their favorite object," he insisted that the Constitution had given the states exclusive authority in appointing electors. If Congress made itself the arbiter in disputes over electoral votes, it would thereby encourage disappointed minorities to invent pretexts for bringing such disputes before that body, where a decision would be made on a partisan basis. The measure passed the Senate but eventually died when the two houses were unable to agree on amendments. Madison, who had followed the course of the bill with great concern, commented to Jefferson: "It is not to be denied that the Constitution might have been properly more full in prescribing the election of P. & V.P. but the remedy is an amendment to the Constitution, and not a legislative interference." In the meantime, however, there was to be no clearly defined procedure for dealing with disputes over electoral votes.[39]

Preparations for the impending presidential election reached something of a climax in May 1800. By that time it was known that the Republicans would control the appointment of electors in New York and that the party had excellent prospects in Pennsylvania, which had elected a Republican governor the previous November. New England was considered to be safely Federalist, although there were some misgivings about Rhode Island. A close contest was anticipated in New Jersey, which elected its legislature in October, and it was forecast that Maryland, with its district elections, would be divided. Virginia, of course, was strongly Republican, as were Georgia, Kentucky, and Tennessee. North Carolina might yield one or two Federalist votes. The great question mark was South Carolina, where party lines were still not sharply drawn and where an appealing candidate might affect the outcome, as had been demonstrated in 1796. It was with such state-by-state appraisals of the political scene in mind that the party leaders approached the task of nominating the candidates.[40]

The Federalists were divided in their allegiance to Adams. Late in 1799 there were attempts to induce Washington to be the party's candidate. When these failed, some of Adams's bitterest opponents talked of running Oliver Ellsworth. "The leading friends of the Government are in a sad Dilemma," reported Hamilton. "Shall they risk a serious scism [*sic*] by an attempt to change [candidates]? Or shall they annihilate themselves and hazard their course by continuing to uphold those who suspect or hate them. . . ?" The dilemma, for the Hamiltonians, was compounded by the fact that Adams's shift in attitude toward France had greatly enhanced his popularity. New England, moreover, remained staunchly loyal to him.[41]

On May 3, 1800, the Federalist members of Congress met for the first full-fledged caucus to decide on candidates for President and Vice President. The agreement reached was "that each member in his state would use his best endeavors to have Mr. Adams and Major-General Charles Cotesworth Pinckney run for President, without giving one preference to the other."[42] The considerations involved in this decision were subtle and complex. Pinckney, a prominent South Carolinian and the brother of Thomas Pinckney, would balance the ticket because of his Southern connections. But the anti-Adams faction had an additional motive for coupling Pinckney with Adams. Knowing that in 1796 South Carolina had voted for Jefferson and Thomas Pinckney, they anticipated that regardless of the party affiliation of the South Carolina electors, they would support Pinckney. Thus, if all the other Federalist electors voted for Adams and Pinckney, the latter would come in ahead of the former. Hamilton, who despised Adams as a "weak and perverse man," was explicit in stating his position. "If I can be perfectly satisfied that Adams and Pinckney will be upheld in the East with intire good faith, on the ground of conformity, I will wherever my influence may extend pursue the same plan. If not, I will pursue Mr. Pinkny [*sic*] as my single object." Here, again, was the now-familiar problem created by that "defect" in the Constitution which Hamilton had detected in 1789.[43]

Adams and his growing body of adherents were angered by the decision that he and Pinckney should be supported "equally," for they correctly suspected a plot. The President reacted by accepting the resignations of Timothy Pickering and James McHenry, who had used their Cabinet posts to further Hamilton's intrigues. At the same time he denounced Hamilton as "the greatest intriguant in the World—a man devoid of every moral principle—a Bastard, and as much a foreigner as [Albert] Gallatin."[44] Throughout the ensuing months, suspicious pro-Adams political leaders debated whether they should throw some votes away from Pinckney while members of the Hamilton faction continued to plead with them to uphold the agreement that had been made at the Federalist caucus.[45]

Party harmony was more readily achieved by the Republicans. There was never any doubt that Jefferson would be the party's candidate for President. The only question was who to name for the second place, and the Republican victory in New York in April determined that the nomination would go to the man who had masterminded that triumph—Aaron Burr. Meeting secretly at Maraché's boarding house in Philadelphia on May 11, Republican members of Congress, and other party leaders, agreed unanimously to endorse him as Jefferson's running mate. No doubt there were some reservations, for Burr's political principles were suspect. Jefferson mistrusted him and had never been intimate with him while they served together in Philadelphia. Burr, in turn, remembering his treatment in 1796, was apprehensive that the southern electors would not vote for him. Even Madison was "not without fears that the requisite concert may not sufficiently pervade the several states." But party discipline was to hold, with frightening consequences.[46]

Overt campaigning, in the sense of activities designed to persuade and activate voters, had been quite modest in 1796 because of the immature development of parties and the short interval between Washington's announcement of his unavailability and the election. It was very different in 1800. Starting late in 1799, even before the formal nominations had been made, both parties endeavored to attract voters to their standards. In most states attention focused on the election of state legislatures, but the campaign had a national dimension as well.

Directing and overseeing the Republican campaign was Thomas Jefferson. He had launched it with the Kentucky and Virginia Resolutions and he remained very actively, though discreetly, in charge until his return to Monticello in the summer of 1800. In letters to prominent party figures he laid down the "platform" of the party. His would be an administration that stressed fidelity to the Constitution, respect for the rights of the states, and opposition to "monarchy." He favored the reduction of the national debt, minimal military forces, peaceful commerce with all nations but political connections with none, freedom of religion, and freedom of the press. He stimulated his associates to disseminate these principles in countless letters to newspapers and in scores of pamphlets, which he often undertook to circulate himself. While in Philadelphia, he conferred constantly with Congressmen and others on party matters, and at Monticello he received reports on the progress of the campaign and served as a clearinghouse for information. He understood the importance of using available media to win converts to his cause. "The engine is the press," he advised Madison. "Everyman must lay his purse and his pen under contribution."[47]

There were by 1800 about two hundred newspapers, many of them newly established, and most of them took a partisan interest in the campaign. Supplementing their efforts at political education were at least a hundred pamphlets, many of which had numerous printings, along with broadsides, handbills, and even cartoons. The barrage of Republican propaganda, in addition to attacking specific measures of Adams's administration—and characterizing the President as a believer in monarchical principles—laid heavy stress on the salient issues of economy and peace. In many localities, well-calculated appeals were addressed to specific ethnic and religious elements. There was also excessive praise for Jefferson, the unblemished republican.[48]

The Federalists in their publications concentrated on defaming Jefferson's character, a tactic that was later to be common in American presidential campaigns. He was variously assailed as an atheist, a coward, an impractical visionary, and a Jacobin. He would destroy the public credit, render the nation defenseless, and undermine the Constitution. He was denounced for making comments derogatory to Washington and for organizing a party to gain control of the government and place himself in the presidency. He was accused of sexual immorality with his own slaves and of fraudulent financial practices. As Charles O. Lerche has described it, he was the victim of a classic smear campaign.[49]

The Federalists as the incumbent party possessed the advantage of a large corps of office-holders, who worked energetically to stave off the threat of a Jeffersonian victory. Like their rivals, they engaged in formal organizing activities, as was evidenced by their use of the congressional nominating caucus and of the legislative caucus in such states as Massachusetts and Virginia. Even President Adams departed from his customary reserve. He used the occasion of a trip from Philadelphia to Washington to address audiences along his route, recalling his contributions to the cause of independence and defending his foreign policy. Somewhat less conspicuously, Aaron Burr spent several weeks traveling through New England, seeking to bolster Republican prospects in that inhospitable region.

It would require a detailed, state-by-state analysis to project adequately the excitement and intensity of the campaign. Some brief glimpses will have to suffice. In Virginia, for example, the Republican caucus had appointed a state central committee, later to acquire the name of the "Richmond Junto." This efficient party agency distributed widely an "Address" to the voters, along with lists of Republican electors and handwritten ballots for the voters' use.

In Maryland, where the campaign actually got under way in March, electoral candidates spent months stumping their districts, speaking at militia musters, race meetings, and ox roasts. Pennsylvania Republicans were unusually busy, writing and distributing thousands of pamphlets. Among them was John Beckley's *An Address to the People of the United States: With an Epitome and Vindication of the Public Life and Character of Thomas Jefferson,* which merits special recognition as the first of a new genre—the campaign biography. In Connecticut, Federalists manifested a sense of outrage when Republicans had the audacity to circulate printed tickets listing their candidates and, even more alarming, send emissaries from town to town soliciting votes. Everywhere there were efforts to involve the electorate in the partisan contest for the presidency.

The most dramatic episode of the campaign, although it had little measurable effect on the outcome, was Hamilton's personal assault on Adams. In June he utilized a trip through New England, made ostensibly for the purpose of bidding his farewell to the troops of the Provisional Army, to try to persuade Federalist leaders to abandon Adams. When this venture proved unsuccessful, he printed and circulated privately a lengthy pamphlet severely critical of Adams. Somehow, Burr obtained a copy, and portions of the diatribe soon appeared in Republican newspapers. At that point, late in October, Hamilton gave the pamphlet general circulation. Even close associates deplored his action, which really reflected the fact that he was no longer the dominant figure he had once been in the party.[50]

As the elections proceeded in state after state, the eventual result remained in doubt. By the end of November it was apparent that the contest hinged on Pennsylvania and South Carolina, which had yet to appoint their electors. Not until December 2, the day before the electors were required to cast their votes, was the deadlock between the two houses of the Pennsylvania legislature broken. After prolonged negotiations, the Republican lower house was obliged to accept an arrangement whereby the legislature chose eight Republican and seven Federalist electors. Leaving aside the votes of South Carolina, it now appeared that Adams and Jefferson would each have sixty-five votes.

In South Carolina, the formidable Charles Pinckney engaged in heroic efforts to secure a Republican majority in the legislature in the October state election, but the balance between the parties was still uncertain when the legislature convened on November 24. During the ensuing week Pinckney worked incessantly to line up votes for the Republican electors. In a tense atmosphere, knowing that the presidential election rested with their decision, legislators were placed under great pressure by rival chieftains. There were rumors of compromise proposals, centered on dividing the state's votes—as in 1796—between Jefferson and General Pinckney. But Pinckney reportedly rebuffed such an arrangement, and in the end party ranks held firm. A full slate of Republican electors, chosen by a narrow margin on December 2, met on the following day to cast eight votes each for Jefferson and Burr.

By mid-December, with the final vote not yet determined precisely, Jefferson felt he had sufficient information to assume that he had been elected. Writing to his running mate, he said that he heard that Burr might be deprived of single votes in South Carolina, Tennessee, and Georgia but that he should still come in ahead of Adams. "However," he added, "it was badly managed not to have arranged with certainty what seems to have been left to hazard." With more concern, perhaps, than he was willing to reveal, he went on to report that several "high flying federalists" had expressed the hope that he and Burr would be tied, in which case they would prevent a choice by the House of Representatives and let the presidency devolve upon the president *pro tempore* of the Senate. A few days later Jefferson realized that he and Burr were equal in electoral votes, and his shrewd calculations of the political complexion of the House convinced him that the Federalists could, in fact, block his election. "The month of February, therefore, will present us storms of a new character," was his ominous prediction to Madison.[51]

Here, indeed, was a major crisis, resulting from the hazards of the dual-vote provision of the Constitution. Now a choice between Jefferson and Burr would have to be made by the lame-duck House of Representatives, in which the Federalists had a majority. It was clear from the outset that the Republicans could count on the vote of only eight states, and nine were required for a decision. Federalist leaders, against the strenuous objections of Hamilton, determined on a course that would either put Burr in the presidency or let it pass to some designated official. The Republicans, for their part, were no less adamant in their commitment to Jefferson.

In an atmosphere charged with tension, intrigue, and excitement, the House began balloting on February 11. As had been predicted, eight states were for Jefferson, six for Burr, and two were divided. Numerous ballots on succeeding days brought no change in the alignment. Meeting repeatedly in caucus, the Federalists held their ranks firm. Jefferson was convinced that they intended to maintain the deadlock and then designate a President by law. "But we thought it best to declare openly and firmly, one and all, that the day such an act passed, the middle States would arm, and that no such usurpation, even for a single day, should be submitted to," he reported to Monroe. He and his associates also threatened to move for a new constitutional convention "to reorganize and amend the government." There were rumors of military preparations in Pennsylvania and Virginia.[52] Finally, on February 17, after thirty-six ballots, enough Federalists yielded to give Jefferson ten states, and the presidency.

Their capitulation was neither graceful nor generous. Chiefly through the efforts of Congressman James Bayard of Delaware, enough Federalist Congressmen from Maryland and Vermont abstained in order to permit those states to move into the Jefferson column. But four New England states remained with Burr, and Delaware and South Carolina cast blank ballots. In Jefferson's view, this obstinacy on the part of the Federalists was "a declaration of war." But he took heart from the observation that the rank-and-file Federalists, "alarmed with the danger of a dissolution of the government," were prepared to desert their "quondam leaders."[53] The conviction that the ultra-Federalists were prepared to go to any lengths to oppose him but that the mass of their followers might be rescued from their delusion was to inspire his appeal for harmony in his inaugural address—"We are all republicans: We are all federalists"—and shape his political strategy in office.

The election of 1800 has been characterized as a "peaceful revolution," transferring power from one party to another through the orderly process of the ballot.[54] Such was the event. A full review of the circumstances, however, suggests that the results might well have been quite different. The intransigence of the Federalist leaders very nearly produced a genuine crisis of succession. Had Burr entered into their intrigues, or had they persisted to the point of refusing to permit any election, or if they had attempted the kind of "usurpation" that Jefferson foresaw, the nation might have been dissolved or been thrown into a tumultuous interregnum. The manner of electing a President was anything but orderly. Instead, it was replete with hazards, and the near-disaster in 1801 was but the latest example of that alarming fact.

The contest between Jefferson and Adams in 1800 added new elements to the developing presidential game and reinforced others. It was, first of all, more than a personal duel, more than a competition involving parties of notables, it was a contest between recently organized political parties. Among the prominent indicators of the presence of parties were the congressional nominating caucuses, the disciplined voting of the electors, the rapid emergence of organizations in the states, and the rigidity of the positions taken during the contingent election by the House. The invention of nation-wide political parties, so evident by 1800, affected in many ways the process of electing the President.

The nominating caucus was a significant innovation. Before a congressional caucus could exert real authority, members of Congress had to be identifiable as partisans. These were *party* caucuses; they implied the existence of partisan alignments in Congress. They provided a convenient means of unifying the sentiments of political leaders from all parts of the nation, and these leaders in turn were linked to political organizations in their states. They could be denounced as cabals or for usurping the privileges of the independent voter—and they were—but they served in their crude fashion as the national agencies of their parties for the very limited function that they performed.

The manipulation by partisan state legislators of laws prescribing how electors should be chosen was another conspicuous feature of the 1800 campaign. The lesson had been learned in 1789, but now it was to be applied with unprecedented zeal. Six of the sixteen states changed the rules of the game for the election of 1800, and others refrained only because the existing mode was congenial to the majority party. The trend was clearly toward consolidating the entire electoral vote of the state, in order to give it maximum weight, and toward having the electors chosen by the legislature rather than by popular vote. Along with these maneuvers, there was the all but universal acceptance of the view that the elector was not a free agent; he was expected to cast his vote in accordance with the dictates of his party. Moreover, he was to vote for both prescribed candidates on his party's ticket.

More than ever before, the decisive political arena was the state election. The results of that election could determine how electors were to be selected and, in eleven states, which party would control the choice of electors in the legislature. Thus there was an additional stimulant to organizational efforts by the parties. There was also a new level of campaign activity. Fervent appeals were made to the voters through newspapers and other media, as well as through personal solicitation. These appeals combined an emphasis on salient issues with inflammatory rhetoric and attacks on personalities as well as direct exhortations to rally to the support of the party.

Among the results of the heightened partisan activity was a marked increase in voter participation. There had been negligible popular interest in previous presidential elections; now the electorate became involved, if only indirectly, through state legislative elections. In Virginia, one of the two states where electors were popularly elected on a general ticket, 25 percent of the adult white males, or roughly half of the potential electorate, turned out. This proportion was not exceeded until 1828. Turnout in Maryland, where the election was by districts, increased by 50 percent over 1796. At the April gubernatorial election in Massachusetts, which had implications for the presidential race, there was also a record turnout, and the gubernatorial election in Pennsylvania in November 1799, the first to be strongly contested on a party basis, brought twice as many voters to the polls as any previous election.[55] These data are admittedly fragmentary, but they are adequate to suggest that partisan campaign efforts were meeting with a positive response. It should again be noted, however, that voters were directly involved in choosing electors in only a handful of states and that even in those states less than a majority of those who were eligible were sufficiently activated to cast their ballots.

Finally, the election of 1800 necessitated, for the first time, a contingent election. Although such an event had been anticipated by the Framers, they could scarcely have imagined the circumstances associated with this one; two candidates of the same party tied in electoral votes. Here was the ultimate predicament created by the dual-vote requirement. Partisanship governed the actions of the House members, and what should have been a routine confirmation of Jefferson's election to the presidency became instead a desperate effort to exploit the rules in order to frustrate the obvious intent of the electors.

Taking a broad view of developments related to the presidential game in the decade after 1790, it can be seen that what most altered the rules of the game was the emergence of political parties, or, more specifically, of two parties. That such parties had not existed previously in the United States and that they were formed in response to national stimuli would now seem to be generally accepted. What remains open to some question is what part the contest for the presidency played in the formation of parties and how parties, in turn, shaped that contest.

The federal Constitution created, in effect, two new arenas of politics, which soon became national arenas. There was the congressional arena, involving competition for seats in Congress, and particularly in the House of Representatives, and there was the presidential arena, where the objective was to win control of the executive branch. When in the early 1790s it became apparent to contemporaries that parties were forming among the notables in the higher circles of government, the most immediate repercussions were visible in Congress. There, under the aggressive leadership of Madison, issues as diverse as the Giles resolutions or relations with Great Britain were exploited in such ways as to compel members to take positions either for or against the administration. By 1795 a fairly distinct two-party alignment was recognized; party leaders could count with reasonable accuracy their adherents and their opponents. Thus, as incumbents identified with one of the congressional parties sought re-election, or as new men were recruited to be candidates, partisanship became an important factor in the elections, and appeals to voters were couched in partisan terms. By 1797 such partisan contests were common, and by 1800 they were all but general.

The arena of congressional politics was in many respects quite separate from the presidential arena. For one thing, members of the House were all popularly elected, whereas in many states electors were not. No less relevant is the fact that in most states congressional elections were not held at the same time as presidential elections, even where electors were popularly chosen. In addition, of course, elections for Congress were biennial and those for President were quadrennial. As a further complication, Congressmen were elected on general tickets in some states and by districts in others. The point to be made is that there was not, as might be supposed, a close connection at the election level between congressional and presidential politics.

It is at least remotely conceivable that parties might have operated in congressional politics but that the election of a President, carried out rigorously within the rules devised by the Framers, would have been outside the party context. What made such a possibility unlikely, if not absurd, was the recognition that the President was no mere figurehead, that as the powerful head of the executive branch he wielded great authority over policy and patronage, and that the office was worthy of a man of the largest talents and highest ambition. Coupled with these considerations was the early discovery that, despite the Framers' contrivances, the process of electing a President could be politicized.

Because of the awesome presence of Washington, the minor skirmishes in 1789 and 1792 over the vice presidency served mainly to show how an "opposition" faction might use the occasion to demonstrate its existence. Even in 1796, with the choice to be made between Adams and Jefferson, the issue was of intense interest only to a relatively small number of notables. Both candidates remained quite aloof from the contest, party organization was negligible, and the anomalous result was accepted with remarkable equanimity.

Jefferson's willingness, indeed his eagerness, to serve as the leader of his party energized the Republican cause after 1796. He followed closely the results of state and congressional elections, now contested increasingly on partisan lines, and did whatever he could to mobilize and strengthen the party. He and his loyal associates were preparing for 1800. Adams, meanwhile, by his vigorous actions early in that year left little doubt that he would seek re-election. To the partisanship that had first been instilled within members of the Congress and then extended to their constituencies there was now added the prospect of a major confrontation of parties over the presidency. That prospect, especially for the Republicans, spurred organizing activity on the state level along with a campaign of political indoctrination oriented toward the presidential election. It was, thus, in the latter part of Adams's administration that the presidency came to play a role in partisan politics comparable with that of Congress.

Although the rapid development of two organized parties can be related to national political stimuli, it is difficult to weigh the relative influence exerted by what may be conceptualized as the separable arenas of presidential and congressional politics. In contrast to the situation two decades later, when presidential politics clearly shaped party formation, the parties that emerged in the 1790s were oriented more toward issues than toward personalities and were stimulated at least as much by the competition for congressional seats as by the contest for the presidency. By 1800 the two stimuli were mutually reinforcing.

The exigencies of presidential politics, however, had independent, identifiable effects on the organization and activities of political parties. The congressional nominating caucus was invented to meet a need exclusively associated with the contest for the presidency, although there had been prior use of the caucus to formulate and secure agreement on policy by party members in Congress. The necessity of mobilizing nation-wide support for presidential candidates obliged the parties to adopt distinctive appeals to the electorate, transcending the more limited, constituency-oriented concerns of individual congressional districts. Too, presidential parties required close collaboration of party leaders from state to state, making them actors in a national arena. Finally, and perhaps of most importance, the new rules of the presidential game had the effect of integrating state politics—especially the election of state legislatures—with national politics. In these ways the contest for the presidency strongly influenced the course of development of American political parties.

Played under uncertain and changing rules, many of them potentially hazardous, the presidential game seemingly had evolved by

1800 to a point where at least its main outlines were predictable for the future. Assuming a kind of linear progression, there would be a tightening and intensification of party organizations, improved mechanisms of national coordination, and enhanced efforts by each party to build intersectional support. As we know, such was not to be the course of events. Why the predicted pattern did not hold leads us to the next chapter.

IV

The Virginia Game

From the inauguration of Jefferson to the re-election of Monroe in 1820, presidential politics were so dominated by Virginians that they can be described most aptly as "the Virginia game." These years formed a distinctive era in the history of presidential elections. Not only did Virginians hold the presidential office for twenty-four unbroken years, they also reshaped the rules of the presidential game to ensure their pre-eminence and to reflect their conceptions of politics. Their ideas and their actions influenced profoundly the course of development—or de-development—of political parties as well as the nature of the presidency. From one perspective, this era might be regarded as an interlude, in the sense that it lacked continuity with tendencies that had seemed to be gathering momentum in the 1790s and was to be followed by a very different kind of presidential politics in the Jacksonian epoch.[1]

Virginia possessed unusual political resources and utilized them effectively in national politics. It was, in the parlance of the times, one of the large states. It stood first in the number of electoral votes in 1800 and ranked second only to New York in 1820. Because it used the general-ticket system regularly from 1800, its electoral vote was cast as a unit. It was a state in which the Republican party held unchallengable dominance and, except for a minor schism between 1806 and 1810, the party was not rent by the kind of disabling factionalism that plagued Republicans in New York and Pennsylvania. Party affairs were smoothly and firmly managed by the Richmond Junto, which functioned as the executive committee of the party. With a remarkably stable membership of influential, if not always conspicuous, men, the Junto was usually successful in harmonizing differences within the party and in organizing the quadrennial state-wide choice of electors.[2]

Virginia capitalized on its position as the foremost southern state; other states in the region followed its leadership, and it had close ties—through its emigrants—with the newer states in the West. Its congressional delegation—large, usually under able leadership, and less subject to change than was the case in most states—amplified its voice in national affairs and especially in the Republican caucuses. It would also seem that Virginia political figures, for reasons not readily elucidated, were more deeply concerned with national politics than their counterparts in other states. Or perhaps it was merely that their energies were not expended in the partisan or factional contests common elsewhere.

There can be little question that Virginia profited from, if it did not exploit, the factional discord that beset the Republicans in New York and Pennsylvania—both large and safely Republican states. New York, at least, was soon disposed to challenge Virginia's hegemony.[3] Virginia, however, had the great advantage of its internal political unity. By placing a New Yorker on the ticket as the vice-presidential candidate—except in 1812—the Virginians were able to hold that state in line despite the uneasiness of the alliance.

Finally, Virginia could present an impressive array of candidates for the first office. The times as well as political circumstances virtually required that the Presidents be selected from an extremely small circle of notables with national reputations for public service. Only later, when parties were so strongly organized as to control the nominating process, might a Harrison, a Polk, or even a Pierce be brought from obscurity to the status of a candidate. On any scale, Jefferson, Madison, and Monroe had acquired national distinction before entering the presidential contest. Their claims to preferment dated back to the Revolutionary era, and all had subsequently filled high stations in the federal government, most conspicuously, in the cases of Madison and Monroe, the office of Secretary of State. There were few, if any, statesmen among their contemporaries who could match their records of service. Under the rules of the Virginia game, their eligibility brought them to the forefront.

The succession of Madison and Monroe was not fortuitous; it was the result of deliberate management. With Jefferson in the presidency, precedent at least implied that Aaron Burr might be next in line, for both Adams and Jefferson had moved from the vice presidency to the first office. But Burr never enjoyed Jefferson's favor, and within a few months after he assumed office his political influence within the Republican party was negligible.[4] His total eclipse was evidenced by his failure to secure a single vote for re-nomination in the 1804 Republican congressional caucus. Meanwhile, Madison had been installed in the prestigious position of Secretary of State, where he could add to the laurels won in the Constitutional Convention and in Congress. Burr's successor in the vice presidency, the aged and infirm George Clinton, was hardly a serious competitor. He died in office in April 1812. As Madison assumed the presidency, the succession was momentarily clouded, for Monroe was out of favor because he had opposed Madison in 1808. Under the skillful guidance of Jefferson, however, Monroe was rehabilitated politically and brought into the Cabinet as Secretary of State in 1811. There his heroic wartime services augmented his reputation. Madison's new Vice President—Elbridge Gerry—posed no threat. Both Jefferson and Madison were scrupulous on the point of avoiding any semblance of interference in the election of their successors, but given the circumstances they had deliberately created by appointing fellow Virginians to high office, they contributed mightily to the perpetuation of the Virginia dynasty. Equally astute was their tactic of rendering the vice presidency a dead-end office.

The views of the Virginia Presidents on political parties are relevant to the strategies they pursued. With most of their contemporaries they shared the opinion that parties were an evil. Here they were drawing on the thought of Bolingbroke, on the "country" ideology of Trenchard and Gordon, and on other republican philosophers. In a well-ordered state, where citizens were imbued with "civic virtue" and where corruption was avoided, there could be neither the basis nor the need for parties. In England, the model most frequently cited, faction was associated with corruption, with the baneful policies of a Walpole, with unseemly rivalry for position and power, and with the machinations of a monied interest. A truly

republican society, freed from contests between a privileged aristocracy and the people and from the other evils inherent in a degenerate
monarchical system, would be united by a common concern for the
public good. Madison, influenced by Hume, was less sanguine that
parties could be avoided, but he felt that their potentially evil effects
could be minimized by proper checks, such as those incorporated in
the Constitution. Jefferson, too, came to accept the inevitability of
parties, and he could condone them if they represented only
moderate disagreements among honest republicans. Monroe held to
the most rigid anti-party position, believing that parties could arise
only under a defective constitution.[5]

Despite the subtle differences in their positions, the Virginians
were in accord on certain key points. They saw the Republican
party as an essential instrument to be used in opposing what they
perceived as a plot by Federalist leaders to subvert the Constitution
and foster what they termed "monarchy." The creation of a large
national debt, the imposition of heavy taxes, the introduction of a
standing army, and the exertion of executive influence on the
legislature all added up, in their eyes, to an approximation of the
worst features of the British system of government. It was therefore
legitimate to organize the republicans of the nation against such a
peril in a Republican party. Once elected, Jefferson expressed the
belief that no real differences existed among the mass of the people—
"We are all republicans: We are all federalists"—and that time
would soon rescue Federalist voters from the delusion into which
they had been led by their "monocrat" leaders. He was prepared
to accept them into the Republican party. Toward their erstwhile
leaders, however, he offered no hope of reconciliation. Only
Republicans would be appointed to office; Federalist politicians
would remain a proscribed sect. Republican candidates might accept
the support of Federalist voters, but they were never to bargain for
it. In short, he refused to recognize the Federalists as a legitimate
opposition and sought by all means to extinguish that party totally.

Madison and Monroe were equally obdurate. They continued the
ban on the appointment of Federalists and never relinquished the
suspicion that Federalist leaders were hostile to republicanism. The
behavior of many prominent Federalists during the War of 1812
did not allay their feelings of hostility. When Monroe came to office

in 1817, he looked forward with full confidence to the final termination of all parties, including the Republican party, but he nevertheless maintained the ban against appointing Federalists. For more than twenty years, the Republicans preached incessantly the doctrine that Federalism was monarchism in disguise, that it was antithetical to republicanism, and that it must be stamped out. Given the great political and rhetorical weight of these charges, the Federalists found themselves almost hopelessly on the defensive.

It is a matter of fact that the Federalists, by themselves, were never able after 1800 to present a serious challenge to the Republicans in national politics and that after 1816 they ceased even the pretense of a contest for the presidency. As a party-in-opposition, they were a failure, and their ineptitude, if such it may be called, was an important factor in the Virginia game. Their rapid decline was hardly predictable, for in 1800 they seemed to be impregnable in New England, to hold at least a strong competitive position in the states from New York to Maryland, and to have respectable bases of support even in Virginia, North Carolina, and South Carolina. Yet they carried only two states in 1804, and by 1807 all of New England had fallen to the Republicans. Opposition to Jefferson's embargo, and even more to "Mr. Madison's war" brought a revival in New England and the Middle States, but by 1817 the party was once again reduced to a remnant, holding on precariously in Massachusetts, Delaware, and Maryland.

Why were the Federalists unable to compete successfully in the Virginia game? The answer is to be found partly in terms of the strategy adopted by the Virginians of denigrating their opponents, of achieving complete supremacy throughout the South and West and commanding as well the support of New York and Pennsylvania, of taking over gradually policies that had earlier been espoused by the Federalists, and of presenting candidates who possessed large, national reputations. But the Federalists themselves were accountable for their downfall.

The Federalist party was unable to produce a leader even remotely matching the stature and ability of Jefferson. John Adams, who might have attempted the role, was totally indifferent toward rebuilding the party, was opposed to parties in principle, and remained aloof from party matters. Rufus King, John Jay, and John

Marshall might have exercised leadership, and all three were of national stature, but none of them was disposed to make the effort. The South Carolina Pinckneys—Thomas and Charles Cotesworth—were hardly qualified, and they could not even sustain the cause of Federalism in their home state. Other worthies—Gouverneur Morris, Oliver Ellsworth, Theodore Sedgwick—lacked essential qualities, and younger men—Harrison Gray Otis, Robert Goodloe Harper, Jared Ingersoll—could scarcely hope to achieve national recognition.

Without a strong leader who might have charted a consistent strategy, the Federalists held a variety of opinions regarding future courses of action. Some, like Rufus King, insisted that the party must retain the purity of its principles, await the inevitable collapse of the Republican-administered government, and then seek essential reforms in the Constitution. Others, of whom Timothy Pickering was the most conspicuous representative, saw little prospect of breaking Virginia's hold on the national government and turned their efforts toward separating New England and the Middle States from the rest of the Union. A more pragmatic school, led by Harrison Gray Otis, of Massachusetts, was prepared to seek alliances with dissident Republican factions to accomplish the defeat of the Virginians and open the way for aspiring younger Federalists to gain office and prestige. William Plumer of New Hampshire was one of the many who soon concluded that the Federalist cause was doomed and who retired from politics until the occasion was propitious to switch to the dominant party. John Quincy Adams was another conspicuous apostate. Such divided councils inhibited effective unified action and weakened the party as a national force.

There were organizational problems as well. Although, as David H. Fischer and James M. Banner, Jr., have shown, the Federalists in many states were diligent in building strong party structures, notably in New England, Delaware, and Maryland, they made only feeble efforts in such key states as New York and Pennsylvania and were quite ineffectual in the South and West. More critical was the lack of an authoritative party agency at the national level. The Federalist contingent in Congress was soon so small, and representative of so few states, that a caucus could serve little purpose. The so-called "national conventions" that met in 1808 and 1812 drew scarcely any delegates from the South or West; indeed, the remnants of southern Federalism after 1800 had slight contact with, or support from, their northern counterparts. This failure was especially serious, for the Federalists were aware of their need to invade the South, as evidenced by their repeated nominations of Charles Cotesworth Pinckney of South Carolina.[6]

However great the advantages may have been for the Republicans over their opponents, the rules of the presidential game could still frustrate their dominance. The problem lay in the requirement that electors vote for two persons without discriminating which was to be President and which was to be Vice President. This "defect," which had been so productive of hazard and difficulty in 1796 and 1800, posed an insurmountable obstacle to partisan management of the contest for the presidency. Reduced to the simplest terms, the Republicans saw that in order to win the presidency, they would have to concede the vice presidency to the Federalists. In 1800, for example, if a single Federalist elector, calculating that neither Adams nor Pinckney could achieve a majority, had thrown one of his votes to Burr, then Burr would have become President. Whenever, in the future, Republican electors voted uniformly for the same two candidates the hazard existed. The only solution would be for Republican electors to focus on a single candidate and cast their second ballots for numerous individuals. But if they followed this course, a mobilization of Federalist electoral votes on one candidate would probably ensure his attaining the second highest number of votes and would therefore make him the Vice President.

The only way to escape from this dilemma was to change the rules of the game—specifically, to require that electors cast distinct votes for President and for Vice President and that a majority be necessary in each case for election. In the three years following the election of 1796, Federalists from South Carolina, Vermont, New Hampshire, and Massachusetts proposed Constitutional amendments to this affect, but no affirmative action resulted. The excitement produced by the Jefferson-Burr tie understandably created heightened interest in the matter, and several state legislatures passed resolutions favoring an amendment. Now, however, it was the Republicans who advocated the change, and it became very much a partisan issue.

It was also an urgent issue, as Albert Gallatin pointed out to Jefferson in September 1801, and it centered on Aaron Burr. As Gallatin analyzed it, the Republican alternatives in 1804 would be "either to support Burr once more [for Vice President] or to give only one vote for President, scattering our votes for the other person to be voted for. If we do the first, we run, on the one hand, the risk of the Federalist party making Burr President . . . ." If, on the other hand, the second tactic was followed, he continued, "we not only lose the Vice-President, but pave the way for the Federal successful candidate to that office to become President." The solution, of course, would be a Constitutional amendment, but because the Republicans did not yet have a two-thirds majority in both houses, the prospects were, at best, uncertain. ". . . I see the danger," Gallatin concluded, "but cannot discover the remedy."[7]

In 1802, late in the congressional session, resolutions were introduced from the Vermont, New York, and North Carolina legislatures calling for what now became known as the "discrimination" amendment. The Republican leadership delayed bringing the matter to the floor until shortly before the session adjourned and when it appeared that the necessary two-thirds majority might be obtained. Then, with minimal debate, the proposed amendment was pushed through the House and sent to the Senate, where it failed of passage by a single vote.[8]

Gouverneur Morris took the credit for casting the decisive negative vote and explained his reasoning to the president of the New York Senate. The Constitutional Convention, he stated, had foreseen that if distinct electoral votes were cast for President and Vice President, candidates for the presidency would connect themselves with popular figures in various parts of the Union to gain their influence, thus, as he colorfully expressed it, "the Vice Presidency would be but as a bait to catch state gudgeons." He even insisted that the Framers had contemplated the possibility that "a person admirably fitted for the office of President might have an equal vote with one totally unqualified, and that, by the predominance of faction in the House of Representatives, the latter might be preferred. This, which is the greatest supposable evil in the present mode, was calmly examined, and it appeared that, however prejudicial it might be at the present moment, a useful lesson would result from it for the future, to teach contending parties the importance of giving both votes to men fit for the first office."⁹ This particular lesson, of course, was not palatable to the Republicans. The amendment was again revived at the following session, but now, realizing they still lacked the requisite votes, the Republicans decided to postpone action.¹⁰

When the new Congress met in the fall of 1803, conditions at last seemed opportune, and with the election of 1804 in the offing, haste was essential. But a delay ensued when De Witt Clinton vacated his Senate seat to assume the mayoralty of New York City, leaving the Republicans again without a two-thirds majority. A month passed before his successor took his seat. Then, late in November, the amendment was brought to the floor. In its final form, it provided not only that electors should give separate votes for President and Vice President but also specified that if no candidate for President secured a majority of the electoral vote, the contingent election by the House of Representatives would be made from among the three highest candidates, instead of five. If no candidate received a majority of electoral votes for Vice President, the Senate would make a choice between the two highest.

The Federalists sought to define the issue as one between the large states and the small states. They argued, quite correctly, that the Constitutional arrangement had resulted from a compromise and that to alter the plan would be to violate the rights of the small states. The scheme of having each elector give two votes for President had been intended to increase the likelihood of a contingent election, where the small states had equal weight with the large, and the original provision for a choice by the House from among the five highest would presumably enhance the chance that a candidate from a small state might be on the list. The new plan, it was asserted, would reduce the possibility of a contingent election and, in the event that one became necessary, curtail the prospect that a small-state candidate would be involved. Thus, it was charged, one of the "inviolable" compromises of the Constitution was to be violated.¹¹

William Plumer of New Hampshire, in a two-hour speech in the Senate, gave the fullest exposition of this position. "For the injury that this amendment will inflict on the small states, and on the eastern states, for the increased weight of influence it gives to the southern and western states at the expense of the former, what equivalent rights do you give to the small States, or to the eastern portion of the Union? You give them none—you do not even pretend it." There was merit to the argument that the amendment would destroy one of the compromises incorporated in the Constitution, but the real issue lay not between large states and small states but between Federalist states and Republican states. Plumer recognized this. He pointed out that three of the largest states— New York, Pennsylvania, and Virginia—were all Republican. "Do not gentlemen on the other side of the House consider the three states as united in one party?" he inquired. "The states east of Pennsylvania, in point of population, will soon become stationary. Those west and south of it . . . are large in territory and increasing in population. To these, add Louisiana, which is a world in itself— and the west and southern states will, on all occasions, decide the election just as they please."[12]

Republican spokesmen were frank in acknowledging their partisan motivation. Unless the amendment were adopted, declared John G. Jackson of Virginia, the Federalists would control the choice of a President. "For, unless we sacrifice the election of Vice President," he explained, "they may vote for him whom we intend for that office, and thereby make him, contrary to the wishes of the majority, the President of the United States." John Taylor of Virginia was equally explicit. It was never the intention of the Constitution, he declared, to create a situation "by which a minor faction should acquire a power capable of defeating the majority in the election of President, or of electing a Vice President contrary to the will of the electing principle." Federalist Senator Uriah Tracy responded to Taylor. "He tells us plainly that a minor faction ought to be discouraged," he observed bitterly, "that all hopes or prospect of rising into consequence, much more of rising into office, should be crushed . . . Have the minority, then, no right left, but the right to be trampled upon by the majority?"[13]

Never before in a congressional debate had the existence of parties been so openly acknowledged and discussed. Senator William Cocke of Tennessee was prepared to avow "that he was actuated by a strenuous wish to prevent a Federal Vice President being elected to that chair." Senator James Jackson of Georgia was no less vehement. "Never will there be a Federal President or Vice President again elected to the end of time," he prophesied. Samuel Thatcher, Federalist Congressman from Massachusetts, professed himself shocked by these partisan references. "We have, I believe, for the first time in this House heard the term federal and republican applied to members of this House," he pointed out regretfully. Senator Pierce Butler of South Carolina, the only Republican to oppose the amendment, chided his colleagues on their partisan motivation. He noted that the objective of the amendment was to prevent the Federalists from electing a Vice President, "When we were as Republicans out of power, did we not reprobate such conduct? Shall we then do as they did; Shall we revive party heat?"[14] His queries went unanswered.

The Federalists put up a strenuous but futile resistance. Senator Jonathan Dayton sought to amend the resolution to eliminate the position of Vice President, which he said would become a mere object of bargaining, but he met with defeat. The amendment then passed the Senate by twenty-two to ten. In the House the vote of the Speaker, Nathaniel Macon, was required in order to produce the necessary two-thirds majority. The proposed amendment then went to the states, where it promptly received the approval of all except the Federalist bastions of Massachusetts, Connecticut, and Delaware. An address to the people of Connecticut summarized the opposition view. "The plan of the amendment," it read, "is to bury New England in oblivion, and put the reins of government into the hands of Virginia forever."[15] This was not an inaccurate assessment.

The Twelfth Amendment throttled what might have been the best opportunity for the Federalists to remain in contention in the presidential game. How the game would have developed if the rules had not been changed is difficult to predict, although the elections of 1796 and 1800 suggest some clues. At the very least, the Federalists in 1804, even if they won in only two or three states, might have expected either to elect a Vice President or to reverse the order of the Republican candidates. We can only speculate about other possibilities and consequences. What would seem to be clear is that the Twelfth Amendment made a fundamental change in the rules, that the change was dictated by the circumstances of party competition, that it was essential to the conduct of the Virginia game, and that in a constitutional sense it meant the recognition and approval of the fact that parties were to operate in the election of the President.

The Twelfth Amendment virtually assured that the President and Vice President would be of the same party. But under the rules of the Virginia game, the second office was to be of little consequence and was not to be a stepping stone to the presidency. It became, as Gouverneur Morris had foreseen, "a bait to catch state gudgeons." In a smilar vein, William Plumer had warned that the office would become a "mere sinecure." "It will be brought as change to the market," he predicted, "and exposed to sale in your Elections, to procure votes for the President."[16] The Virginians used the office to gain support in critical states outside of the South, and they placed in it men who would not constitute a threat to the Virginia succession.

Burr, whom they regarded as dangerous, was treated like a pariah and became a party outcast. In 1804 the nomination was given to George Clinton, who had served seven terms as governor of New York and was an opponent of Burr. Clinton, at sixty-six, was well past his prime. William Plumer, who was personally fond of him, described him with compassion: "He is an old man—time has impaired his mental faculties as much as it has the powers of his body. He is too old for the office he now holds; little as are its duties—he is from age rendered incapable of discharging them."[17] Nevertheless, Clinton was re-elected in 1808 and died in office in his seventy-third year. Because New York was in revolt against Virginia in 1812, the vice-presidential nomination was offered to the venerable John Langdon of New Hampshire, then in his seventy-second year. When he declined on the grounds of his age and infirmity, the nomination went to Elbridge Gerry, who was only three years his junior. Gerry, who had been a Signer, a member of the Constitutional Convention, and, more recently governor of Massachusetts, was in frail health and died after less than two years in office. The Republicans returned again to New York in 1816, selecting Daniel D. Tompkins, who had served four successive terms as governor. Broken in health by his heroic exertions during the War of 1812 and beset with financial problems resulting from his inability to account properly for personal expenditures he had made to aid the military effort, he was a pathetic figure. Rarely sober, he seldom presided over the Senate and spent most of his time in New York. Despite his failings, in 1820 he was continued in office. Clinton alone had presidential ambitions, which he manifested in 1808, but they were more the product of choler—he despised Madison—than of realism. Politically shrewd though the Virginia tactics may have been, it is appalling to consider what might have been the fate of the nation had any of these Vice Presidents been obliged to assume the responsibilities of the presidency.

With their skillful strategy, their overweening strength, and their successful revision of the rules, the Virginians nevertheless were not unassailable. There were three threats to their continued hegemony. There was the danger of internal discord, both within Virginia and within the ranks of the party nationally. There was the possibility that a formidable alliance might be formed between the Federalists and dissident Republicans. Most of all, there were the emotions of envy and jealousy that could be exploited to form combinations to topple the Virginians from their lofty eminence. All of these threats became realities and lent excitement to the otherwise one-sided Virginia game.

The future seemed tranquil and bright as the Republicans prepared for the election of 1804. The prospect of the early ratification of the Twelfth Amendment was encouraging, as was the growth of Republican strength in all sections of the nation. Jefferson was willing to run for a second term; it remained only to designate a vice-presidential candidate to replace Burr. The Republican congressional caucus met on February 25, 1804, well in advance of the early state elections, to choose a nominee. Previous to the meeting, certain Virginia Congressmen had obtained George Clinton's consent to be the candidate, and a letter from him to that effect was read at the caucus. In a formal ballot, Clinton received sixty-seven of 108 votes; Jefferson's nomination was unanimous. There was some muttering against the choice of Clinton. New England Republicans complained that they had not been consulted, and some westerners were unhappy that John Breckinridge of Kentucky had not been selected.[18]

In an innovative action, the caucus appointed a thirteen-member committee to "devise measures to promote the success of the republican candidates." Because the adoption of the Twelfth Amendment was not yet assured, it was understood that the com- mittee would endeavor to manage the electoral vote given for Clinton in such a way as not to endanger the election of Jefferson.[19] The ratification of the amendment in September obviated the necessity for such arrangements.

The Federalists were utterly dispirited as they approached the uneven contest. They saw no prospect of victory, and the Louisiana Purchase, which forecast the addition of several new Republican states, dampened their hopes for the distant future. At a dinner to observe Washington's birthday in 1804, leading Federalists agreed to support Charles Cotesworth Pinckney and Rufus King as their candidates, but not until some later time was it understood that Pinckney would head the ticket. No publicity was given to the nominations, even after Federal electoral tickets were nominated. Indeed, the Republicans taunted their opponents on their reluctance to disclose the identity of their candidates. The reason, no doubt, for this tactic was that the Federalists clung to the remote hope that if the Twelfth Amendment was not ratified in time, their electors could influence the outcome of the election. Meanwhile, Timothy Pickering and his confederates looked to a victory by Burr in the New York gubernatorial election as the prelude to efforts to divide the Union. When that plan had to be abandoned because of Burr's defeat, they had only further weakened and divided their party.[20]

Against such furtive and disorganized opposition, the Republican ticket triumphed easily. Pinckney and King received only the elec- toral votes of Connecticut and Delaware, plus two from Maryland. William Plumer was persuaded that the Federalists would never rise again, and he resolved to remain silent with respect to politics. "By this means," he reasoned, "opposition will cease, and the rage of party be no more . . . The general government may then desist from their wars against our institutions."[21] On his part, Jefferson viewed with undisguised satisfaction the fulfillment of his frequent prediction that the Federalist would quickly shrink to a small, irreconcilable core of "monocrats."

Such expectations of political tranquility were soon disappointed. As the strength of the Federalist opposition diminished, Republicans indulged in the dubious luxury of factional discord. Even Virginia was not immune. Jefferson's refusal to consider a third term meant that for the first time the Republican party would have to confront the problem of leadership succession, thereby putting to a test the vague authority of the congressional caucus. The political scene was also agitated by rising debates over foreign policy, associated with the inconclusive efforts of the administration to remain aloof from the Napoleonic wars while at the same time asserting American rights on the seas. The passage of the Embargo Act late in 1807, with its disastrous effects on American commerce, escalated controversy and stimulated a marked Federalist revival, especially in New England. Because of altered circumstances, the election of 1808—in contrast to 1804—was to be enlivened by discord, confusion, and opportunism.

Most Republicans assumed that Madison would succeed Jefferson. The President's long-held esteem for his Secretary of State was well known, and although he made no overt efforts in Madison's behalf, he had given him the dominant role in the administration. Madison, however, had enemies within the party, the most vocal of whom was John Randolph. The mercurial Virginia Congressman had emerged as the administration's brilliant floor leader in 1803, but by 1806 he had broken with Jefferson and headed a small faction of Old Republicans—also known as Quids—who were especially vociferous in their assaults on Madison. Shrewd observers, like John Quincy Adams, saw in these developments a movement to set Madison aside for another candidate—James Monroe. Monroe, then engaged in delicate negotiations in London, was bombarded with letters from Randolph reciting the failings of the Secretary of State and urging Monroe to seek the presidency. Jefferson warned Monroe against Randolph's intrigues—"You must not commit yourself to him"—but when Jefferson and Madison refused to submit to the Senate the unsatisfactory treaty with England that Monroe and his associate, William Pinkney, had negotiated, Monroe was deeply offended. When he returned to

America in December 1807 he was alienated from his former close friends.[22]

Aware of Monroe's disaffection and potential candidacy, Madison's managers decided to convene the Republican congressional caucus early in the hope of forestalling a movement to Monroe in Virginia. Accordingly, a call was issued for a meeting on January 23. In the meantime, however, matters came suddenly to a head in Richmond. On January 21, rival factions of legislators supportive of Madison and of Monroe held separate caucuses. Those "friendly to the election of Madison"—about 120 in number—met in the Bell Tavern, nominated an electoral ticket pledged to Madison, and initiated the usual elaborate campaign preparations. Meeting at the same time in the capitol, the dissidents voted fifty-seven to ten to endorse Monroe, and at subsequent meetings they named their electoral slate and appointed state and county campaign committees.[23] Previously the Virginia caucus had deferred making specific nominations until after the congressional caucus had met. Now that precedent was abandoned and a new one—that of state-sponsored nominations—inaugurated.

The congressional caucus met on January 23 in ignorance of what had taken place in Richmond. Most of Monroe's supporters, knowing that they would be outnumbered, absented themselves, as did all but one Republican Congressman from New York. Thus the meeting—attended by about eighty-nine of 149 Republicans in Congress—was less a party caucus than a mobilization of Madison's adherents. Without discussion, those in attendance gave eighty-three votes for Madison and three each for Monroe and George Clinton. In the balloting for a vice-presidential nominee, Clinton got seventy-nine votes, with nine other votes scattered. As in 1804, the caucus appointed a committee of "correspondence and arrangement" representing all of the states except Delaware and Connecticut, which had no Republican Congressmen. Reports of the caucus were widely published and included the cautionary statement that the members had acted "only in their individual characters as citizens" out of a "deep conviction of the importance of the union to the Republicans" and because the caucus was "the most practicable mode of consulting and respecting the interest and wishes of all."[24]

The absence of all but one representative from the key state of New York was ominous. The Republicans of that state, divided into three warring factions, were restive under Virginia's dominance and disaffected toward Madison. George Clinton entertained hopes for the presidency, and his enterprising and ambitious nephew. De Witt Clinton, was looking to exploit any opportunity. Several weeks after the results of the caucus were known, a letter of George Clinton's, revised by his nephew, was published in the Clinton organ in New York. It denounced the caucus, stated that Clinton had not been consulted on his nomination for Vice President, and barely intimated that he was not receptive to the nomination. Soon the Clinton presses, led by James Cheetham's *American Citizen*, were booming the ancient hero for the presidency, proposing Monroe as his running mate, and viciously attacking Madison. Behind the scenes the Clintonians made overtures for Federalist support and counted on the backing of Pennsylvania, where one wing of the divided Republican party was cool toward Madison.[25]

The Federalists, as was their wont, were vacillating and tardy in their preparations for the contest. In June a committee designated by a party caucus in Massachusetts began to make arrangements for a meeting of leaders from several states that would determine strategy and agree on candidates. "I think the Federalists were never more united or more encouraged than at present," Christopher Gore wrote exultantly to Rufus King. The conference, attended by about thirty representatives from only eight states, was held surreptitiously in New York during the third week in August. Some of the Massachusetts men were in favor of throwing the party's support to Clinton, but he was anathema to many of those present. "I cannot endure the humiliating idea," Theodore Sedgwick wrote prior to the conclave, "that those who alone from education, fortune, character, and principle are entitled to command should voluntarily arrange themselves under the banners of a party in all respects inferior, and in many odious, to them." With little enthusiasm, the decision was made to run C.C. Pinckney and Rufus King again.[26]

Most Federalist newspapers failed to mention the names of these candidates; in some states it was announced that their electoral ticket was unpledged. Not until mid-September did the *National Intelligencer*, the leading Republican newspaper, become aware that

Pinckney and King were in the field, and the discovery prompted a cry for all Republicans to be "vigilant and assiduous" and to unite behind Madison against such insidious foes. In many states Federalists were uncertain whether to back their party's candidates, align themselves with Clinton or Monroe, or leave the choice to their electors. The main body of Virginia Federalists formally endorsed Monroe, to the dismay of a minority faction that clung to Pinckney and King. Still leaderless and divided, the party was quite unable to exploit the divisions among the Republicans or even mount a forthright effort in behalf of its own candidates.[27]

The campaign was waged furiously in the press. Here Madison had the advantage of the support of the leading party organs—the *National Intelligencer*, Thomas Ritchie's Richmond *Enquirer*, and James Duane's Philadelphia *Aurora*. They undertook the task of repelling the charges that Madison was a tool of Napoleon, that he was, in fact, a French citizen, that he had been corruptly implicated in the Yazoo scandal, that he was committed to the destruction of American commerce, and similar pleasantries. They were also burdened with defending the caucus, which was brought under attack by Clintonians and Monroeites for having usurped a privilege that belonged to the people, or to their legislatures. In addition, they published interminable documents related to Madison's conduct of foreign policy, which did not enhance Monroe's reputation. And, of course, they held Madison up as the "regular" nominee of the party and stressed the need for unity against the renascent Federalists.

As the date of the election approached there were so many imponderables in the political situation that Monroe could even foresee the possibility of victory. As he assessed his prospects in a letter to one of his Virginia confidants, it was likely that Clinton would withdraw in his favor, giving him New York. "That arrangement," he explained, "can only be made after the Electors are chosen." The key state, as he saw it, was Massachusetts, which had a Federalist legislature and a Republican governor. "If Massachusetts supports me, the Eastern States generally will probably join her in it." The danger was that if he courted Federalist support, the mass of discordant Republicans would unite behind Madison. Somehow they must be persuaded that the continuance of the administration's policies would "involve in one common ruin everything that is dear to us." He had, he said, offered to withdraw from the contest, but his friends had prevailed on him to continue on the grounds that "the cause of free govt. would be advanc'd, not injur'd."[28]

Monroe's calculations were both faulty and overly optimistic. The New England Federalists, concluding that neither Monroe nor Clinton could be elected, stayed with Pinckney and King. The rival Pennsylvania Republican factions at the last moment arranged a "harmony" electoral ticket pledged to Madison. In New York, the Clintonians proved to be unable to control the legislature, which chose the electors. Exaggerated rumors of a Federalist resurgence gave urgency to calls for party unity, and Madison swept to an overwhelming victory. Pinckney and King carried Massachusetts, New Hampshire, Rhode Island, Connecticut, and Delaware and picked up three votes in North Carolina and two in Maryland for a total of forty-seven votes. Clinton got only six of New York's nineteen votes. Monroe received none. Madison was the choice of 122 electors; the reluctant Clinton had 113 votes for Vice President, losing six Republican votes in Vermont and three in Ohio. The Virginia electors had considered dropping Clinton because of his antagonism to Madison, but they decided to support him as the caucus nominee in the interest of future party harmony.[29]

The presidential contest of 1808 saw numerous challenges to the rules of the Virginia game. There was the division within the ranks of the Virginia Republicans, represented by Monroe's stubborn candidacy. There was, as well, the apostasy of the New York Clintonians, threatening the tenuous Virginia-New York alliance. There was the irregularity of the state-sponsored nominations of Madison and Monroe prior to the convening of the congressional caucus. The refusal of 40 percent of Republican Congressmen to attend the nominating caucus was a serious challenge to the authority of that agency, as were the violent attacks made on it subsequently by disaffected partisans. The openness with which the Monroeites and the Clintonians greeted possible Federalist support was violative of the rules. So, too, was the publication of Monroe's 24,000-word "letter" explaining and defending his negotiations with

England and the release by Jefferson of Madison's diplomatic correspondence, both actions intended to influence the election.

But despite these deviations, the game retained familiar elements. Madison—whose supporters in Virginia outnumbered Monroe's more than four to one—secured the status of the "regular" Republican candidate through the endorsement of the Junto and the caucus. The South and West followed Virginia's lead; Pennsylvania and New York pursued their usual querulous but subservient course. The inept Federalists posed a sufficient threat to give some credence to appeals for party unity. And Madison, with his luminous if somewhat battered reputation, took his destined place in the succession.

Madison's administration was anything but tranquil. Diplomatic problems with England and France defied resolution. Petty factional bickering marred party harmony. A weak and discordant Cabinet seriously impaired the effectiveness of governmental operations. Discontent with Madison's policies, especially as they affected commercial and maritime interests, found expression in a strong Federalist revival in New England and contributed to divisions within the Republican party, especially in New York and New Jersey. On the positive side, the breach with Monroe was healed, and he entered the Cabinet as Secretary of State in March 1811, thus taking his place as the heir presumptive.

When the Twelfth Congress met in a special session in November 1811 there was a general sense that fateful decisions impended. The failure of all efforts to secure American objectives either through diplomacy or economic coercion was confronted, and belated and inadequate military preparations were begun. On June 1, 1812, Madison sent a message to Congress reciting the nation's grievances against England and, in effect, presenting war as the only remaining option. The House voted promptly, seventy-nine to forty-nine, for war, and two weeks later the Senate acted by the close vote of nineteen to thirteen. All forty Federalists in Congress voted against the war, together with twenty-two Republicans, including several from the key state of New York. The war found the nation divided; it was opposed by the Federalists and was generally unpopular in the North, except in Vermont and Pennsylvania. It was against this background that the presidential election of 1812 was to be contested.[30]

Anticipating opposition to Madison's renomination, his supporters in Virginia took the initiative and late in February 1812 arranged a meeting of the Republican legislative caucus, which named a slate of electors pledged to vote for him. A similar action was taken early in March by the Republican members of the Pennsylvania legislature, thus assuring Madison of party support in these two large states. When the congressional nominating caucus met on May 18, Madison was the unanimous choice of the eighty-two Republicans who attended, but nearly forty Republicans—including most of the New York delegation—absented themselves, either because they were opposed to the caucus in principle or because they favored another candidate. John Langdon was nominated for Vice President, but after he declined because of his advanced age and infirmities, the caucus reconvened on June 8 and named Elbridge Gerry as his replacement. Adding a new feature to the developing ritual, Gerry stated his formal acceptance of the nomination in a widely published letter. At this second caucus, "a ballot was opened for such persons as were not present at the former meeting," and ten Congressmen added their endorsement of Madison. Subsequently these nominations were applauded by Republican caucuses in several states.[31]

New York, however, was again determined not to play the Virginia game. The Clinton faction there had manifested its insubordination in 1808, and now, with the assistance of other elements in the party, it supported the ill-considered pretensions of De Witt Clinton, then serving as mayor of New York City and lieutenant governor. Late in May at a caucus of ninety of the ninety-five Republicans in the legislature, Clinton was nominated unanimously for the presidency. This decision was influenced by the presence of several Congressmen, who reported critically on Madison's ineptitude and urged that Clinton be brought forward to replace him. The caucus adopted resolutions hostile to the congressional nominating procedure and appointed a General Committee to correspond with other states and take appropriate measures to advance Clinton's candidacy. Following the meeting, a delegation waited on Clinton and informed him of the nomination. As dictated by the prevailing etiquette, he responded that "he sensibly felt and duly appreciated so distinguished a proof of their confidence."[32] These actions, with the rationale that accompanied them, were significant as marking out a pattern for the state-sponsored nominations that were to be much in vogue in the years between the demise of the congressional caucus and the emergence of the national convention.

Clinton was, and remains, a political enigma. Oscillating between the heights and the depths of New York politics, relying more on personal charisma than on organizational loyalties, he has been credited with such various achievements as the invention of the spoils system and the construction of the Erie Canal. "His objects were always magnificent," in the estimation of his contemporary, Jabez D. Hammond, "his ends were always such as evinced an elevated and lofty mind, but he did not seem to be aware of the necessity of providing ways and means to accomplish those ends."[33]

Clinton's nomination, in addition to reflecting his own extravagant ambition, is best understood as representing the intense antipathy of New York politicians toward the long dominance of Virginia. George Clinton had made a feeble effort to topple the dynasty four years earlier; now, with the times apparently more propitious, his nephew would make the challenge. If the Federalists could be brought to co-operate, and if the sentiment opposed to the war—and to Madison's conduct of the war—could be mobilized, the prospect was not hopeless. As the war proceeded, and disaster followed disaster, culminating in August with the humiliating surrender of Detroit, opposition to the administration mounted.

Much depended on the course the Federalists would take. Beginning in June, and moving in their customary leisurely fashion, leading Federalists discussed and corresponded on the subject. Some were for backing Clinton, others insisted on maintaining the purity and integrity of the party, and some proposed forming a new party. Early in August, after delicate preliminaries, the high command of the New York Federalists—John Jay, Rufus King, and Gouverneur Morris—deigned to meet with Clinton, but only with the firm understanding that the sole topic to be discussed would be the formation of a Peace party; there was to be no mention of Clinton's candidacy. At the conference, Clinton stated that he had broken forever with the Madison administration and that he was personally in accord with the views of those present on the war, but he admitted that he could not yet express these sentiments publicly. Neither was he prepared at that time to participate in the organization of a Peace party, suggesting that such plans be deferred for several weeks. When he attempted to outline his own presidential prospects, he was cut off by Morris, who said that any "general or continental measures" must await discussion by the Peace party throughout the Union.[34]

No alliance resulted from this meeting. Instead, the New York high command proceeded with vague plans to launch the new Peace party. A large and enthusiastic meeting in Washington Hall on August 18 of the "Friends of Liberty, Peace, and Commerce" adopted resolutions—drafted by Morris—denouncing the war as unjust, unwise, and untimely and calling on all citizens "to lay aside party distinctions, to banish party feelings, to unite" in overthrowing the national administration. Meetings were to be held in each county, at which representatives of the "friends of peace" would be chosen. They would confer with one another and with like-minded men in other states on measures to rescue the nation from impending calamity.[35] This plan was not entirely original. New Jersey Federalists had already taken the initiative in holding a state convention of Friends of Peace in June, and the tactic was being adopted elsewhere. What remained to be determined was who would be the Peace party, or Federalist, candidate.

This fateful question was addressed by a secret Federalist "convention" held in New York City in mid-September. With more than sixty delegates in attendance from eleven states, the meeting grew out of discussions among party leaders from Massachusetts and Pennsylvania. Most of the delegates favored an outright nomination of De Witt Clinton, but Rufus King was vehement in his opposition. On the other hand, efforts to induce John Marshall or Bushrod Washington to be candidates, with a view to gaining support in the South, had come to naught. After three days of heated discussion, it was agreed that it would be inexpedient to nominate a Federalist candidate. Instead, the party would support such candidate "as would be likely to pursue a different course" from Madison. A five-member committee—all Pennsylvanians—was appointed "to ascertain the result of the elections for Electors, and the candidates whom they would be inclined to support and to communicate the same as expeditiously as practicable to the Electors of the several states."[36]

The Federalist conclave, and the ambiguous decision at which it arrived, was intended to be kept secret. Almost inevitably, there were leaks, and garbled reports of what had taken place soon appeared in Republican newspapers. On October 15, the *National Intelligencer* published a lengthy and not entirely accurate version of the meeting, adding the powerful charge that the conspirators had conferred with Clinton and reached an agreement with him. Immediately Clinton's General Committee in New York branded the account as "entirely false," adding that Clinton's sentiments were "decidedly Republican." With something less than full candor, Gouverneur Morris and others who were involved issued their denials. But the *National Intelligencer* persisted in the accusation that Clinton was the candidate of a "coalition" of Federalists and dissident Republicans, and the Republican press generally took up the cry.[37]

The Clinton strategists faced a dilemma: they were dependent on Federalist support but could not openly embrace their old opponents without offending their Republican adherents. In a like vein, they could not adopt the extreme Federalist position on opposition to the war. Neither were they prepared to abandon entirely their claim that they were true Republicans by entering wholeheartedly into the organization of the Peace party, which was viewed as Federalism in disguise. The most authoritative expression of their position was set forth in an "Address" issued by the Clintonian General Committee on August 17, 1812.

This statement first sought to justify a state-sponsored nomination by attacking the validity and propriety of the congressional caucus, repeating arguments which had by now become familiar. More to the point, the Address sought to justify New York's claim to the presidency. Noting that Virginia had held the office for twenty of the first twenty-four years and was now seeking to extend that span, the authors acknowledged that such dominance had aroused jealousy. Even worse, the persistence of the "Virginia influence" had embittered relations between the agricultural and commercial states, with consequences detrimental to the Union. New York, as a Middle State, could moderate this ominous cleavage. With respect to the war, the Address blamed the administration for failing to make adequate preparations and for incompetence in the direction of the military effort, as well as for imposing onerous and unpopular taxes. In a subtle bid to the Federalists, it was stated that Clinton would "select the best talents in the nation to fill the high stations of government." "From his energy we anticipate vigor in war, and a determined character in the relations of peace."[38]

This rather mild manifesto was answered point by point in a lengthy pamphlet issued by the Pennsylvania State Republican Committee in mid-September. The whole thrust of this rejoinder was that Madison was the only regular Republican candidate, that he had been nominated in accordance with the usages of the party, that his nomination had been warmly endorsed by Republican caucuses in eight states, and that he should not be proscribed merely because he was a Virginian. Clinton's reputation was limited; "the nation have not tried, proved, and found him honest and capable." Outside of New York, he was supported only by Federalists. Madison and Gerry, by contrast, were known throughout the nation; the mention of their names "would call forth panegyrie, and interesting recollections of important public events in which they have borne distinguished parts."[39] The message was clear. Stand by the party; place your confidence in men of exalted reputation.

In those states where the Federalists held control the campaign was relatively quiet until mid-October, when it was finally revealed that the party would back Clinton. In doubtful states, and especially in New Jersey, Pennsylvania, and Ohio, the Clintonians were active in establishing newspapers, distributing bundles of pamphlets, and dispatching emissaries to arrange meetings and enlist local activists. Clinton, himself, issued no statements and engaged in no overt electioneering. Thus his adherents could interpret his views, especially on such critical issues as the war and his relations with the Federalists, as suited the occasion. Madison, however, departed from precedent by responding publicly to laudatory addresses from New Jersey and South Carolina Republicans, using the opportunities to make dignified appeals for patriotic support of the war.

These epistles were given extensive notice in the Republican presses.[40]

The Federalists generally sought to remain in the background during the campaign, adopting in most northern states the Peace party label. In Massachusetts their electoral ticket bore the heading: "Friends of Peace, Commerce, a Naval Defence, and the Constitution." But late in October, Federalists were advised that "the votes of every Federal Peace-maker Elector chosen in Massachusetts will be given for De Witt Clinton, Esq." Only by such a course, which obliged Federalists to "choose between Caesar and Pompey," could the Virginia dynasty be ended and New England commerce be revitalized. In Pennsylvania, where the Clintonians made valiant efforts to gain support, even to the extent of placing Jared Ingersoll of that state on the ticket as Clinton's running mate, they met with little success among traditional Republican voters. The Federalists —who styled themselves as Federal Republicans—endorsed Clinton in mid-October but brought little energy to the cause. Virginia Federalists followed a distinctive course by holding a convention at Staunton in late September and forming an electoral ticket pledged to Rufus King and William R. Davie of North Carolina.[41] The Clinton campaign generally was not well co-ordinated because of the lack of a firm alliance between the Clintonians and the Federalists.

In three states manipulation of the laws affecting the appointment of electors had a bearing on the results. In Massachusetts, which changed the mode of election prior to every presidential election, there was a conflict between the Federalist lower house and the Republican Senate that was not resolved until late in October. Then, in what was regarded as a victory for the Federalists, it was determined that electors would be chosen from the six Common Pleas districts. In New Jersey, where the general-ticket system had been instituted in 1804, the Federalists—or Friends of Peace— obtained an unexpected victory in the October legislative election. In a singularly brazen act, they repealed the general-ticket law on the day the voters were to go to the polls, enacted a new law vesting the choice in the legislature, and proceeded to appoint electors pledged to Clinton. A comparable tactic was employed by the Republicans in North Carolina. That state had used the district system since 1796, and as recently as 1808 the Federalists had been able to carry three districts. In 1811, over widespread protests, the Republican legislature repealed the district law and took upon itself the appointment of electors. The result was that all of the state's votes went to Madison. Had these changes not been made, it is likely that Madison would have gained the total electoral vote of New Jersey, and possibly some votes in Massachusetts, but that he would have lost votes in North Carolina.[42]

Informed estimates prior to the election had Clinton assured of about ninety votes from New England, New York, New Jersey, Delaware, and Maryland, with 110 votes required for victory. His adherents hoped that additional votes might come from Pennsylvania, Ohio, or North Carolina. Pennsylvania was the first state to vote—on October 30—and it gave nearly a two-to-one plurality to Madison. In Ohio, despite the fact that rival Republican factions ran electoral tickets pledged to Madison, the Clintonian ticket was resoundingly defeated. Attention then turned to North Carolina, where the Republicans had only a narrow and unstable majority in the legislature. Rumors circulated that emissaries of Clinton were on the scene offering bribes to doubtful legislators. But when the electors were at last chosen on November 21, the Madison slate secured an overwhelming vote.

Once again the South and West had remained firm, and in the "Keystone State" of Pennsylvania the Republicans had patched up their internal differences and rallied to the support of the Virginia candidate. New York was lost. The youthful Martin Van Buren, making his first appearance in the legislature, assumed command of Clinton's forces, outmaneuvered the Republican faction that was now supporting Madison, and gained the total electoral vote of the state for Clinton. In the final tally, Madison received 128 electoral votes to 89 for Clinton. Gerry ran ahead of Madison, picking up one vote in New Hampshire and two in Massachusetts. It was a close contest, but in actuality Clinton had been able to add only New York and New Jersey to the states that in 1808 had gone for Pinckney and King, and it is at least questionable whether he could have carried New Jersey in a popular election.

There were many notable features to this election. It was the first wartime election. It was the first to have a major state-sponsored candidate in the person of Clinton. It occasioned the first public statements by a candidate, bland though Madison's letters were. It involved the first attempt at the formation of a fusion party—the Peace party. It produced a rudimentary form of party platform, represented by the "Address" of the New York Clintonians. Most of all, however, it exemplified the perils of the Virginia game.

The very success with which the Virginians managed the presidential game provoked a challenge to their dominance. The common bond of New York Clintonians and the Federalists was less the war issue than their shared hatred of Virginia, and the Virginia dynasty. The most persistent and clamorous theme in the opposition newspapers was that of overthrowing the Virginians, with all that they represented in terms of southern and western influences and of actions prejudicial to the northern commercial and maritime interests. The electoral vote reflected this feeling. Clinton mobilized the states north of the Potomac, except for Vermont and Pennsylvania; the South and the West spurned him.

The Virginians could rely on their strong sectional base, but in addition they could count on the strength of a party loyalty that had been nurtured for nearly twenty years and that could be aroused— as in Pennsylvania—by the barest rumor of a threat from the Federalists. These were obstacles that the Clintonians and the Federalists could not surmount, even with the assistance of an unpopular war. Until the sectional alignment should be broken or Virginia's leadership should falter, the Virginia game would continue.

In 1816, as Madison's second term drew to a close, the succession was again at issue. His presumed heir was James Monroe. After his insurgent candidacy in 1808, Monroe had undergone a process of political rehabilitation, supervised and encouraged by Jefferson, that restored him to the good graces of the party and brought him in 1811 to the key post of Secretary of State. His achievements during the war had been generally admired, and with a record of almost continuous public service dating back to 1776, he felt entitled to advance to the presidency. Not without some difficulty, he obtained the backing of Virginia's political managers—the Richmond Junto—and the support of the extremely influential administration and party organ, the *National Intelligencer*.[43]

His path was not, however, free of obstacles. Jealousy of the Virginia dynasty now surfaced not only in New York, but even more significantly in the South and the West. Younger politicians in those regions, chafing under their continued subordination to the Old Dominion, were determined to make an effort to upset the succession. The candidate around whom they proposed to rally was William H. Crawford of Georgia, who enjoyed considerable personal popularity among Congressmen and who had acquired stature through serving as Minister to France and as Secretary of the Treasury. The New York Republicans, divided as usual, played a devious game, with one faction favoring Crawford and another—led by Van Buren—ostensibly promoting Governor Daniel D. Tompkins.[44] There was considerable potential in the Crawford movement; what was lacking was firm commitment on the part of the candidate.

Virginia again seized the initiative. On February 14 the Republican legislative caucus appointed a slate of electoral candidates which, though not formally pledged to Monroe, were understood to be his supporters. Within the next few weeks, Monroe's candidacy was endorsed by the Republican legislative caucus in Pennsylvania and by state conventions in Massachusetts and Rhode Island. In mid-February the *National Intelligencer* came out strongly for Monroe, and its lead was quickly followed by those Republican newspapers that were favored with administration patronage from Massachusetts to Georgia. All sounded the theme that Monroe was the "statesman of the *longest tried*, and most proved integrity, without regard to geographical lines." Opposition to him was based on unjustifiable "local prejudices" against his Virginia connection, and this sentiment, it was alleged, was chiefly propagated by Federalists. In the meantime, several dissident papers had disclosed a preference for Crawford, and the New York Republican legislative caucus had recommended Tompkins.[45]

Crawford supporters were in a quandary. Their soundings revealed that they could probably get a majority of votes in the congressional nominating caucus. But Crawford, himself, told his intimates that he did not wish to challenge Monroe, and rumors of his reluctance spread. The result was indecision on the part of those opposed to Monroe. Should they attempt to force a nomination through the caucus, at the risk of dividing the party, when they were unsure of Crawford's willingness to be a candidate? Some were disposed to move forward. On March 10 an anonymous, printed notice circulated through Washington announcing that the customary Republican nominating caucus would be held on March 12. The *National Intelligencer* promptly warned that the call did not originate with Monroe's friends and that they would not attend. Only fifty-seven Congressmen, mainly Crawford men, heeded the call, and they prudently decided not to proceed with a nomination. Instead, they issued a call for another meeting to be held March 16.

When this caucus met, 119 of the 141 Republicans in Congress were in attendance. Despite the rumors that Crawford would be withdrawn, Monroe's managers were anything but confident. They sponsored two resolutions intended to prevent a caucus nomination, both of which were defeated. Then, by a vote of 65 to 54, Monroe was nominated over Crawford. For its vice-presidential candidate, the party turned again to New York, selecting Governor Tompkins by a wide margin over Governor Simon Snyder of Pennsylvania. Perhaps recalling the incident in 1812, when Langdon had declined the nomination, a committee appointed by the caucus addressed letters to both Monroe and Tompkins, asking whether they would serve if elected. Both signified their willingness in brief, dignified public letters. "I can only say," responded Monroe, "that, should the suffrages of my fellow-citizens call me to that trust, I should feel a duty to enter on it."[46] This was his only public utterance of the campaign.

Crawford's interests had been badly managed. He was genuinely reluctant to contest the nomination of Monroe, and he had instructed his friends, when the caucus convened, to make a magnanimous statement of his refusal to be a candidate. His leading backers, however, absented themselves from the caucus, and, as Crawford explained to Albert Gallatin, "deprived themselves of the right to make the proposed statement." Thus, in the public eye, Crawford was denied the credit he had hoped to gain by standing aside, although he continued to feel strongly that his behavior placed Monroe in his debt and entitled him to anticipate Monroe's support when the presidency next became available.[47]

Later, the maneuvers in the 1816 caucus were to be held up as clear proof of the iniquities of the caucus system. Monroe, so went the argument, was overwhelmingly the popular choice among Republicans. That he had very nearly been denied the caucus nomination was the consequence of nefarious intrigues among the members of Congress. Had Crawford been nominated, the presidency thereafter would be determined by such congressional plotting; the people's role would be usurped. The use of the caucus was justifiable only when it gave voice to the general sentiments of the people; it was illegitimate when it sought to impose a President on the people. There was merit in these charges. New England, where Monroe enjoyed general favor among Republicans, had only five Republican Congressmen, so its sentiments were not represented adequately in the caucus. Moreover, the Crawford movement was carried on largely behind the scenes by politicians whose leading motive was to end the Virginia dynasty. But the fact that important political figures in New York, New Jersey, Pennsylvania, Maryland, North Carolina, Georgia, Kentucky, and Tennessee were prepared to oppose Monroe is indicative of the strength of the anti-Virginia feelings.[48] They had had enough of the Virginia game.

Once assured of the "regular" nomination, Monroe faced negligible opposition. The Hartford Convention and Jackson's victory at New Orleans ended the Federalist revival, and Madison's belated espousal of such old Federalist measures as a national bank and a protective tariff deprived that party of any semblance of a program. Yet another blow to its slim hopes was the defeat of Rufus King for the governorship of New York in April 1816. "I presume that the failure will, as I think it should, discourage the Federalists from maintaining a fruitless struggle," King wrote to one of his closest friends. "Federalists of our age must be content with the past."[49] When a committee of Philadelphia Federalists sought to arrange another secret conference to prepare for the presidential contest, Gouverneur Morris discouraged the effort. Leave the Republicans unchallenged, he advised, and they will soon divide.[50] Still, there were diehards in Massachusetts who would not yield, and they roused themselves to change the election law once more, this time to place the appointment of electors in the legislature. As Jefferson had predicted, some Federalists could never be reconciled. The remnant was small, however. Only Massachusetts, Connecticut, and Delaware went counter to the tide; their legislatures chose Federalist electors, who gave thirty-four votes to Rufus King.

With the perception that the Virginia dynasty would end with him, Monroe devoted much thought to the composition of his Cabinet. He reported his conclusions to Jefferson late in February 1817. It would produce a bad effect, he had decided, to name anyone from the South or the West as Secretary of State. "You know how much has been said to impress a belief, on the country, north and east of this, that the citizens from Virginia, holding the Presidency, have made appointments to that dept. to secure the succession, from it, to the Presidency, of the person who happens to be from that State." If he were to follow the traditional pattern, he would array against the administration "the whole of the country, north of the Delaware, immediately," and the states south of the Potomac in due course. Accordingly, he looked to "the Eastern States" and selected John Quincy Adams for the post. "I can hardly hope, that our Southern gentlemen, who have good pretentions, will enter fully into this view of the subject," he concluded, no doubt with Crawford in mind.[51] Crawford remained, somewhat irritably, as Secretary of the Treasury. When Henry Clay and other westerners refused to accept the office, John C. Calhoun was appointed Secretary of War. Benjamin Crowninshield continued briefly as Secretary of the Navy and William Wirt became Attorney General. There were no Virginians in the Cabinet.

With his Cabinet arranged on this new principle, Monroe looked forward to an end of partisan strife. Although he was unwilling to adopt Andrew Jackson's recommendation that the long-standing ban against the appointment of Federalists to high offices be removed, he saw no need for parties in a properly constituted republic and perceived himself not as the head of a party but as the head of the nation. Crawford took a less elevated view of the political scene. Aware as early as March 1817 that rival candidates were maneuvering to capture the presidency on the retirement of Monroe, he foresaw the breakup of the old parties and the formation of new combinations. Clay, in his opinion, would emerge as the leader of the West. Adams would compete with De Witt Clinton for the favor of the North. Crawford, himself, would have a strong base in the South. In its broad outlines, his assessment was valid; a new game was in the offing, and it got under way as soon as Monroe took office.[52]

None of the aspirants was prepared to challenge Monroe in 1820. Despite the frightening controversy over Missouri and the difficulties arising from the economic crisis that developed in 1819, the surface aspect of presidential politics was remarkably dull. A call was issued for a congressional nominating caucus early in March, addressed now to "such republican and other members of congress as may think proper to attend," but when fewer than forty Congressmen turned out, they decided that it was "not necessary" to make any nominations. John Quincy Adams understood why the call had been issued. "This is the result of caballing," he recorded in his diary. His information was that Clay wanted to supplant Tompkins in the vice presidency, thereby advancing his move toward the presidency. Ahead, Adams foresaw an alliance between Clay and Clinton. The decision of several state delegations to boycott the caucus frustrated Clay's gambit, and by common agreement, Monroe and Tompkins were regarded as the party nominees.[53]

The Federalists offered no opposition. Although a total of thirteen Federalist electors were chosen in Massachusetts, Delaware, and Maryland, they all voted for Monroe. William Plumer, a Republican elector from New Hampshire, sounded the only discordant note. Having a low opinion of Monroe, and admiring John Quincy Adams, he cast a solitary vote for the rising statesman from Massachusetts. An era that had begun with the intensely exciting and divisive election of 1800 drew to a close as the "Era of Good Feeling."

A whole generation elapsed between the inauguration of Jefferson and the departure of Monroe, and although the Virginia dynasty constituted a fixed element in the political scene and dominated the presidential game, some obscure currents of change were flowing beneath the surface of events. Their cumulative effect was not to be fully apparent until 1824—or later—but then the character of the presidential game was to be altered drastically.

The most important of these developments had to do with the method of choosing presidential electors.[54] Throughout these years, partisan legislatures in several states engaged in the practice of manipulating the mode of election. The most glaring example was Massachusetts, which changed its system for every election. In 1800, 1808, and 1816, the choice of electors was made by the legislature; in 1804, 1812, and 1820, different forms of the district system were used. In some years, as in 1812, the specific plan adopted resulted from a compromise between the opposing parties; in other years, as in 1808, it represented the determination of the dominant party in the legislature to control the electoral vote. New Jersey, too, gained notoriety for this practice, especially in 1812, when the Federalist legislature abruptly took upon itself the naming of that state's electors. Also conspicuous was North Carolina, which shifted from the district plan in 1808, to legislative choice in 1812, restored the district plan in 1813, and then adopted the general ticket in time for the 1816 election.

Manipulation was one problem; another was the variety of methods from state to state. In 1800, electors was chosen in ten states by the legislature, by general ticket in two, and by districts in three. By 1824 the general ticket was used in twelve states, six employed some form of the district system, and six vested the choice in the legislature.

It is not a simple matter to explain this diversity, but some generalizations are possible. All the older states, from Vermont to Georgia, had by 1812 adopted either the legislative or general-ticket method, with the exception of Maryland. Under either plan, there was the assurance that the electoral vote of the state would be cast as a unit, thus giving the state—or its dominant party—the maximum weight in the election. Partisan motives operated strongly to favor such a winner-take-all approach, and it is not coincidental that it was so generally adopted in the older states, where parties were more firmly rooted than in the newer states. Where either the legislative or general-ticket system was used, a state-level party agency—usually the legislative caucus—would prepare a slate of electors; in the absence of such an agency, it would have been all but impossible to employ the general-ticket plan, for it is difficult to conceive how voters, especially in the larger states, could have prepared their own electoral tickets. Even in the legislature, some confusion would have resulted if, in the absence of a party agency of some kind, each legislator had prepared his own electoral ticket. There was, in short, a close relationship between parties and the winner-take-all electoral modes; parties found such modes most adaptable to their purposes, and such modes, in turn, were dependent on parties.

There was some tendency for the newer states—those admitted to the Union after 1790—to favor the district system. It was used at various times by Kentucky, Tennessee, Illinois, Maine, and Missouri. Where party competition was negligible and most voters at least nominally Republican, and state-level party agencies weak or non-existent, the district system was tolerable. On the other hand, Ohio and Mississippi from the first used the general ticket, and Louisiana and Indiana opted for choice by the legislature. There was, then, no clear pattern of preference; local circumstances determined.

Despite the variety and instability of practices, the most notable trend over the period was toward the general-ticket system. Between 1800 and 1824 the number of states adopting this mode increased from two to twelve. It was consistent with the partisan, winner-take-all ethic and had the additional popular virtue of admitting the mass of the electorate to participation in the presidential contest. Among the larger states, only New York clung to the legislative method, until it capitulated to the demands of its outraged citizenry in 1828. Pronounced though this trend was, it was not decisive. No clear and overwhelming consensus had yet formed on this crucial question of how the President should be elected. As Senator Mahlon Dickerson of New Jersey put it in 1817, scarcely any public official was "elected or appointed by a rule so undefined, so vague, so subject to abuse, as that by which we elect the Chief Magistrate of the Union."[55]

No Constitutional topic more frequently engaged the attention of Congress than that of attempting to fix a uniform and proper method of electing the President. Between 1800 and 1822, scores of amendments in this vein were proposed and debated. The plans that received the most attention and enlisted the strongest support involved the choice of electors by districts. On four occasions, such proposed amendments were carried by the necessary two-thirds vote in the Senate, but they fell short in the House. At almost every session of Congress after 1812 the issue of reforming the method of presidential selection provoked extensive discussion and revealed significant but often ambiguous thoughts about the American political process and the presidential system.[56]

The general-ticket system was brought under heavy attack. It had been adopted reluctantly by many states only because others had instituted it, thereby enhancing their political power. Such had been the rationale for its adoption by Virginia in 1800. The only justification for it, in the view of most critics, was self-defense. Similar arguments applied against the legislative mode, with the added indictments that it mingled improperly state and national concerns, created inducements to corruption, and deprived the people of their voice in the election. The only way to eliminate these improper methods of choosing electors would be by a Constitutional amendment requiring the district plan.[57]

Three major arguments were consistently advanced in support of the district system. There was, first of all, the need for uniformity, in order to remove the elements of manipulation and instability. Second, the district system was to be preferred because it lessened greatly the likelihood of sectionally based parties, which were fostered by the legislative and general-ticket methods. Finally, the adoption of the district system would lessen the influence of caucuses, thereby freeing the citizen-voter from the improper control of political managers.

The case for uniformity was a strong one. "Sir," declaimed Congressman Jabez D. Hammond, "the power of the States to choose, or direct the manner of choosing Electors for the President, is a rotten, a gangrenous part of our Constitution, which if not removed will infect and poison the body politic."[58] Senator Mahlon Dickerson agreed, pointing to the numerous instances where the method of election had been changed "according to the dictates of the interest, the ambition, the whim, or caprice of party and faction."[59] "It illy comports with the dignity or the real interests of this great Confederacy to suffer this struggling among the States for the advantage over each other," argued Representative Israel Pickens. "Yet so long as the subject is left at large, contending parties will resort to it for present purposes."[60] Speaker after speaker called in similar terms for uniformity. The standard opposition position was that the Framers clearly intended that the matter should be left to the states, and their rights in this regard should not be impaired.[61]

The point made most insistently in favor of the district plan was that it would reverse or moderate the dangerous tendency of the other methods to foster geographically based parties. "A reason against any mode of giving the individual votes of states, of all others the most important, and most affecting the vital existence of the Union," explained Representative Pickens, "is its tendency toward a geographical severence of parties." He pointed out that in 1812 "a whole section of the Union, with a small exception voted for one individual [Clinton], while the opposite section supported his opponent [Madison]." Had the district system prevailed in that election, he argued, electors in most states would have divided their votes. "This would exhibit a promiscuous division of sentiment extending itself over the whole nation, and not capable of being delineated by State lines or the course of rivers." District elections, declared one of Pickens's colleagues, would promote the co-operation of individuals in different parts of the Union. "Their joint exertions . . . must create one of the strongest bonds of union." With the district plan, maintained another speaker, "All dangers from geographical divisions and jealousies on the approach of an election would be done away with. The Chief Magistrate would consequently be, as was intended, emphatically the choice of the whole people, and of all the different interests throughout the Union."[62]

The response to those attacks on the general-ticket system was equivocal. In his typical fashion, John Randolph denounced any interference with the rights of the states. His fellow Virginian Senator James Barbour charged that the general ticket had been first introduced by "the Eastern States" to serve their purposes, and the southern states had been obliged to adopt it in self-defense. The proposed amendment "deranged the compromise in which the constitution had its being." In his view, the popular will had always prevailed in past elections. "There was . . . no danger to the liberties of the people from the present mode of electing a President of the

United States." Others simply took the position that the Constitution should be maintained inviolate. No one, it seemed, was prepared to offer a reasoned defense of the merits of the general-ticket system.[63]

Proponents of the district plan maintained that its general adoption would go far toward eliminating what they saw as the baneful aspects of parties. Reflecting their ambivalence toward parties as legitimate agencies and sounding on occasion much like the Progressives of a later generation, most of them accepted the inevitability of parties but sought to cure their "excesses." Their chief targets were the congressional nominating caucuses and the state legislative caucuses and their political managers. So long as states cast their electoral votes as units, and so long as success in the presidential contest depended on forming combinations of states, political management would rest with the few who controlled the caucuses, and the people's role would be minimized.

William Gaston of North Carolina, after describing the intentions of the Framers and the safeguards they had sought to erect against cabal and intrigue, satirized the prevailing practices:

> The *first* step made in the election is by those whose interference the Constitution prohibits. The members of the two Houses of Congress meet in caucus, or convention, and there ballot for a President and Vice President . . . The result of their election is published through the Union under the name of a recommendation. This modest recommendation then comes before the members of the respective State Legislatures. Where the appointment ultimately rests with them, no trouble whatever is given to the people . . . When, *in form*, however, the choice of Electors remains with the people, the patriotic members of the State Legislature . . . back this draft on popular credulity with the weight of their endorsement. Not content with this, they benevolently point out to the people the immediate agents through whom the negotiation can be most safely carried on, make out a ticket of Electors, and thus designate the individuals who, in their behalf, are to honor this demand on their suffrages. Sir, the whole proceeding appears to be monstrous.

Gaston's conclusion was that while the district plan would not totally end improper influences in presidential elections, it would "deprive cabals of facility in combination, render intrigue less systematic, and diminish the opportunities for corruption."[64] Others echoed this analysis. With the district plan, it was argued, "no caucus or self appointed committee will be required to form a ticket for the State." "The people will be free from the imposing influence of a nominated ticket and will be able to fix on their own candidates with a fair prospect of success."

The proponents of district elections did not advocate or anticipate an end to parties, but they did foresee a moderation of sectional alignments and evil practices. "The amendment now proposed," explained Senator Dickerson, "will neither increase nor diminish the relative strength of parties which now divide, and which, in all probability . . . will continue to divide the United States." He acknowledged, however, that particular parties would gain weight in some states and lose it in others. "Faction cannot but exist," conceded Gaston, "but it will be rendered tolerant." "Do gentlemen fear that party concert cannot be preserved, if Electors of President and Vice President be chosen by districts?" inquired a Representative from New York. His answer was to point out that in the House, most of whose members were elected from districts, there was no lack of partisanship.[65]

Year after year these arguments in favor of the district plan were persuasive to the majority of both houses of Congress. The prevailing variegated system had relatively few defenders. But although the Senate acted favorably on four occasions, the amendment could not secure the necessary two-thirds vote in the House. In a representative vote in 1821 it failed by a small margin, 92 to 54.[66] Thirty-one of the negative votes came from Pennsylvania and Virginia, where there was an obvious reluctance to give up the vast power those states wielded through their general-ticket system. Ironically, a method of election condemned by representatives of the overwhelming majority of the states was to continue because two large states opposed a change. Even more ironic was the fact that by 1836 every state but one—South Carolina—had capitulated in "self-defense" to the abhorrent general-ticket system. In this way a key rule of the presidential game acquired acceptance.

The issue of the mode of election was related to the matter of voter participation in presidential elections, and here, too, there was an undercurrent of change. Throughout the era of the Virginia dynasty, three factors inhibited popular involvement. One, of course, was the practice in nearly half the states of entrusting the choice of electors to the legislature. A second, which was especially apparent after 1812, but which operated in some states even earlier, was the lack of any real contest. A third factor was restrictions on the suffrage.

Between 1790 and 1824, in what may be termed a "quiet revolution," all but three states—Rhode Island, Virginia, and Louisiana—eliminated those property or tax-paying requirements that had previously barred a segment of adult while males from the polls. For the reasons mentioned previously, this liberalization of the franchise was not immediately reflected in presidential voting; its full impact was not to be felt until 1840. But as suffrage restrictions were reduced and as the proportion of states confining the choice of electors to the legislature declined, the conditions were created for transforming the contest for the presidency from one in which only a very small minority of voters was directly involved to one that could call forth 80 percent of adult white males. All that would be required to achieve such participation was vigorous competition between closely balanced parties.[67]

There had been other changes since 1800 that were to contribute to the reshaping of the presidential game. They are so obvious as to require only brief notice. Eight new states entered the Union between 1800 and 1824, altering and complicating sectional influences on politics. The relative voting weights of the states changed. Virginia sank to third place behind New York and Pennsylvania; Ohio's electoral vote exceeded that of Massachusetts; Kentucky outstripped South Carolina. A new, post-Revolution generation of politicians came to maturity—Clay, Adams, Jackson, Calhoun, Van Buren, Crawford—and in their attitudes and behavior they differed from their predecessors. The people, too, were changing, casting off habits of deference and vigorously assuming participant roles. The old party system was crumbling, with the Federalists after 1815 recognizing the futility of their position and the Republicans dividing into factions preparatory to a contest over the succession.

The Virginia game was over. Many of its distinguishing features were to disappear after 1824. There was not to be another Virginia candidate for the presidency. The political unity of the Old

Dominion, effectively marshalled and guided for so long by the Richmond Junto, was shattered in the 1830s. The congressional nominating caucus, so prominent a feature of the Virginia game, was but a vestigial and discredited remnant when it held its final meeting in 1824. The solid sectional alignment of the South and the West, which provided the secure base for Virginia's nominees, fell apart. The pattern of using the vice presidency to soothe the obstreperous New Yorkers while installing the heir apparent in the post of Secretary of State was disrupted. The opportunities to manipulate modes of election ended as the general-ticket system acquired acceptance. The limited access of the electorate was soon broadened. The rigid code that had inhibited candidates for the presidency from even appearing to intervene in the election process was to be relaxed. All this is not to say that every trace of the Virginia game vanished or that there were no elements of continuity, but it is to emphasize the distinctive qualities of that game and to suggest that by 1824 the time had arrived to experiment with new and very different rules.

V

The Game of Faction

As President Monroe entered on his second term in 1821, he reviewed with satisfaction the progress of the republic and exulted in the near-perfection of its tested political institutions. Grave foreign threats had been met and repulsed. Menacing internal divisions, confronted most recently in the controversy over Missouri, had been resolved. A broad consensus had been achieved on major elements of domestic policy, except for some fine-spun theoretical differences related to internal improvements and the tariff. The nation, he observed, was free from the defects that had brought down the ancient republics, where aristocracies had been pitted against the people or where popular rule had degenerated into the tumult and disorder of anarchy. That republican principles and soundly contrived institutions had proven their efficacy was demonstrated, above all, by the subsidence of party strife.

Even the presidency, it seemed in 1820, had ceased to be an object of contention. The future, as always, was inscrutable, but there was some basis for believing that the high expectations of the Framers might be realized. Now the first office might be conferred by the people on that citizen whose exalted reputation for long and distinguished public service, unblemished character, and conspicuous talents had placed him foremost among his countrymen. Such, it might be argued, had been the case with Monroe. With the great policy issues adjusted, with sectional rivalries muted, with Virginia no longer exerting its claim to dominance, and with old party distinctions fading, on what basis could the presidency be contested?

The answer, soon to be revealed, was that many ambitious

aspirants of the rising generation, supported by their "friends" and by their native states and regions, would contend for the prize. Around these men factions would form, not on old party lines or on explicit issues of principle or policy, to contest the succession. The factional competition represented a radical departure from the Virginia game and from the hazardous experiments that had preceded it. In these circumstances, the old rules and codes of behavior no longer applied; it was to be a new kind of game.[1]

In retrospect, we know that this era was brief. It began in 1822 and by 1832 the outlines of yet another format were emerging. In the interval there were to be extraordinary innovations. Former rules, inhibitions, strategies, and organizational mechanisms were cast aside as the protagonists groped for acceptable and effective means to reach their objectives. Brief though the game of faction was, it was not ephemeral; it left enduring influences on the larger shape of the presidential game. Moreover, it produced alarming tensions between the old republican ideal of a non-politicized presidency and the actuality of political behavior.

In order to focus attention on certain themes, or common influences, that characterized the game of faction, it is appropriate to recapitulate in only the sketchiest fashion the narrative of the elections of 1824, 1828, and 1832. In part, no doubt, because they all featured the intriguing figure of Andrew Jackson, as well as because of their unusually dramatic elements, these elections have received more than ordinary treatment by historians. They are best understood, however, not as discrete incidents but as related elements in an unfolding pattern of innovation and development.

Contemporary observers became aware of the new game of faction early in Monroe's second administration. The astute Hezekiah Niles noted in January 1822 that an unprecedented number of presidential candidates—he listed eight, not including Jackson—were already in the field. How they differed from one another, except as personal rivals, was not clear. "The former great landmarks have been destroyed," Niles remarked, "and the great measures of policy with which gentlemen will be guided, if elected to the presidency, are left to speculative opinions and indefinite presumptions."[2] By 1823 the number of aspirants had been reduced to five. The leading figure, until he was disabled by a protracted illness in September, was

William H. Crawford, the Secretary of the Treasury. Next in favor was John Quincy Adams, who had switched from the Federalists to the Republicans in 1808 and, after a varied diplomatic career, was now Secretary of State. Rising rapidly in popular favor was the Hero of New Orleans, Andrew Jackson. Henry Clay, brought into prominence by his brilliant career in Congress, and John C. Calhoun, soon to drop out of the race and settle for the vice presidency, were the other contenders. Except for Jackson, they were all "insiders," enmeshed in intricate maneuvers and intrigues in Washington to advance their interests. All were Republicans.

It soon became apparent that the traditional congressional nominating caucus would not be able to unite the disintegrating Republican party behind a single candidate. At a rump session attended only by his supporters, Crawford received the caucus nomination, while his rivals, denouncing the discredited institution, were placed in nomination by caucuses or conventions of their "friends" in various states. With four candidates in the field, it was a confusing contest. Adams could count on the solid backing of New England, where, although he was not personally popular, he was regarded as a favorite son. Crawford's strength was in Georgia and Virginia, and he expected that New York, where Van Buren was his able advocate, would aid his cause. Jackson, somewhat surprisingly, was taken up with great enthusiasm in Pennsylvania, had widespread support in the South, and vied with Clay and Adams for the western states.

In some states, such as North Carolina, the contest was between Crawford and Jackson, in others, like New Jersey, it pitted Jackson against Adams, while in Ohio and Indiana, Adams, Jackson, and Clay all had respectable constituencies. In only a few states— notably New Jersey, Maryland, North Carolina, Ohio, Indiana, and Illinois—were there close contests. Elsewhere, one candidate or another enjoyed overwhelming popularity, essentially on the basis of his standing as a state or regional favorite. Jackson alone, by his victories in Pennsylvania and New Jersey, showed a capacity to transcend a purely sectional appeal. Because of the lack of intense competition in most states, campaign efforts were modest and voter participation was low; only about one-quarter of the eligible voters were drawn to the polls.

As had been anticipated, no candidate received a majority of the electoral votes. Jackson led with 99, followed by Adams with 84, Crawford with 41, and Clay with 37. Although the figures are relatively meaningless, Jackson was also the leader in popular votes. The House of Representatives, with each state having a single vote, now had the responsibility of choosing the President from among the top three candidates. Between December 6, when Congress convened, and February 9, when the fateful ballot was taken, Washington seethed with intrigue and rumors of corruption. While Jackson remained aloof, refusing to engage in any conversations on the "presidential question," Adams held lengthy discussions with Clay and other key figures, seeking to win over the requisite number of states. When the ballots were counted, Adams had the votes of thirteen states—of which four had given the majority of their electoral votes to Jackson and three had been carried by Clay—to seven states for Jackson and four for Crawford.

While the election was pending, it was reported that Clay had been offered, and had accepted, the post of Secretary of State. The charge was made that the appointment was the result of a "corrupt bargain" to secure Adams's election. "So you see," Jackson pointedly remarked to one of his confidants, "the *Judas* of the West has closed the contract and will receive the thirty pieces of silver."[3] His view of the House election was that the voice of the people had been denied by the intrigues of a few. Adams was conscious of the awkwardness of his situation. He referred in his inaugural address to the fact that he had been chosen over one who had "a larger minority of the primary suffrages than mine," but he could see no useful purpose to be served by declining the office.

The questionable circumstances of this election set the stage for a sharper contest in 1828. An "Administration party," in which Clay figured prominently, rallied around Adams, who was expected to be a candidate for a second term. Jackson, who had been remarkably restrained in the 1824 campaign, left no doubts about his eagerness to challenge Adams and vindicate himself—and the people. In October 1825 he was put in nomination by Tennessee and gained endorsements elsewhere. In Washington, Vice President Calhoun and Van Buren, a member of the Senate, collaborated effectively in organizing opposition to administration measures.

Jackson campaign committees were organized, subsidized presses were established, and the "corrupt bargain" charge was chanted incessantly. Meanwhile, old party distinctions were ignored as political leaders and voters took upon themselves the designations of "Adams men" or "Jackson men." Not without some misgivings, especially in Virginia, former Crawford activists moved into the Jackson camp, while Adams sought to extend his base beyond New England.

In a campaign that featured personal villification, along with subtle sectional appeals, unprecedented efforts were made to arouse the electorate. Jackson was portrayed variously as the people's choice, the blameless victim of intrigue, or as a headstrong military chieftain lacking in all the qualities essential to a statesman. Adams, with equal variety, was depicted as his father's son—a monarchist at heart—or as a man with the experience and talent to meet any challenge. The candidates themselves remained discreetly silent, although it was only with the greatest difficulty that Jackson's advisers prevailed on him not to respond to the malicious personal attacks on his wife and his mother, as well as himself.

In a pattern strongly reminiscent of 1812, Adams and Jackson divided the electoral votes of the states very much along sectional lines. Jackson carried every state south of Maryland and west of New Jersey. Adams swept New England, along with New Jersey and Delaware, and took nearly half of the electoral votes of New York and Maryland, where the voting was by district. In several of the states Jackson won, especially in the South, his pluralities were greater than two to one; Adams achieved similarly lop-sided victories in four New England states. With relatively close competition between the candidates in a third of the states, and with all but two of the states choosing electors by popular vote, participation was double that of 1824. The final tally of electoral votes gave 178 for Jackson to 83 for Adams. Calhoun was re-elected as Vice President.

The simplicity and the clarity of the contest between Adams and Jackson in 1828 was in marked contrast to the political scene that was to be exhibited four years later. The forces that rallied behind Jackson in 1828 hardly constituted a party in any meaningful sense of that term, and the same may be said of the Adams supporters.

The Jacksonians lacked a name—other than that of Jackson party —and they were lacking as well in any articulated program or even any national nominating agency. In many states they confronted no organized opposition. Such unity as they possessed derived from their desire to install Jackson in the presidency.

During Jackson's first administration, the process that was to transform a faction into a party was soon under way. Jackson's break with Calhoun and the subsequent shake-up of his Cabinet, his designation of Van Buren as his heir apparent, his sharp position in opposition to rechartering the Bank of the United States, and his calculating use of his patronage powers, all contributed to shape the leadership, the constituency, and the policies of the emerging party. The introduction of the national nominating convention in 1832 and the increasing, but not yet general, use of the label "Democrat" further established the identity of the party. At the same time, especially in the Middle States and New England, strong state party organizations formed to challenge what had been the dominant Adams party and to support the Jackson administration.

As the Jacksonians sought to solidify their position, the opposition struggled with formidable problems. With Adams on the sidelines, Clay became the most conspicuous opponent of the administration, but he could not expect the kind of sectional backing Adams had received in New England and he enjoyed little popularity in the South. As a further complication, a new party, the Anti-Masons, became a potent factor. It had emerged in New York in the aftermath of the mysterious disappearance in 1826 of one William Morgan, who it was believed had been assassinated by the Masons because he had revealed the secrets of the order. By 1830 it had assumed the status of a major party in New York, Pennsylvania, and Vermont and had some importance in several other states as well. So promising did its prospects appear to many of its shrewd leaders that plans were made to enter the arena of presidential politics. Meanwhile, the nation was agitated by the revival of debates in Congress over large issues of domestic policy—the Bank, the tariff, and internal improvements—by controversies over Jackson's exercise of his presidential prerogatives, and by unprecedented attacks on slavery by William Lloyd Garrison and his fellow abolitionists.

The campaign featured the appearance of a major innovation, the national nominating convention. The Anti-Masons led the way in September 1831 by holding such a convention of delegates, which nominated William Wirt of Maryland, a former Attorney General under both Monroe and Adams. Adopting the name "National Republican," Clay's adherents held a similar convention three months later and unanimously presented the Kentuckian to the country as their candidate. Last to meet were the Democrats, who convened in Baltimore in May 1832, primarily for the purpose of securing agreement on Jackson's running mate. Calhoun had separated himself from the party and his rival, Martin Van Buren, received the highly coveted vice-presidential nomination. Although there were outward appearances of harmony, some southern delegations were unhappy with the selection of Van Buren, for they shared the general understanding that he was being groomed as Jackson's successor and the prospect did not please them.

Despite the attempts to give prominence to the issue raised by Jackson's veto of the recharter of the Bank, the campaign was in many respects less exciting than that of 1828. With the opposition to Jackson divided in some states because of the candidacies of both Clay and Wirt, with the South—except for South Carolina—and most of the West still faithful to Jackson, and with Maine and New Hampshire shifting to the Democratic column, the Old Hero scored an easy victory. Clay captured only Massachusetts, Rhode Island, Connecticut, Delaware, and Kentucky, and shared the electoral vote of Maryland. Wirt's lone victory was in Vermont. Voter participation remained close to the 1828 level; approximately 55 percent of the eligibles went to the polls. In terms of its implications for the future, the most interesting aspect of the election was the manifestation of strong anti-Van Buren sentiment among the professed Jacksonians in Virginia, North Carolina, Georgia, Alabama, and Mississippi. In those states, tickets were arranged that were headed by Jackson but which substituted Philip P. Barbour of Virginia for Van Buren as the General's running mate.

The elections of 1824, 1828, and 1832, which have been dealt with so cursorily, can not be understood as representing contests between parties or as constituting referenda on explicit policy choices. They focused on personalities, and it was around those personalities—Jackson, Crawford, Adams, Clay—that factions formed. A party did not select Jackson to run for President, rather, Jackson's candidacy gave rise to the formation of a coalition in support of his election. The same generalization would apply to Adams and to Clay.

This is not to say that these candidates represented nothing more than their individual personal qualities. On the contrary, each embodied special appeals. Adams was perceived as a northern man, with all that that implied in terms of sectional attitudes, and as one who would extend the sphere of the federal government. Clay projected the image of a strong nationalist and, with less vigor, a spokesman for the West. Jackson, in addition to being the nation's greatest military hero since Washington, was identified with southern and western interests and, after 1824, took on the mantle of a tribune of the people. Politicians and voters responded in terms of these appeals. This game of faction, with its orientation toward expressive personalities, was carried on in a changing and unstable context of rules, practices, and codes of behavior. It was a distinctive but dynamic type of game, whose characteristic features, and especially its enduring elements, now require delineation.

To an extraordinary degree, presidential politics in this era centered on personal rivalries, elaborate intrigues, and calculated plots to "destroy" opponents. All the prominent actors on the presidential scene engaged in these tactics, and all were made the victims of treachery, deceit, and slander. Each was obliged to be on his guard for such assaults, often from unexpected quarters, as well as to be in a position to launch counterattacks. In 1824 and 1828 the plots revolved around the presidential candidates; after 1828 the most elaborate and ominous intrigues were related to Jackson's designation of his successor.

The maneuvers preceding the 1824 election were intricate in the extreme.[4] Crawford, regarded as the front runner because of his strong showing in the congressional caucus in 1816, was eyed with hostility by all his rivals, and especially by Adams and Calhoun. In 1823 his administration of the Treasury department was attacked in a series of letters—signed A.B.—published in a Washington paper friendly to Calhoun. When Senator Ninian Edwards of Illinois was revealed as the author of the letters, he expanded on his charges, and Crawford was forced to defend himself in an ensuing congressional investigation. This attempt to "destroy" Crawford was typical of the savage tactics being used, but it failed; he was exonerated of any wrongdoing. In a similar incident, Adams's conduct at Ghent was called into question on the basis of a cleverly altered letter of Jonathan Russell. Adams, in a widely publicized rejoinder, denounced the document as a forgery and recorded privately his suspicion that Clay was behind the whole affair.

As the election approached, there were devious efforts to effect, or frustrate, alliances. At one point, both Crawford and Adams factions made overtures to Clay, proposing that he accept the vice presidency. Adams intimated that he would be glad to have Jackson as his running mate, noting "his fitness for the place, the fitness of the place for him, and the peculiar advantage of the geographical association." When Crawford's prospects faltered, Van Buren consulted with his friends in Virginia about the possibility of shifting their support to Adams. Crawford's friends, determined to proceed with their plans to have him nominated by a congressional caucus, dangled the vice-presidential nomination before Clay and Adams in an effort to induce the backers of these aspirants to join in the caucus. As Jackson appraised his rivals, he expressed strong enmity toward Clay and Crawford, some regard for Calhoun, and admiration for Adams. The references could be multiplied, but they would only reinforce the point that Washington seethed with intrigue as the rival candidates played the game of faction.[5]

The climax of these behind-the-scenes dealings was, of course, the House election in February 1825. Hints of the sorts of negotiations that went on can be gleaned from contemporary correspondence, but because we can never learn what took place in face-to-face discussions, the full story can scarcely be told. It is sufficient to observe that Jackson was deprived of the votes of states that he had carried in the election, that Clay's influence was exerted in Adams's favor, and that Clay received the top post in Adams's cabinet.

Jackson was later to charge that, through Representative James Buchanan of Pennsylvania, he had been offered Clay's support in return for a Cabinet appointment, but Buchanan, when pressed, did not fully substantiate the General's version of the incident. In

January 1825, on the eve of the House election, an unsigned letter in a Jacksonian newspaper accused Adams of having already offered Clay the Secretaryship of State in return for his assistance. Clay immediately issued a public denial, at which point Representative George Kremer of Pennsylvania gained undying fame by revealing himself as the author of what was to become known as the "corrupt bargain" charge. Attempts were made to have the accusation investigated by a congressional committee, but Kremer refused to appear. Nevertheless, the general impression had been created that Adams's victory was the result of intrigue, even that the legitimacy of his accession to the presidency was tainted, and the Jacksonians would not let the issue die.

Adams correctly forsaw that the circumstances associated with his election would produce a determined opposition to his administration. Within a few days of the House election, he predicted in his diary the objective of his opponents. "It is to bring in General Jackson as the next President. To this end the administration must be rendered unpopular and odious, whatever its acts might be, and Mr. Calhoun avows himself prepared to perform this part."[6]

Calhoun and Van Buren overcame past differences and "united heart and hand to promote the election of General Jackson."[7] Through their joint effort an opposition faction was mobilized in the Senate. It was extremely effective in harassing the administration, most notably by attacking the Panama Mission that constituted such a key element in Adams's foreign policy. Calhoun, in turn, was made the target of abuse by administration supporters and even by some within the Jackson camp who wanted to deny him the place of Jackson's running mate in 1828. Meanwhile, despite Jackson's aversion to Crawford, Crawford's hatred of Calhoun, Calhoun's mistrust of Van Buren, and Van Buren's hesitancy about making a public declaration of his support for the Old Hero, the disparate elements that were to form the Jackson coalition joined warily together in anticipation of ousting the beneficiaries of the "corrupt bargain."[8]

Vicious in-fighting and intrigue did not cease with Jackson's victory in 1828. Even before he took office, dissension was brewing over the succession. Calhoun, as Vice President and as one who had helped to construct the Jackson coalition, thought of himself as the heir apparent. But he had powerful enemies, the most active of whom were the embittered Crawford, Secretary of War John H. Eaton, and presidential confidant William B. Lewis, and they planted suspicions in Jackson's receptive mind about the Vice President's loyalty. The unseemly social crisis created by Eaton's wife—the notorious Peggy O'Neale—added to the strain, as did Calhoun's extreme views on the tariff and state rights. As he saw his influence wane, Calhoun was aware that the person now highest in the President's favor was his erstwhile ally, Secretary of State Martin Van Buren.

In the spring of 1830, Calhoun was "destroyed." Through the efforts of Crawford and James A. Hamilton, known to be a close friend of Van Buren, Jackson was informed that Calhoun, when Secretary of War, had favored censuring Jackson for his conduct in 1818 during the Seminole War. This was an extremely sensitive point with the General, and when Calhoun was unable to present a satisfactory answer to the charge, Jackson broke all relations with him. Months later, in February 1831, Calhoun took the extraordinary step of publishing a bulky volume of letters and documents on the controversial incident, seeking to justify himself and to place the blame for the rupture on Van Buren. Van Buren promptly issued a statement denying any complicity in the affair, and for the next several years his relations with Calhoun were those of "undisguised hostility."[9] The culmination of these internecine feuds was the reorganization of Jackson's Cabinet, the purge of Calhounites from the administration, and the general recognition that Van Buren was now the President's designated heir.

Calhoun did not yield easily. When Van Buren's nomination as Minister to England came before the Senate early in 1832, the Vice President broke a tie by casting the deciding vote against confirmation. Van Buren would now be "destroyed." "It will kill him, sir, kill him dead," Calhoun exulted. "He will never kick, sir, never kick." Jackson appraised the consequences of this act differently, confidently predicting that it would result in Van Buren's elevation to the vice presidency.[10]

When he submitted his resignation as Secretary of State, Van Buren was aware that he had become the "heir-apparent to the succession." In his sagacious view, recent developments had demonstrated "the great evils to which an Administration was exposed whose chief Cabinet officer occupied that position." With a keen sense of how presidential politics had changed since the era of the Virginia dynasty, he contrasted the old game with the new. "In those days," he observed, "the selection of candidates was confined to comparatively few individuals and the republican party was not the theatre for Presidential intrigues upon any thing like the same scale as that since in vogue." He sensed that access to the presidential contest, once narrowly restricted, had now broadened.[11] As access broadened, intrigues among the rivals multiplied. Thus the prize might go not to the most illustrious of citizens but to the one who was most skilled in the political arts.

Presidential politics in this new and turbulent era involved not only intrigue but also calculation. Because candidates, or would-be candidates, could not look for support to well-organized parties, sustained by loyal and disciplined cadres of voters, they tended strongly to base their calculations on the response they could expect to elicit from particular geographical sections of the country. How did they stand with the South, the North, the West, or New England? By 1828 these crude calculations took on somewhat more explicit meaning as sectional interests came to be identified with positions on such issues as the tariff, Indian removal, or slavery. Similar considerations applied in 1832, although by then there were such additional factors as Anti-Masonry, Calhoun's revolt, and the established record of the Jacksonians to be weighed. Throughout the decade political allegiances—both among leaders and among the electorate—were shifting and unstable, with the result that the game of faction was not readily predictable.

The commonest terms employed in political analyses were geographic. Jefferson's appraisal of the developing presidential contest in 1822 was typical. "The candidates . . . seem at present to be many; but they will be reduced to two, a Northern and a Southern one, as usual," he predicted to Albert Gallatin. Rufus King, from a quite different vantage point, saw Adams as "the only northern Candidate; and as between him and Black [southern] Candidates, I prefer him." In an excessively optimistic appraisal of his prospects in 1823, Clay reasoned that if New York would support him, Pennsylvania, New Jersey, and Maryland would follow suit "and those four states united to the Western and South western states, secures the election." Adams, he believed would be "supported by New England alone." In the same year Jackson revealed his hopes: "Should the people take up the subject in the south, and west, as they have in Pennsylvania, they will soon undeceive Mr. Clay's friends."[12]

Soon after his election by the House, Adams was told by one of Calhoun's friends "that the Administration would be supported only by the New England states—New York being doubtful, the West much divided, and strongly favoring Jackson as a Western man, Virginia already in opposition, and all the South decidedly adverse." Working actively against Adams in 1825, Calhoun endorsed "the blending of the Slave with the Indian question, in order, if possible, to consolidate the whole South." In numerous letters, he emphasized that the South, headed by Virginia and with Pennsylvania as a reliable ally, would resist the Adams administration and rally behind Jackson.[13] Quite obviously, these sectional calculations had validity, as evidenced by the voting patterns manifested both in 1824 and 1828.

While candidates and their "friends" sought to construct majority coalitions, having due regard for sectional factors and critical issues, the ultimate shape that these coalitions—or parties—would assume remained uncertain. Hezekiah Niles late in 1826 started a new section in his *Register* entitled "Elections and Electioneering." His intention was to follow "the new political designations that have sprung up and the strange mixtures of old parties which the new state of things has brought about."[14] It was not an easy assignment, for the designations and the mixtures were, indeed, bewildering. In some states Republicans sought to maintain the fiction that they were divided only on the "presidential question" and that they would soon be reunited against their traditional Federalist foes. As Calhoun reported to Monroe in 1826, old enemies were new friends, and vice versa. Former Federalists assumed prominent roles as adherents of Jackson or Adams; old Republicans found themselves in opposing camps.

The vagueness of party designations provides one useful indicator of the degree of confusion. Down to 1832, rival factions sought to cling to the name "Republican," even though some erstwhile

Federalists were uncomfortable with the label. Practice varied from state to state, but the commonest names used in 1828 were Jackson party, Jackson Republican party, or—in Pennsylvania—Jackson Democratic party. On the other side was the Adams party, Administration party, Adams Republican party, or—in rare instances —National Republican party. To the Jacksonians, their opponents were "the Coalition" or the "Federalists." In like manner, Adams men referred to the "Opposition" party. After 1828, when it could no longer be termed the Adams or Administration party, Jackson's opponents half-heartedly adopted the National Republican label, which was soon to be discarded in favor of Whig. The Jacksonians, meanwhile, most commonly described themselves as Republicans in 1832 and only gradually adopted the name of Democrats. Lacking clear labels, these parties were most appropriately designated by the names of their presidential candidates.

The Jackson-Adams contest in 1828 had presented a sharp choice to politicians and voters, but such clarity soon gave way to change and confusion. The Adams party, so overwhelming in New England, suddenly weakened, and by 1830 the Jacksonians controlled New Hampshire and Maine and showed respectable strength in Rhode Island and Massachusetts. The rapid emergence of the Anti-Masons in Vermont, New York, and Pennsylvania made them a factor to be reckoned with. Growing restiveness in the South, centering on the tariff and nullification, and involving as well the ambitions of Calhoun, raised doubts about the future political course of that region. As Jackson approached the midpoint of his first term, there was great uncertainty about the shape of developing political alignments.

Calhoun's course at this time can serve to illustrate this confusion. In 1830 he was being urged by his friends to seek re-election as Vice President with Jackson. Late in the summer, when many knowledgeable politicians had concluded that Clay was fading and that John McLean of Ohio would be Jackson's opponent, Duff Green suggested to Calhoun that he should run for Vice President on both tickets. Then, following the open rupture between Calhoun and Jackson and the Cabinet upheaval, Calhoun set his sights on the presidency. Governor John Floyd advised him that he would have Virginia's support against Jackson and that he shared Calhoun's opinion that the General was "ruined" and Van Buren "dead." Calhoun was confident that he could carry the South, except for Georgia, and looked to a possible alliance with the Anti-Masons in the North. "I never stood stronger," he boasted to one of his supporters in May 1831. But at that point the pressure exerted on him by the dominant State Rights party in South Carolina, which in its fury against the Tariff of 1828 had embraced the doctrine of nullification, became too great for Calhoun to withstand. On July 26 he issued his Fort Hill Address, setting forth an extremist position in opposition to the tariff and defending nullification. His supporters outside South Carolina were appalled. Even the loyal Duff Green recognized that it meant an end to Calhoun's presidential hopes. Many of Calhoun's followers were left in limbo; they could support neither Jackson nor Clay in 1832, but they could—in time—rally to oppose Van Buren.[15]

If there were strains, soon to become fissures, in the Jackson coalition, the opposition was even more fractured. It was, first of all, divided between Anti-Masons and the shrunken remains of the old Adams party. There was uncertainty as to whether these contingents would coalesce behind a single candidate, and if so, whether that candidate would be Clay or McLean. If Calhoun had carried through with his plan to enter the contest, instead of taking his stand with South Carolina, the House might well have had another opportunity to choose a President.

This was, as later developments were to disclose, a transitional period. Old party distinctions faded, new and unstable coalitions were formed for each presidential contest, national parties had yet to assume definite shape. The towering personality of Jackson provided a rallying point for his adherents, but it was far from certain that his impressive constituency would remain united behind any successor. Neither was it apparent what would serve to consolidate an opposition.

The unsettled state of the presidential game and the gradual transition to a radically different format was reflected in the means now used to nominate candidates and arrange electoral slates. Without some authoritative agency to secure agreement on candidates, a political party can have no meaningful existence. The lack of such a mechanism in 1824 and 1828 was a distinctive characteristic of the game of faction, and the first experiment with a new device in preparation for the election of 1832—the national delegate convention—signaled a fundamental change in the presidential game.

The congressional nominating caucus had never been a strong institution. It had served mainly to express the consensus among Republicans on their presidential candidate and, more importantly on most occasions, to secure agreement on his running mate. It remained weak in part because the Republicans possessed such overwhelming strength and such obvious candidates for the succession that no more potent agency was required. Moreover, the Presidents of the Virginia dynasty, with their ambivalent views toward political parties, were not disposed to work for the development of a stronger national party organization. That its authority could readily be challenged was evidenced in 1808 and 1812, just as its potential for manipulation was revealed in 1816. Among its notable deficiencies were its failure to provide representation for states that lacked Republican Congressmen, its inability to secure even the full attendance of all who were eligible to participate, and its omission of influential state party leaders. Of even greater consequence was the fact that its legitimacy was constantly challenged by those who insisted that it was quite improper for Congressmen to assume the prerogative of intervening in the selection of a President, even though they purported to act in their capacity as private citizens.

With the approach of the 1824 election, the question of what should be the proper mode of nominating presidential candidates excited tremendous interest and controversy. Hezekiah Niles, who carried on a year-long denunciation of the caucus system, followed the discussions attentively. The Tennessee legislature formally condemned the congressional caucus and sent its resolutions to other states for their reactions. Although only Maryland fully endorsed the Tennessee statement, and four legislatures specifically opposed it, publicists and politicians fanned the issue. The Republican legislative caucus in New York upheld the congressional caucus, at the same time deploring the fact that nominations by individual states tended to "disturb the harmony of the great republican family, by creating and strengthening individual predilections and local feelings . . ." Niles, in rebuttal, insisted that with old party distinctions ended and principles of government no longer in dispute, there was no justification for a caucus. Crawford's rivals joined heartily in denunciation of the caucus, for they owed their nominations to other agencies.[16]

Despite the widespread condemnation of the traditional practice, Crawford's supporters decided to proceed with their plan for a caucus nomination. On February 7, 1824, they published a notice inviting "democratic members of Congress" to meet a week later to recommend candidates. On the same date another notice was printed over the signatures of twenty-four Congressmen, announcing that 181 of the 261 members of Congress were agreed that it would be "inexpedient, under existing circumstances, to meet in caucus."[17]

Heedless of this warning, sixty-six Congressmen assembled on the evening of February 14 in the House chamber while more than a thousand interested and generally hostile observers filled the galleries. Only fourteen states were represented, and over half of the members present were from New York, Virginia, and Georgia. Crawford was duly nominated, with the venerable Albert Gallatin as his running mate. In an attempted defense of their action, the members of the caucus published an "Address," in which they insisted that old party lines had not been obliterated and that therefore the Republicans should adhere to "the ancient usages" to maintain their supremacy.[18] From every point of view, the caucus was a well-publicized disaster, and along with his other liabilities, Crawford had to bear the stigma of being the "caucus candidate."

Long before the caucus met, the other candidates were securely in the field as state-sponsored nominees. The South Carolina legislature led off by nominating Senator William Lowndes on December 18, 1821, and later—after Lowndes's death—conferred its blessing on Calhoun. In July 1822, Jackson was put forward by the Tennessee legislature, and in November, Clay was nominated by the legislatures of Kentucky and Missouri. Adams was first recommended to the nation by a caucus of Maine legislators in January 1823, and a week later similar action was taken in Massachusetts. Thus all of the candidates had received some sort of "official" nomination nearly two years in advance of the election and more than a year before the fateful congressional caucus convened.

Subsequently, caucuses or conventions in most of the states endorsed one or another of the candidates and, in many instances, arranged electoral slates pledged to their favorites. Although there had been previous instances of such state-sponsored nominations, notably in 1808 and 1812, suddenly this had become the generally accepted mode.

The practice of state-sponsored nominations undoubtedly contributed to the fragmentation, indeed the destruction, of the old Republican party. Moreover, it strongly encouraged the nomination of sectional favorites. In those states where substantial support appeared for more than one candidate—as in Ohio, New Jersey, or Louisiana—it was necessary for the rival factions to try to construct ad hoc organizations to arrange electoral tickets and conduct a campaign. In the course of such efforts, it was common to hold delegate conventions, especially to oppose the faction represented by the majority in the legislative caucus, thus giving an impetus to the convention system. The state nominations were represented as expressing the voice of "the people," whereas the congressional caucus was condemned for usurping the right of the people to name their candidates. This new emphasis on the role of "the people," together with the increased use of the delegate convention, were important by-products of the novel maneuvers associated with the state-sponsored nominations.

Events in Pennsylvania illustrate the new style and its attendant rhetoric. A delegate convention of "democratic republicans" convened in Harrisburg for two days early in March 1824. After nominating Jackson by a vote of 124 to 1, naming Calhoun for the second place on the ticket, and selecting an electoral slate, the convention published a stirring "Address" condemning the congressional caucus and noting that for twenty-four years the succession to the presidency had been limited to the person occupying the position of Secretary of State. "The period has surely arrived," declared the Address, "when a president should be elected from the ranks of the people . . . Andrew Jackson comes pure, untrammelled and unpledged, from the bosom of the people."[19] Never before had such a claim been so boldly made in behalf of a presidential candidate.

Formal nominations for the presidency were scarcely necessary in 1828, so obvious was it that the contest would be between Jackson and Adams. But there was a need for state-level agencies to arrange electoral slates, create the rudiments of state-wide party structures, and manage campaigns. In a pattern reminiscent of 1824, Jacksonians and Adamsites constructed what were essentially ad hoc organizations in most states to perform these essential functions. Where the Adams forces controlled the legislatures, as in New England, the Jacksonians of necessity turned to the device of the state convention. In the South, for similar reasons, the convention system was introduced by Adams's supporters. Thus the delegate convention swiftly developed as an alternative to the legislative caucus as an instrument for coordinating and directing state party affairs. Prior to 1824, it had been used commonly only in New Jersey, Delaware, and Pennsylvania; by 1828 it had been introduced into all but a handful of states. As it acquired acceptance, it not only gave a new structure to party organizations, it also enhanced greatly the sense, and even the actuality, of popular participation in party affairs. Again, the game of faction had contributed to an important innovation in the conduct of politics.[20]

Of even greater moment was the birth of the national nominating convention. There had been mild suggestions as early as 1822 that a convention should replace the traditional caucus, but the times and circumstances were not propitious. However, in 1826, as Van Buren wrestled with the problem of welding together a coalition behind Jackson that could assert the claim that it represented a continuance of the Old Republican party, the idea of holding a national convention received serious consideration. In his discussions with Calhoun, the two agreed "to go at the next Presidential election for a nomination by a national convention." The next step was to enlist the support of Thomas Ritchie, member of the Richmond Junto and editor of the very influential Richmond *Enquirer*. Ritchie was impressed by Van Buren's vision of reconstituting a union of "the planters of the South and the plain Republicans of the North," and he had been among the advocates of a convention in 1822. The *Albany Argus*, Van Buren's organ in Albany, broached the proposal in January 1827, and the response was favorable, if unenthusiastic, in other quarters.[21]

As the political situation developed, however, the project was dropped. There were many reasons, but chief among them was the concern that harmony within the coalition might be disrupted by controversy over a vice-presidential nomination. Calhoun had powerful enemies. Crawford and De Witt Clinton were his rivals for the coveted nomination, and a fight over the issue in a convention could only impair Jackson's prospects for victory. Accordingly, the vice-presidential nomination was prudently left to the states, and in time only Georgia held out against Calhoun.

Looking ahead to 1832, the Jacksonians did not plan for a national convention. In April 1830, the Democrats in the Pennsylvania legislature caucused and resolved that the "unanimity and harmony of the great democratic party" would be promoted by placing Jackson before the people for re-election. Two weeks later, there was a similar endorsement from New York, and this was echoed in due course by caucuses or conventions in other states.[22] It seemed that the format that had been followed in 1828 would again maintain. But two considerations intervened to make a national convention desirable. One was the adoption of the convention plan by the Anti-Masons and the National Republicans. Even more influential was the necessity to secure agreement on a vice-presidential candidate.

The story of the origins of the three national conventions that met in 1831 and 1832 has been told admirably by James S. Chase, so it need not be detailed here. The Anti-Masons provided the model. Buoyed by their success in several states, they arranged for the first national party convention in Philadelphia in September 1830 to lay plans for a major effort in the 1832 election. The main outcome of their deliberations was a call for a convention to meet in Baltimore on September 26, 1831, for the purpose of nominating candidates for President and Vice President. Because their strength was restricted to relatively few states in 1830, the Anti-Masons could scarcely rely on state-sponsored nominations. Moreover, their more ambitious leaders held the vision that the new party might be built into the chief opponent of the Jacksonians, and for these reasons a national convention would best serve their purposes. Their fatal problem, however, was the lack of a viable candidate. After receiving a cool response from Clay, being rebuffed by John McLean, and setting aside Adams, they were left with William Wirt, an admirer of Clay and former Attorney General. It was not an auspicious choice, but some hopes were entertained that the National Republicans might be induced to unite behind Wirt.

The movement for a National Republican convention originated in Kentucky, although there is no evidence that it was instigated or encouraged by Clay. In December 1830 a state convention meeting in Frankfort took the unusual step of naming delegates to a national convention, in the event that one should be held. Congressional leaders and others who were desirous of promoting Clay's candidacy appreciated the need for some form of national party organization, and they saw the merits of a national convention in that light. The project assumed specific form on February 17, 1831, when Maryland legislators opposed to the Jackson administration issued a formal call to delegates from all the states to meet in Baltimore in December.[23] The prospect of such a convention spurred organizational activities in the states, as conventions, caucuses, or mass meetings were arranged in order to select the delegates who would go to Baltimore.

The National Republican convention was a well organized, tightly controlled affair.[24] With 156 delegates from seventeen states in attendance, it convened on December 12 and continued in session for five days. No controversial issues were permitted to come before the delegates; such matters were decided in secret caucuses off the floor. Clay was nominated without opposition, as was his running mate, John Sergeant of Pennsylvania. Clay promptly accepted the nomination in a brief formal letter, as did Sergeant. Much of the time of the convention was actually devoted to measures designed to encourage the formation of party organizations in the states in order to advance the campaign effort. On the final day, without any discussion, the delegates adopted an "Address," which was in the nature of a party platform, and ordered that 10,000 copies be printed and distributed.

The "Address" was almost entirely devoted to attacking Jackson and his actions. More in sorrow than in anger, the statement expressed the belief that "placed in a situation for which he was by education and character wholly unfit, worn out by the tasks, infirmities, and natural progress of age, he acted under influences which, morally speaking, he could not well control." Specifically, he was condemned for his unprecedented abuse of patronage, his equivocal stands on the tariff and internal improvements, his ill-informed attacks on the Bank of the United States, his assaults on the judiciary, and his inhumane policy toward the Indians. Clay and Sergeant were depicted as ardent, fearless, and consistent friends of liberty and republican institutions and supporters of the American System. Their success was assured "beyond the possibility of doubt." As an "opposition" party, the National Republicans were understandably more disposed to assail the incumbents than to detail an alternative program.

The Jacksonians were motivated to hold a national convention when it became apparent that Jackson's re-election might be imperiled by contention over the vice presidency. Early in 1831 the loose coalition that had put Jackson in the presidency was anything but harmonious or unified. In addition to the rupture with Calhoun and his adherents, there were sharp differences over tariff policy, sectional strains among southern, western and northern wings, and personal rivalries related to the vice presidency and to the larger question of who would be Jackson's successor. There was the danger that several state or regional favorites would be nominated for the second place on the Jackson ticket, creating at least the strong possibility that the ultimate choice would devolve upon the Senate.

Worried by the portents of discord, Jackson's intimate adviser, William B. Lewis, decided that the only way to attempt to hold the party together was a national convention. Accordingly, he arranged with Amos Kendall and Isaac Hill for the New Hampshire Jacksonians to issue the call in June 1831 for such a convention. The announced object was "the adoption of such measures as will best promote the re-election of Andrew Jackson, and the nomination of a candidate to be supported as Vice-President at the same election."[25] The convention was to meet in Baltimore on the third Monday in May 1832, and each state was invited to send delegates equal to the number of its electors.

By the time the convention met, several candidates were in the field. Richard M. Johnson of Kentucky, who had gained fame in the West as the reputed slayer of Tecumseh, had been nominated in Kentucky and Missouri and had considerable backing in the Old

Northwest as well. Virginia was favorable to Judge Philip P. Barbour, who appealed to anti-tariff Jacksonians in other states. Pennsylvania was pledged to Congressman James Wilkins, a native son and high-tariff advocate. New Jersey's favorite son was Mahlon Dickerson. Meanwhile, Van Buren's rejection by the Senate had suddenly catapulted him into the prominence of a party martyr, and he gained endorsements from several northern states, along with the blessing of the President and some of his closest advisers.

At first reluctant to be considered, Van Buren in March 1832 yielded to the entreaties of his friends and agreed to accept the nomination if it came his way.[26] His prospects were anything but assured, however, with Pennsylvania and Virginia opposed, much of the South hostile, and the West cool. Many Jacksonian loyalists felt that he would be a liability to the ticket; others who were less loyal opposed him because he was suspect on the tariff issue, a northerner, and the likely heir apparent. His supporters, however, were extremely energetic in portraying him as one who deserved vindication by the party for whose cause he had labored and suffered.

On May 21, 1832, the Baltimore Athenaeum was packed with 320 delegates representing every state except Missouri, as well as a large crowd of spectators and journalists. The next day the meeting was transferred to the larger quarters of the Universalist Church, in order to accommodate the vast throng. Some of the delegations had been chosen by state party conventions, some by legislative caucuses, and others by district or county meetings. Several states sent delegations far in excess of their number of electors, and a few had only token representation. In an opening address, Frederick A. Sumner of New Hampshire explained why the democracy of his state had issued the convention call. It was not to impose on the people "any local favorite, but to concentrate the opinions of all the states." The coming together of "representatives of the people from the extremity of the union, would have a tendency to soothe, if not to unite, the jarring interests, which sometimes comes in conflict, from the different sections of the country." He concluded by expressing the hope "that the people would be disposed, after seeing the good effects of this convention in conciliating the different and distant sections of the country, to continue this mode of nomination." Sectional differences must be muted in the interest of party harmony.

The convention then proceeded to organize by electing a chairman *pro tem* and appointing committees to report on the names of the authorized delegates and to draft rules to govern the proceedings. On the next day, a permanent chairman—Robert Lucas of Ohio—was chosen, and rules were adopted. Of special importance were those specifying that each state should be entitled to cast votes equal to its electoral votes, that one person in each delegation should be designated to report the vote of the state, and that two-thirds of the whole number of votes in the convention should be necessary for a nomination. The last provision, which was retained by Democratic party conventions until 1936, was adopted after some debate on the grounds that it would ensure that the nominees had the overwhelming support of the party. Involved as well was a compromise between those who opposed granting full voting privileges to those states that were unlikely to support any Democratic candidate and those who favored nomination by a simple majority. Under the formula that was adopted, no one section of the party could dictate the choice of a candidate, but, on the other hand, a minority might block the selection of a nominee to whom it was strongly opposed.[27] Contrary to some accounts, the convention did not impose the unit rule; states could—and did—divide their vote, although the vote was announced by each state's representative rather than being cast by each individual delegate. The significance of this arrangement, of course, was that it treated the state delegations as voting blocs, thus enhancing their tendency to respond to the dictation of state party leaders.

The convention next proceeded to the nomination of a vice-presidential candidate. In order, no doubt, to avoid any statements that might disturb the harmony of the session, the rules forbade any nominating speeches. Instead, the state delegations were simply called on to report their votes. On the first ballot, Van Buren received 208 votes—more than the required two-thirds—to 49 for Philip P. Barbour and 26 for Richard M. Johnson. The Virginia delegation, which had given all its votes to Barbour, announced that it concurred in the nomination of Van Buren, whereupon the

Kentucky delegation, which had supported Johnson, moved that Van Buren's nomination be made unanimous. Then, almost as an afterthought, the convention voted unanimously to "concur in the repeated nominations" that Jackson had received in various parts of the Union. The officers were directed to inform Van Buren of his nomination.[28]

In the meantime, a committee consisting of one delegate from each state had been instructed to draft an address to the people of the United States. When the convention met for its final session on May 23, this committee made a remarkable report. They were, they said, in full agreement on the principles that ought to be embodied in such an address. Nevertheless, they deemed it advisable "under existing circumstances," to recommend to the several delegates that they make, "such explanations by address, report, or otherwise, to their respective constituents of the objects, proceedings and result of the meeting as they may deem expedient." As its final act, the convention appointed a general corresponding committee, ordered the printing of its proceedings, adopted appropriate resolutions of thanks, and then adjourned to pay its respects to the last surviving Signer, Charles Carroll.

On the surface, at least, harmony was exhibited. How the nomination of Van Buren was actually arranged still remains an unresolved question. No doubt the delegates were aware of Jackson's decided preference, and Major Lewis was later to imply that his influence was exerted in behalf of Van Buren, but elements of mystery remain. In any event, any semblance of an open rupture was avoided, and the party appeared to be united behind its candidates. We can only assume that prudence dictated the decision not to issue an address, for differences of opinion would surely have emerged, particularly with respect to the tariff and the Bank. Although its future as a party agency remained uncertain—a motion to hold another convention four years hence was withdrawn after some discussion—the convention had achieved the announced purpose of securing agreement on a vice-presidential nominee. Future conventions would confront sterner tests, notably in adjusting contests over presidential nominations and platforms, but important precedents had been established by this first Democratic National Convention.

That there was not entire harmony within the Jackson party, despite the clear verdict of the convention, soon became apparent. In the South, dissident elements sought to organize opposition to Van Buren. Some were former Calhounites, most were avid in their opposition to the tariff, and others rebelled at the prospect of having a northern man placed in the position of heir apparent. In Virginia, North Carolina, Georgia, Mississippi, and Alabama, electoral tickets were arranged with Barbour as Jackson's running mate. At first receptive, Barbour at the last moment renounced his candidacy, with the result that the movement foundered and showed little voting strength in the election.[29] South Carolina, despite having sent a delegation to the national convention, exhibited its peculiar political orientation by throwing away its electoral votes on Governor John Floyd of Virginia, a Calhoun partisan. There was dissatisfaction, too, in Pennsylvania, where Senator William Wilkins was coupled with Jackson, but this action represented mainly the pique felt by the Keystone State at never having had a candidate for national office. Quite obviously, party discipline was not firm, but the institution of the national convention provided a device for resolving internal differences and maximizing agreement within the party.

In this turbulent era, the contest for the presidency centered more on personalities than on parties. Voters rallied to the standards of a Jackson, an Adams, or a Clay, rather than to the appeal of a party label. It becomes important, therefore, to understand the role that the candidates themselves played in the political drama. It was, in brief, a rigidly prescribed role, dictated by the constraints of republican ideology, by tradition, and by prudence. Candidates were governed by a code that defined their behavior.

The republican creed, especially as it applied to presidential candidates, discountenanced any actions that implied the use of intrigue, corruption, or demagoguery to obtain office. Elective positions should not be sought after; rather, they should come unsolicited from the people in recognition of superior service, talent, and virtue. In its most exalted form, the creed frowned on the formation of parties, except to preserve the republican system from the threat of subversion. Once in office, the successful candidate for the presidency should in no way influence the popular will with respect to the selection of his successor. The ideal republican candidate, as exemplified best of all by Washington, was one who disdained the political arts, identified himself with no faction, acquired a reputation for distinguished and patriotic service, and responded to the call of his fellow citizens.

The ideal, needless to say, could not be fully realized. There were, moreover, extenuating circumstances. Jefferson could work actively behind the scenes to build a party and secure his election in 1800 because the Federalists were, by his lights, moving toward monarchy. Monroe in 1808 could join with his friends to attempt to block Madison's succession because of his conviction that the principles of the Republican party were in danger. Or Madison in 1812 could make dignified responses to formal communications from New Jersey and South Carolina because there was a need for national unity. But the ideal survived, and the code of conduct was generally respected.

Jackson, who liked to believe that his life was regulated by rules that could be invoked to govern every contingency, found the republican code congenial. When Henry Baldwin, an influential political figure in Pennsylvania, inquired whether he would "acquiesce" in a nomination for the presidency, Jackson responded in classic style. "The course ever pursued by me and which I have always thought congenial with the republican principles of my country," he wrote, "was on no occasion to solicit for office; but at the same [time] not to decline any public demand on my services." It was his "political creed that the services of every man belonged to the country, when that country demanded it." To others who made similar inquiries, he answered with the same formula. In obedience to this "creed," he felt obliged to accept, very uncomfortably, his election to the Senate from Tennessee in 1823.[30]

Jackson was eloquent in voicing the republican view that the elective will of the people should not be influenced by intrigue and was especially severe in his denunciation of caucuses. "I am happy to see the good people of America are putting their faces against those congressional caucuses," he wrote to his friend, General John Coffee, "and I do hope that one last held will put these unconstitutional proceedings to sleep forever, and leave to the people their constitutional right of free suffrage." He expressed his concern about "a sistematic system of intrigue and corruption, first secrete and last, open and undisguised, that will ultimately destroy the liberty of our country." For himself, he would not resort to "any sort of combination, management, or intrigue" to secure his election. Neither would he be a party man. "If I am elected to fill the Presidential chair," he confided to his nephew in 1824, "it must be done by the people; and I will be President of the nation, and not of a party." He authorized the publication of his correspondence with Monroe in 1816–17, when he had suggested that a former Federalist should be appointed to the Cabinet, to illustrate his views on parties. Other candidates were violating the code, transgressing the republican creed, but Jackson would remain aloof from such actions and rest his case with the people.[31]

As his interest in the presidency intensified, Jackson amplified, modified, and even departed from his code. In April, 1824 a supporter in North Carolina, L. H. Coleman, solicited his views on the tariff. Jackson then enunciated a new rule. His name having been brought before the nation, it was incumbent on him to declare his opinion "upon any political or national question pending before and about which the country feels an interest." Accordingly, he responded by declaring himself in favor of "a careful Tariff," and his judiciously worded letter was immediately given wide publicity. Subsequently in other letters designed for publication he set forth in guarded terms his positions on internal improvements and on the expediency of paying off the national debt, as well as reiterating the views he had expressed in the Coleman letter.[32] Such candor, not to say such public declarations, was all but unprecedented for a presidential candidate.

Jackson's "rule" about responding to inquiries was modified at the insistence of his chief campaign advisers. In preparation for the 1828 campaign, Jackson drafted a statement of his position on public issues, which he discussed with John H. Eaton. Eaton strongly advised against its publication, arguing that his friends knew his views and that only his enemies would seek to draw him out. "Be still—Be at home is the great and open path to tread," cautioned Eaton. On another occasion, when Jackson was eager to respond to the charges made against him by Clay, Eaton urged a policy of "retirement and silence." Jackson should be quiet and let his friends manage whatever had to be done. James K. Polk was equally explicit. He pointed out that "the ground taken for you by your friends . . . that you live in retirement on your farm, calm and unmoved by the excitement around you, taking no part in the pending canvass for the Presidency, but committing yourself into the hands of your country, would seem to superficial observers to be inconsistent with any appeal to the public made by you at this juncture. . . ." Van Buren endorsed the injunction against any utterances. "Our people do not like to see publications from candidates," he warned Jackson.[33]

The General did not entirely heed their advice, although he was more restrained than he had been in 1824. He responded "in a laconic style" to a request from the Indiana legislature for his tariff views. "Note I only write when called upon by the Legislature of a State," he explained somewhat lamely to Polk, adding that he suspected Clay was behind the inquiry.[34] He also felt obliged to deny any implication in the Burr conspiracy when that awkward question was raised in 1828, but otherwise, despite incredible provocation, he held his tongue in public.[35] In 1832, having absorbed the lessons of the two previous campaigns, he remained mute as a candidate, although by then his positions on the issues were apparent from his actions.

As President, Jackson modified his code. In 1824 he had said that "the very moment I proscribe an individual from office, on account of his political opinion, I become, myself, a despot."[36] As he proceeded with his policy of "reforming" the civil service, rewarding his friends and ousting his enemies, he was soon accused of despotism. Another grievous breach of republican etiquette was his interference in the choice of his successor. Jefferson, Madison, and Monroe had been scrupulous on this point, for if the executive used his influence to such an end, the people's will could be set at naught. As early as December 1829, Jackson had indicated his preference for Van Buren, and by 1831 he was assuring him that if re-elected he intended to resign, whereupon Van Buren as Vice President could succeed him. In other statements, public and private, Jackson urged Van Buren's nomination as Vice President and made it plain that he was the heir apparent. Jackson even altered his views toward parties. Following his re-election in 1832, he told Van Buren that he intended to administer the government "in such a way as to strengthen the democratic party, unite the whole and produce the greatest prosperity to our beloved country."[37]

The attitudes of other candidates were consistent with those of Jackson, especially with regard to overt electioneering. Adams in 1828 permitted himself to make a formal, non-political speech on the occasion of ground breaking for the Chesapeake and Ohio Canal and responded stiffly to the greetings of the people while traveling through Philadelphia and New York. He also wrote letters, which were published, to the Baltimore weavers and to New York Anti-Masons, but he could scarcely be accused of demagoguery.[38] Clay was also scrupulous. In declining an invitation to a public dinner at his Virginia birthplace, he said that to do so would violate a rule that he had prescribed to himself. In something of a departure from strict propriety, however, he did address the Young Men's National Republican Convention when it met in Baltimore in 1832.[39] Van Buren acknowledged the right of citizens to be informed about his stand on the issues of the day, and in accordance with this rule, he responded at some length in 1832 to inquiries from a public meeting held in Shocco Springs, North Carolina. He also seized the opportunity, when responding to an address from supporters in New York City, to deplore the "artful misrepresentations" of his enemies. "Whatever temporary success may occasionally attend the seductions of wealth, and the assaults of calumny," he exhorted his admirers, "let nothing impair your confidence in the people."[40]

In subtle but important ways the code that constrained the behavior of presidential candidates was relaxed in those years. Jackson was the innovator. By announcing publicly that he would accept the nomination offered by his Pennsylvania supporters and, even more, by responding to inquiries about his political views, he departed from custom. In both cases he was able to justify his actions in terms of republican principles. But the notion that the people had the right to know where candidates stood on the issues opened a new perspective on the contest for the presidency.

Previously it had been sufficient to judge candidates on their established reputations; now, if Jackson's rule were to gain acceptance, candidates must declare themselves on public questions. There were two dangers raised by this innovation. One was that candidates might open themselves to the serious charge of electioneering, of engaging in an unseemly solicitation of votes. Even more serious was the hazard that candid statements would provide ammunition for opponents or create divisions among supporters. Accordingly, and chiefly with the latter consideration in minds, candidates were to be extremely cautious in their public utterances. Their roles during a campaign would long remain severely circumscribed.

If the candidates themselves were restrained, their managers and active adherents recognized no limitations as they sought to influence the electorate. Consequently, no aspect of the presidential game changed more spectacularly after 1824 than did that element known as the campaign. Except in 1812, there had been little semblance of a campaign associated with the contest for the presidency since 1800, and because—among other reasons— electors had been chosen in many states by their legislatures, the art of mobilizing mass electorates on a national scale had scarcely developed. But after 1824, with the revival of the contest for the presidency, with popular elections the rule, and with improved means of communication, the presidential campaign was to assume a new form. Voters must be activated, excited, persuaded, organized, and brought to the polls. To these ends were campaigns planned and conducted.

With the numerous sectionally based candidates, backed by minimal organizations, the election of 1824 did not greatly arouse the electorate, but it did engender some interesting innovations in campaign practices. There were the unprecedented public statements by Jackson, signalling changes in the code of behavior for candidates. There was the modest use of conventions and mass meetings to foster enthusiasm, issue addresses, and solicit support. There were, too, the first semblances of modern campaign managers in the persons of Josiah S. Johnston, who assumed the direction of Clay's efforts in the summer of 1824 with remarkable sophistication, and John H. Eaton, who filled a comparable role for Jackson.[41]

Of greater significance, however, was the new emphasis given to designing and propagating appealing images of the candidates. This endeavor can best be illustrated with reference to Jackson, whose image was less than favorable. One of his admirers, writing to the General in June 1823, noted that his detractors were giving the impression that he was governed by passion and impulse and inquired whether something could not be done to counteract this perception. One remedy was soon available in Eaton's *Life of Andrew Jackson.* Running to more than four hundred pages and devoted mainly to Jackson's military campaigns, the work had been started by one of Jackson's military aides, Major John Reed, and after his death was completed by Eaton. A scant twenty pages were devoted to Jackson's life before 1812, and only the last ten pages dealt with his character and personality. There Jackson's virtues were glowingly delineated.[42]

"No man has been more misconceived in character," Eaton insisted. Rather than having "a temper irritable and hasty," there were "none who reasoned more dispassionately." "Easy, affable, and familiar," he treated all men equally and was beloved by his troops. Benevolent, honorable, "scrupulously attached to his promises," his moral qualities were unassailable. A Republican from the first, he was not, however, "one of those blind infatuated partisans, who holds the opinions of others in derision." In his view, "party rancour was carried much too far, both for our own and the honour of our country." Thus, in what may be regarded as the first substantial campaign biography, was Jackson eulogized.

Contributing even more to the shaping of the Old Hero's image, and setting something of a model for later campaign literature, were Eaton's *Wyoming Letters.*[43] First published in a Pennsylvania newspaper in 1823 and subsequently issued in pamphlet form, these pieces depicted Jackson as a man of the Revolution who, like Washington, was the embodiment of republican virtue and unblemished patriotism. True, he was a military man, but so had Washington been. He was uniquely qualified to restore cherished republican values as "the Washington of his age." Now, when intrigue rather than virtue and faithful service was becoming the pathway to high office, he would return to the traditions of the Founders. He would, in short, epitomize the heroic republican ideal. This effective appeal to the common man was not couched in the rhetoric of democracy; instead, it called for a return to older values.

In time, of course, this image was to change, and in an especially poignant way, Jackson came to symbolize the tension between the republican ideal and the popular politics of the party game.

It was in preparation for the election of 1828 that campaign activities rose to an unprecedented level of breadth and intensity. Because the Jacksonians were the "outs," they were far more vigorous and innovative than their opponents. Moreover, the very circumstances of Jackson's defeat in 1824—by a "corrupt bargain" —induced him and his managers to adopt the strategy of appealing to "the people" for vindication. Never before had such emphasis been given to the people's role and majesty in a presidential contest, with the result that 1828 produced what can well be termed the first popular-styled campaign.

The Jacksonians devoted more than three years to organizing, managing, and conducting their campaign against Adams. The effort was formally launched in October 1825, when Jackson was nominated by the Tennessee legislature. He then resigned his seat in the Senate and, in a communication to the legislature, set a new tone for his campaign by endorsing an amendment to the Constitution that would vest the election of the President directly in the people. In addition, he would bar Congressmen from accepting appointments to office by the President in order to prevent the demoralization and corruption of the legislative branch. Further, he assured the Tennessee legislators—and the nation—that in his dual role as Senator and presidential candidate he had not degraded the trust reposed in him "by intriguing for the Presidential chair." With its thinly veiled attack on the "corrupt bargain" and its manifestation of confidence in the people, it was a brilliant campaign document.[44]

Soon a remarkably effective campaign organization was created. Jackson's closest advisers in Tennessee had formed themselves into what became known early in 1823 as the Nashville Central Committee. With William B. Lewis, John Overton, and Alfred Balch as its most active members, its announced purpose was to respond to the calumnious attacks on the General, but it provided as well a model for the establishment of similar committees in other states, with which it maintained an active correspondence. Much of the direction of the campaign, especially with respect to disseminating propaganda and encouraging extensive organizational efforts, stemmed from this committee. It can scarcely be called a party agency; rather, it represented the personal campaign organization of Andrew Jackson, and he took an active role in its operations.

In Washington, a Jackson Correspondence Committee, headed by an influential banker, John P. Van Ness, was a key element in the public-relations apparatus, raising funds to subsidize newspapers and aiding Congressmen in the distribution of relevant documents. This committee collaborated with the caucus of Jacksonian Congressmen, mobilized by Van Buren, which directed legislative attacks against the administration and through speeches—liberally distributed under the franking privilege—augmented the barrage of propaganda. These three agencies worked well together, sharing a common goal, and collectively they enlisted the talents of an extraordinary array of politicians and publicists throughout the nation.[45]

As had been the case since Jefferson's time, enormous emphasis was placed upon newspapers to reach and persuade the electorate.[46] Early in 1826 funds were raised by John H. Eaton to establish a new paper, the *United States Telegraph*, in Washington, and under the vigorous editorship of Duff Green it was quickly recognized as the official organ of the Jacksonians. Through the efforts of party activists, and especially Congressmen, scores of papers were started and editors of older presses were induced by subsidies to lend their pens to the cause. They took their cues from the *Telegraph*, or directly from the Nashville and Washington committees. In March 1828, Green introduced the *Telegraph Extra*, a weekly that ran for thirty-six numbers and was devoted exclusively to campaign materials. Featuring enthusiastic accounts of Jacksonian meetings throughout the country, engaging in charges and counter-charges against the Adams party, and printing documents favorable to its interest, it furnished Jacksonians everywhere with the ammunition required to wage the great battle.

Spurred by the Nashville Committee, by energetic Congressmen, and by the effective appeals of the *Telegraph* and its growing battery of local papers, campaign organizations sprang up in states, counties, and towns. Conventions, mass meetings, correspondence committees, vigilance committees, and the like drew increasing numbers of individuals into active participation in the campaign. As commitment and enthusiasm mounted, the political scene was enlivened with barbecues, parades, banners, songs, and huge rallies. Fastening on the General's nickname, Hickory Clubs were formed, and they vied with one another in raising ever larger hickory poles to signify their identification with their hero. Most of the frivolous but engaging techniques for arousing the voter had been employed previously in local campaigns, but now they marked the beginning of the transformation of the presidential election into a quadrennial folk festival.

No event of the campaign quite compared with Jackson's visit to New Orleans. Invited by the Louisiana legislature to receive the homage of the city that had been the scene of his greatest triumph, Jackson in his characteristic fashion concluded that he might accept without appearing to deviate from his stern rule against electioneering. He set out from Nashville in late December 1827 on a steamboat filled with friends and admirers from many parts of the Union. Stopping briefly at Natchez to receive the plaudits of the crowd assembled there, he arrived at New Orleans to a thunderous reception on January 8, the anniversary of his victory. For four days he was feted and eulogized. Avoiding any semblance of a political statement, he conducted himself with great dignity and reserve. He well knew how to play the role of hero. The nation's presses carried extensive, and almost uniformly favorable accounts of his pilgrimage. Had the country required anything to remind it of the debt it owed to General Jackson, the need had been met.

In terms of its substance, the campaign was as coarse, vile, and vituperative as any in our history. The presses of both parties spewed forth personal abuse almost to the exclusion of anything else. Jackson was depicted as an ignorant military chieftain, a duellist, a bigamist, an adulterer, a slave trader, an accomplice of Aaron Burr's, the murderer of his own militia troops, and the son of a prostitute. "The whole object of the coalition is to calumniate me," he complained. "Cart loads of coffin hand-bills, forgeries, and pamphlets of the most base calumnies are circulated by the franking privilege of members of Congress, and Mr. Clay. Even Mrs. J. is not spared, and my pious Mother . . . has been dragged forth by [Charles] Hammond and held to public scorn as a prostitute who intermarried with a Negro, and my eldest brother sold as a slave in Carolina . . . I am branded with every crime."[47] Adams met with similar treatment. In addition to being a partner in the "corrupt bargain," he was charged with being a pimp, with having used public funds to buy gambling equipment for the White House, with cherishing his father's fondness for monarchy, and other equally heinous offenses.

The Nashville and Washington committees devoted considerable effort to countering the attacks on Jackson, while Jackson spent much of his time collecting documents to be used by them for his defense. It was the Washington Committee that published a lengthy response to Clay's denial of the "corrupt bargain," while the Nashville Committee undertook to rebut the accusation of adultery, as well as the assertion that Jackson had been involved in the Burr conspiracy.[48] The numbers of pamphlets and handbills that disseminated these atrocious libels ran into the hundreds of thousands, and they reverberated in the party newspapers and on the hustings.

The Adams forces, although they were far less effectively mobilized, employed the same tactics as their rivals. With Adams remaining perversely aloof from any semblance of electioneering, Clay, with some assistance from Daniel Webster, assumed the leadership of the administration forces. He campaigned personally in several states, addressing public dinners and huge rallies and induced other members of the Cabinet to follow his example. Using his authority as Secretary of State to designate and subsidize newspapers to print the public laws, he marshalled press support for Adams, headed by the *National Journal* and the *National Intelligencer* in Washington. John Binns of Philadelphia, who publicized the execution of eight mutinous militiamen on Jackson's orders through his notorious "coffin hand-bills," and Charles Hammond of Cincinnati, author of the adultery charge, were two of many effective propagandists in the Adams camp. But there was no adequate counterpart to the Nashville Committee, no large corps of skilled advisers and managers to match Lewis, Eaton, Van Buren, Calhoun, Green, Benton, Kendall, and Hill, and Adams lacked the charismatic appeal of Old Hickory. The Jacksonians had much the better of it in their campaign appeal.

Oddly enough, the campaign of 1832 was less flamboyant than that of 1828. Jackson took little part in its direction, confidently assuming that he would be re-elected. The National Republicans faced a disquieting prospect because of the competition from the Anti-Masons in several key states, and although fusion electoral slates were arranged in New York, Pennsylvania, and Ohio in an attempt to consolidate the anti-Jackson forces, enthusiasm was muted. The presence of Van Buren on the ticket cooled the ardor of southern Jacksonians. The Democrats no longer harped on the "corrupt bargain" charge, standing instead on calls for party unity and on the defense of Jackson's record. In turn, the National Republicans attacked Jackson's policies, especially with respect to the Bank, denounced his dictatorial assertions of executive authority, and focused their personal abuse on Van Buren, the "wily magician."[49]

The campaign was not devoid of innovation. There were, first of all, the national party conventions. Important for producing party unity, they contributed to the general campaign effort by generating enthusiasm, stimulating organizational activity, and, in varying degrees, defining the parties' appeals. A notable auxiliary to the national convention was the "Young Men's" convention. In response to a proposal made at the National Republican Convention, 316 "young men" representing seventeen states convened in Washington for five days early in May 1832 to endorse the nominations of Clay and Sergeant, hear a brief but moving address by their presidential candidate, pay their respects to Charles Carroll, and make a pilgrimage to Mount Vernon. In addition, they adopted ten resolutions in the nature of a party platform, setting forth their views on a host of issues but not mentioning the Bank. This Young Men's National Republican Convention was clearly intended to inspire those in attendance to enhanced efforts in the campaign. It was modeled on young men's conventions that had been held in New York as early as 1824 by rival parties, and it later became a characteristic feature of campaign activities in many states.[50]

What most distinguished the campaign of 1832 from its predecessors was the relative clarity of the issues. As never before, or at least since 1800, there was now the sense that the Democrats and the National Republicans presented a choice not only between men, or even between sectional favorites, but of public policies as well. The Democrats had not adopted a formal platform, and they were not yet fully in agreement even on such staple issues as the Bank, the tariff, or internal improvements, but Jackson, at least, had confronted these issues and established points of reference. The National Republicans, through the "Address" adopted at their convention, by the resolutions of their Young Men's Convention, and by the well-known statements of Clay, projected some definition of their orientation. How operative the apparent differences between these two parties were in influencing the judgments of voters is difficult to ascertain, but at least issues had been introduced as an important element in presidential campaigns, along with appeals related to party loyalty, sectional identification, and personality.[51]

The new campaign style contributed to producing a heightened level of popular involvement in the presidential game. The proportion of eligible voters participating more than doubled between 1824 and 1828, and dipped only slightly in 1832. In 1824 there were only two states in which as many as fifty percent of the eligibles had voted; in 1832 eleven states exceeded that mark and in four of those—New Hampshire, New York, Kentucky, and Ohio—the turnout was over 70 percent. In the South, where Jackson met with little opposition, participation remained low—around one-third—but elsewhere the contests engaged the interest of the electorate.[52]

Still, the presidential game failed to arouse the voters as much as did state or local elections. With relatively few exceptions, more voters were attracted to the polls by gubernatorial elections—or the election of sheriffs—than by presidential elections in this period. Among other reasons, national issues and personalities were remote. Opportunities and incentives for popular involvement in presidential elections had been very limited prior to 1828. The resources devoted to activating and mobilizing voters in those contests had been minimal. Old party identifications had atrophied. Now, with the revival of the contest, with the creation of partisan organizations and alignments, along with important changes in the general environment affecting political behavior, presidential elections at last began to take on a large popular dimension.

Crucial to determining the eventual character of the presidential game was the decision arrived at in these years in favor of the general-ticket system as the accepted mode for choosing presidential electors. Between 1813 and 1822 the issue of amending the Constitution to provide for the choice of electors by districts had been debated at almost every session of Congress, and the majority sentiment had favored such a change. The minority that upheld the general-ticket system, and successfully blocked any amendment, had relied chiefly on the arguments of "self-defense" and state rights to justify their position. The debate continued between 1823 and 1826, although within an altered context and with different emphases. It was strongly influenced by the events leading up to, and resulting from, the factional contest for the presidency in 1824, and particularly by the concerns aroused by the House election. It was shaped, as well, by the perception after 1824 that new parties were forming. The ultimate outcome of the debates was the failure of all amending efforts and, concomitantly, the extension of the general-ticket plan, now reinforced by an explicitly stated doctrine.

With the prospect that a contingent election would be necessary in 1824 because of the multiplicity of candidates, Congress considered several plans for amending the Constitution to avert such an event in the two years prior to the election. Senator John Taylor of Virginia proposed early in 1823 that if no candidate received a majority of the electoral vote, there should be a second meeting of the electors to choose between the two men with the highest votes.[53] An alternative plan was devised by Senator Mahlon Dickerson of New Jersey. He revived his earlier amendment that called for the election of electors by districts, but added two features. If no candidate received an electoral majority, the contingent election should be made by joint vote of both houses, with each member voting individually. He would also limit a President to two terms. He viewed his scheme as a compromise, whereby the large states would yield the great weight that they exerted under the general-ticket arrangement and the small states would relinquish their equal status in the contingent election. "Although the district system would not have a tendency to diminish the power of the great states," he argued, "it would have a tendency to diminish the power of the great men of the great States. But for that consideration the proposed amendment would long since have been adopted." After a brief debate, the amendments were tabled.[54]

The Eighteenth Congress, which convened in December 1823, featured discussions of novel plans put forward by Thomas Hart Benton of Missouri in the Senate and by George McDuffie of South Carolina ·in the House. Benton advocated district elections but upheld the existing Constitutional provision for the contingent election. He would, however, eliminate electors, merely assigning one vote to the candidate receiving a plurality of votes in a district. In a lengthy, carefully researched speech, he denounced the general-ticket system on the grounds that it served only the interests of political managers in the large states. "It was adopted by the leading men of those States to enable them to consolidate the vote of the State." It disregarded the rights of the minority, alienated the states from one another, and "produced apathy among the voters." But he defended the contingent election by the House as representing one of the inviolable compromises of the Constitution.[55] Debate on Benton's plan, and a host of variations put forward by other Senators, extended over two months, but soon degenerated into attacks on, and defenses of, the congressional caucus. Finally the whole question was simply postponed indefinitely.

McDuffie, as chairman of a select committee appointed to devise an amendment that would provide for a uniform method of electing both electors and Representatives and for preventing the presidential election from devolving on the House, produced yet another ingenious plan. Electors would be chosen by the voters in congressional districts, with two electors assigned to the state at large. If no candidate secured an electoral majority, there would be a second popular election, restricted to the two highest candidates. If this election resulted in a tie vote, Congress would by joint ballot choose the President. As part of his plan, all Representatives would be elected from single-member districts.

Under the prevailing diverse practices, McDuffie pointed out, "we have no Constitutional provision at all." In favoring the district over the general-ticket system, he argued eloquently that the former mode favored the people, and the latter the politicians. If the general-ticket system became widely established, he predicted, "a central power would spring up in almost every state, consisting of the ruling politicians of the day, who would be bound to the people by no tie of regular responsibility and be, in every respect, more liable to cabal, intrigue, and corruption than the Legislature itself." He favored a second popular election as "the only effectual mode of preserving our government from the corruptions which have undermined the liberty of so many nations." We must, he declared, "confide the election of our Chief Executive to those who are farthest removed from the influence of his patronage." He did not want the President chosen "by cabals of politicians, having views and interests alien from those of the people . . . ." Like many others, he was especially concerned to avoid a contingent election and to take any other steps necessary to prevent Congress from being converted "into a theatre for the Presidential canvass." At the conclusion of McDuffie's brilliant speech, the House adjourned and no further action was taken during the session.[56]

Meanwhile, James Madison, whose prominent role in the Constitutional Convention gave great authority to his views, lent his sanction to the amending effort. In particular, he supported the district plan. "The district mode," he wrote in 1823, "was mostly, if not exclusively, in view when the Constitution was framed and adopted; and was exchanged for the general ticket and legislative election as the only expedient for baffling the policy of the particular states which had set the example." He even reached the point where he felt that the best plan would be to have popular elections by districts, with a contingent election by a joint ballot of both houses of Congress, "and as the smaller states would approve the one, and the larger the other, a spirit of compromise might adopt both." Another surviving Framer, Rufus King, disagreed. He opposed any change in the contingent election, reasoning that the small states had been granted this feature in 1787 as part of an inviolable compromise.[57]

What proved to be the decisive debate on this vexed issue took place early in 1826 on a resolution by McDuffie that merely called for the appointment of a select committee to devise a plan that would provide for district elections and prevent a contingent election by Congress. McDuffie opened the debate by repeating his earlier arguments, again stressing the theme of the people *versus* the politicians. In the course of the discussions, twenty-one amending proposals were brought forth, representing every conceivable variation of earlier plans. Needless to say, no consensus emerged, but several able advocates now put forward a plausible rationale for the general-ticket system, focusing on what was termed the "federative principle."

The case was made most explicitly and effectively by Andrew Stevenson of Virginia, soon to be named Speaker of the House. Citing the Constitutional provision that "Each *State* shall appoint, in such manner as the Legislature thereof may direct" electors to choose a President, he argued that the election of a President was intended to be made "by the states in their political characters." The election was to be both federal and popular. The Constitution gave to the states, through their legislatures, "a wise and salutary check upon the President, instead of making him responsible to the People of a consolidated nation." This was the essence of the federative principle. At the same time, Stevenson coupled his defense of the general ticket with a defense of parties, and even of caucuses. "They enable the views and wishes of the people to be carried into effect, and not scattered and broken . . . Without such parties, what should we have been, or what shall we become?"[58]

The federative principle, as defined by Stevenson was enunciated by numerous other spokesmen including ardent supporters of the Adams administration, who opposed McDuffie for partisan reasons, and small-state representatives, who insisted on the inviolability of the original Constitutional compromise. Henry R. Storrs of New York, an Adams man, denounced the theory that the President should represent "the people." Rather, he should represent the people of the several states. Edward Everett of Massachusetts advanced the extraordinary argument that to amend the Constitution was one thing; to change it as McDuffie proposed, thereby destroying the federative principle, was quite another. One of Stevenson's Virginia colleagues was especially ingenious in upholding both the federative principle and the virtues of political parties, extolling the "adaptability" of the existing system. Ralph I. Ingersoll of Connecticut connected the general ticket with the sovereignty of the states; the proposed amendments would be "destructive of the great principles on which our Constitution rests." A New Hampshire Congressman, in defending the general ticket, applauded its tendency to energize parties. "For this reason alone I would adhere to the present system. This Government has nothing to fear from party excitement, but much from the want of it," he declaimed. "It is essential to the existence of our institutions."[59]

In contrast to earlier debates, the proponents of the district plan were now outnumbered by the defenders of the general ticket, whose leading argument was their insistence on the federative principle. In addition, they rebutted the criticisms of parties made by many who favored the district plan and took strong state-rights positions. McDuffie, no doubt sensing defeat, attempted to answer his antagonists, but he soon shifted to a scathing attack on the "corrupt bargain" and the "unprincipled coalition" that supported Adams, and the whole debate was transformed into a partisan squabble. At its conclusion, the section of McDuffie's resolution calling for district elections was beaten, 90–102. Represented in the majority was a diverse array of Adams men, small-state advocates, southern defenders of state rights, and sophisticated large-state politicians.[60]

In the Senate, Benton chaired a committee dominated by Jacksonians that brought forth a plan consistent with the position the General had taken in his communication to the Tennessee legislature and with McDuffie's plan. There would be district elections in August, and if no candidate received an electoral majority, a second popular election would be held in December, involving the two highest. In case a tie resulted, the choice would be made by the House, voting by states. There was little discussion of this scheme because the Senate decided to await the outcome of the House debate.[61]

Although Jackson sought to keep the issue alive, nearly three decades were to pass until there would again be a serious discussion of altering the method of electing the President. In his first annual message to Congress, Jackson remarked that the American people "will never be satisfied with any ruler who is not the choice and selection of themselves." He accordingly urged the adoption of an amendment similar to that proposed by Senator Benton, adding his recommendation that Presidents be limited to a single term of six years. His objective was to ensure "that the office of Chief Magistrate may not be conferred upon any citizen but in pursuance of a fair expression of the will of the majority."[62] Year after year until his retirement, Jackson repeated this plea to Congress, but it aroused no response. The reform impulse was dead. In the political context that was developing, those who sought to revive it were obliged to recognize that the general-ticket system had triumphed.

The progress of the general-ticket-system was rapid after 1824. In that year, it was employed by twelve states, while six elected by districts and six by the legislature. By 1828 six more states had adopted the general ticket, and by 1836 the lone holdout was South Carolina, which clung to the legislative mode down to the Civil War. For the most part, the transition was accomplished state by state with little controversy, except in New York. There the efforts of Van Buren's Regency to retain choice by the legislature provoked a popular rebellion which forced the adoption of the district plan in 1828. Four years later, with the Regency again in power, political expediency dictated a shift to the general ticket. Thus, after nearly half a century of diverse practices, there was at last a uniform mode for choosing electors, South Carolina excepted.

The single most important rule governing the presidential game had acquired acceptance. The game was not to involve the people of the United States, but the people of the several states. No longer would manipulation of electoral methods be an element in the game, as it had been in the past, nor would the electorate be excluded, as it had been in the many states where electors were chosen by the legislatures. Assuming that the people were to be arrayed in parties under the management of skilled politicians, each state could be expected to cast an undivided bloc of electoral votes in presidential elections. Party organizations—and their leaders—would now be extremely influential in conducting the game in every state.

It will be apparent that the uniform adoption of the general-ticket system was not the result of a formal, Constitutional decision and that as late as 1824 the issue of whether it would be preferred to some form of district plan remained in doubt. It therefore becomes important to offer an explanation of how and why the decision was reached, and why it came at the time that it did.

During the congressional debates, the proponents of district elections employed the rhetoric of republicanism and even of mild anti-partyism in attacking the general ticket, expressing as well their concerns about geographical parties, the role of political minorities, and voter apathy. The themes most emphasized by those opposed to any amendments and supportive of the general ticket were in quite a different vein. They expounded on the federative principle, insisting on the political character of the states. They spoke of the inviolability of the large-state, small-state compromise embodied in the Constitution. They upheld the doctrine of state rights. And they were candid, even vehement, in repelling attacks on political parties. They succeeded in developing a rationale for the general ticket that went far beyond the earlier somewhat apologetic argument of self-defense. Whether this rationale was fully persuasive is very doubtful, but even if it was not, the system that it sought to justify came to prevail.

No less interesting than what was said was what was not discussed. The debates centered on process, the process by which the President was to be elected. Virtually no consideration was given to the matter of how the process would affect the nature of the office. Rather, there was concern with how the process would affect the political roles of the states, how it would affect parties, how it would affect the electorate, or how it might affect the role of Congress. Whether it would enhance or weaken presidential authority, enlarge or reduce the independence of the office, contribute to or militate against the expression of a national consensus on public policies, or attract or repel statesmen of exalted reputations were questions that were not addressed. Even those who were most advanced in championing a genuinely popular process, such as Benton and McDuffie, based their case on the grounds that the people were less subject to corruption than any intermediaries, rather than by arguing that the President should represent a national constituency. The Framers had designed an office—the presidency—and then had sought to contrive a process of election that would produce precisely the type of person they invisioned to fill that office. They were keenly aware of the connection between the process and the office. That awareness was lacking in the debates that preceded the adoption of the general ticket.

Even the misgivings about the legitimacy of the process were not resolved. With the circumstances attendant on the House election in 1825 fresh in their minds, and with the full knowledge of the near disaster in 1801, the majority of the members of Congress was apprehensive about the contingent election provided for in the Constitution. But they were unable to agree on an acceptable alternative, and the danger remained.

The triumph of the general ticket was less the product of constitutional theory than of political reality. The proponents of change found it difficult to agree on an amendment that would meet their various requirements. More to the point, the re-emergence of parties, and especially of state party organizations formed to support the pretensions of Adams or Jackson, strengthened the appeal of the general ticket in those states where it had been in vogue and made it all but obligatory in those that had favored district elections. Legislative elections succumbed to the example of popular participation in most states and to the rhetoric of democracy. Like the adoption of the Twelfth Amendment, the acceptance of the general ticket represented in the broadest sense the accommodation of the electoral process to the requirements of political parties, or to the kind of parties that were to be characteristic of the American political system.

The presidential game, as it altered during these years, created strains between the ideal of how politics should operate in a republic and actuality. The savage intrigues in which candidates and would-be candidates engaged, the divisive sectional calculations, the "corrupt" involvement of Congressmen in the making of Presidents, the relaxation of inhibitions on electioneering by candidates, the extension of political management represented by the convention system, and even the re-emergence of parties supportive of "men rather than measures" occasioned alarm. A New York Congressman sounded a typical note of anxiety in 1826: "Faction is at war with the vital principle of freedom," he declared. "It destroys independence of sentiment, and the freedom of election; it subjects the understanding of the People to the influence of their passions; its tendency is to render them venal, to accustom them to leaders and prepare them for a master. It accelerates the corruption of manners, leads to civil broils, to political changes and revolutions; and, in its progress, leads us directly to despotism as gravity to the center."[63]

For professed republicans, the novel shape that politics, and especially presidential politics, had assumed could not but engender feelings of guilt and concern. Still faithful to an inherited ideology that stressed the need for disinterested public officials, devoid of unseemly ambition and disdainful of demagoguery, and for an elective system that was immune to corruption, politicians of the era could not entirely escape the feeling that they had somehow failed to sustain their heritage. But there were new circumstances to be recognized, which in turn could produce rationales for different behavior. The people, meaning those who possessed the franchise, were now to be acknowledged, courted, appealed to, and heard as never before, and parties, traditionally viewed as suspect and transitory, acquired increasing acceptance as permanent and even essential features of the American political system. The rules of the presidential game were altered to accommodate these considerations despite the dissonance between ideal and actuality.

VI

The Party Game

The game of faction had invigorated the contest for the presidency and engendered innovations in behavior and procedures. The patterns so long characteristic of the Virginia game had been discarded. A new version of the contest for the presidency had emerged, featuring popular participation, the all but universal adoption of the general-ticket system, the tentative appearance of national conventions, vigorous campaign styles, and attempts to organize broad coalitions in support of rival candidates. Although the course of future developments could scarcely have been predicted in 1832, we can view that turbulent and experimental era as marking the prelude to what was now to become the party game.

The party game evolved between 1832 and 1844, incorporating and building on the novel elements that had been introduced in the previous decade. After 1832, the process of party formation begun earlier was brought to completion. By 1844 the contest for the presidency was to be waged by two parties that were both national in scope. In the interim, and not without the expression of ambivalent and even hostile views, political parties acquired qualified acceptance as appropriate agencies for mobilizing the electorate of the republic. The convention system, the key device of the new party organizations, was adopted after furious debates and with lingering misgivings. A popular campaign style, forecast by the appeals made in 1828, was fully elaborated in 1840, when a pattern was fixed that was to persist into the twentieth century. The office of the presidency reflected the changes in the game produced by the contest of parties. The presidency was to be not only the prize for which the contest was waged and the axis on which the politics of the nation revolved but also an office whose incumbent was expected to acknowledge and reward the party to whom he was indebted for his election.[1]

The period during which the party game was assuming its distinctive and durable form has been generally recognized as one marked by unusual vitality, excitement, instability, and change. John Higham characterized it as the age of "boundlessness." Tocqueville perceived it as the time when "individualism" came to dominate the orientation of Americans. Others have emphasized the weakening of institutional controls, the growing disrespect for authority, and the rise of egalitarian attitudes. The varied influences of nationalism, romanticism, and rationalism were all operative, along with the powerful forces of religious revivalism and humanitarian reform. Economic development entered a new phase, with expanded markets opened up by improved transportation and served by a growing manufacturing establishment. Westward expansion and the rapid development of urban areas brought massive shifts in population. At the beginning of the era, railroads were a novelty; by its end, the telegraph was a reality.

The task confronting those who would seek to impose the orderliness of a party system on the politics of this turbulent period was indeed formidable. New and very diverse interests had to be accommodated, sudden excitements or enthusiasms had to be recognized, attitudes resistant to discipline and authority had to be confronted. The simple calculus of the old North *versus* South sectionalism had to be adjusted to take into consideration the claims of "the West," a vaguely defined but self-conscious and rapidly growing entity. The unprecedented assault on slavery launched in the 1830s by militant abolitionist organizations, and the equally militant defense of the institution by outraged southerners, had ominous political implications. Conflicting views regarding the role that the federal government should play in economic matters found political expression, as did disagreement over the issue of geographical expansion. There was, in addition, the problem of adapting to the federalized nature of the American political system, with its separate but related arenas of state and national politics. Beyond all these difficulties in the way of political parties, there was the anti-party attitude inherent in traditional republican ideology. Such were the obstacles faced by those who would make the contest for the presidency a party game, and in taking note of them we can better appreciate why success was limited.

The most important factor in transforming the contest for the presidency into a party game was, quite obviously, the formation of a comprehensive party system. As it developed by 1844, it was basically a two-party system, although it was not entirely impervious to third-party movements. Unlike the parties of the Jeffersonian era, these new parties—Democrat and Whig—were intersectional, extended to every state, and—for a brief period of less than two decades—competed on fairly even terms. They were most effective as what can be termed electoral parties. That is, they functioned best in securing agreement on candidates, conducting campaigns, mobilizing their partisans in the electorate, and sustaining and rewarding a large and effective corps of organizers. They were less successful in articulating issues, formulating programs, and enforcing discipline on elected officials.[2]

As of 1832 the game of faction had not resulted in the creation of a party system. The Jacksonians were represented in strength throughout the nation; only in New England and Kentucky were they a decided minority. The opposition, divided into National Republicans and Anti-Masons, was quite ineffective in the South and the West. Where the Jacksonians faced significant competition, notably in the Middle States and New England, they had developed party organizations and gained the allegiance of activists and voters, as had their opponents. In the South and West, where overt opposition to the Old Hero ranged from modest to negligible, symptoms of partisanship were scarcely visible beyond the presidential contest. Party organization was weak or ephemeral, state and even congressional elections were conducted with little or no reference to party labels, and doctrinal positions remained vague. Neither National Republicanism nor Anti-Masonry exerted a strong appeal to those sections, nor did Henry Clay, and there was at least the prospect that, like the Federalists, these opposition parties were doomed to remain in the minority, awaiting another Era of Good Feelings.

Quite suddenly, between 1832 and 1835, the political scene

altered drastically. Parties in opposition to the Jacksonians emerged in the southern and western states, sufficiently formidable to challenge and even defeat their once invincible foes. In the North, the Anti-Masonic frenzy subsided, except in Vermont and Pennsylvania, and the opposition coalesced under the name Whig, a label that appeared first in the 1834 spring elections in New York City and quickly displaced the short-lived National Republican designation.[3] Although the Democrats actually increased their strength in the North during those years, especially in New England, they suffered large-scale defections among the nominal Jacksonians in the rest of the country. By 1836, Martin Van Buren faced strong opposition in virtually every state, in stark contrast to the conditions Jackson had confronted in 1832.

The bases for the appearance of opposition parties in the South and West were many and varied and can scarcely be dealt with exhaustively here. In the South, Jackson had been looked upon as a fellow southerner and slaveholder, and it had been expected that he would be zealous in defending southern interests. His failure to take a strong stand in favor of tariff reduction, his break with Calhoun, and his dismissal of southerners from his Cabinet all occasioned misgivings, as did his support for Van Buren for the vice presidency, but there was no major revolt in 1832. Then, early in his second administration, his stinging rebuke to South Carolina in his Nullification Proclamation, his advocacy of the Force Bill, and his extraordinary exercise of executive authority in removing government deposits from the Bank of the United States raised issues on which an opposition could rally. Leaders of the movement, many of whom were personally disaffected toward Jackson or who were antagonistic to the dominant Jacksonian faction in their states, raised the cries of state rights and executive usurpation. They were emboldened in their endeavors by the prospect that Van Buren would be the Democratic nominee in 1836, and they were aware that the South had never given its support to a northern candidate for President. They exploited the mounting southern concern about the security of the institution of slavery, now under attack by northern abolitionists, arguing that the interests of their region could be safe only with a southern President. These appeals were effective. By 1835 there were opposition parties in every state, some adopting the name of Whig, some employing the State Rights label, and others simply calling themselves the Anti-Van Buren party.[4]

In the western states, where the issues of state rights and slavery were of minor interest, opposition factions emphasized "executive usurpation," decrying especially Jackson's removal of the deposits and his determination to dictate the choice of his successor. Van Buren enjoyed little personal popularity, and when a western candidate in the person of William Henry Harrison emerged, he provided a rallying point for anti-administration elements. Disaffection in the West assumed form somewhat later than in the South, but by 1835, Whig or Anti-Van Buren parties were clearly recognizable.

While these opposition parties were taking shape from state to state, the "presidential question," as it was commonly termed, was constantly under discussion. It was conceded that Van Buren would be the administration candidate, but who would oppose him? There were opposition parties in every state, but could they be welded into a national coalition in time to agree on a single candidate? Would a national leadership emerge to give direction to the discordant elements that shared in common only an aversion to "executive usurpation" and to Martin Van Buren? Would the presidential game in 1836 be a two-party contest, or would it signal the disintegration of parties and a return to the factionalism of 1824, with the ultimate decision to be made by the House of Representatives?

There was no prospect that the transitory National Republican organization that had been contrived to support Clay's candidacy in 1832 could be revived to mobilize the opposition. but there was the possibility that leaders of the opposition in Congress, who marshalled a strong and fairly coherent following to contest Jackson's banking policy and even secured the passage by the Senate of a resolution censuring the President, might function as the organizers of a national opposition party. However, the most conspicuous of these leaders—Calhoun, Clay, and Webster—were all hopeful of winning the presidency in 1836 and viewed one another as rivals, rather than collaborators. No consideration could be given to arranging a national convention to organize the opposition and produce agreement on a candidate because denunciation of the convention system was a conspicuous element of the anti-Van

Buren rhetoric and because it was apparent by 1835 that candidates already in the field would not yield. Contrary to the common assertion, there was no "Whig strategy" for 1836.[5] There could be no Whig strategy because there was no national Whig party. Instead, there was an inchoate opposition made up of Whigs, Anti-Masons, State Rights men, Calhounites, and anti-Van Buren Jacksonians.

In the absence of unified management, either through a congressional caucus or a national convention, opposition candidates proliferated. Calhoun, who early in 1834 believed that the Jacksonians faced destruction, planned to mobilize the "State Rights party of the South" and, with anti-administration support in the North, mount a successful candidacy. His hopes were dashed when the Virginia election in 1835 demonstrated his lack of support in that crucial state.[6] Clay, too, saw himself as the most formidable opponent of Van Buren, but in January 1835 when Ohio Whig legislators nominated a native son, Supreme Court Justice John McLean, he recognized the hopelessness of his cause.[7] Webster was placed in nomination by the Massachusetts legislature in January 1835, but his candidacy aroused little enthusiasm elsewhere, despite his efforts to enlist the backing of the Anti-Masons. None of these three "great figures" could provide a rallying point for the opposition.[8] Instead, Van Buren's major challengers were to come from unexpected quarters.

William Henry Harrison was an unlikely candidate. A native of Virginia, he had served as governor of Indiana Territory, represented that state in Congress, and been minister to Colombia. He enjoyed a fine military reputation derived from his achievements as a major general during the War of 1812. Best of all, he had won modest fame for his victory over the Indians at the Battle of Tippecanoe. Now, advanced in years and in straitened circumstances, he held the modest position of Clerk of the Court of Common Pleas in Hamilton County, Ohio.[9]

He emerged from obscurity to public notice when a letter of his protesting the undue attention given to Colonel Richard M. Johnson's military exploits was widely reported in the press late in 1834. Soon after, he was nominated for President by a public meeting in Harrisburg, Pennsylvania. Within the next few months, similar meetings in Cincinnati, New York, Indiana, Kentucky, and elsewhere added their endorsements. Backed by a small coterie of Ohio friends, Harrison took his candidacy seriously, writing numerous letters for publication and making a personal tour to win support in Indiana. His prospects brightened in December 1835 when he was nominated by both the Whigs and the Anti-Masons in Pennsylvania. Meanwhile, he had received the grudging support of Clay, who regarded him as the most eligible candidate to unite northern and western opponents of the administration. Ohio, its original nominee, McLean, having withdrawn from the contest, conferred its blessing in February, and other western and northern states, except Massachusetts, soon fell in line. The opposition parties of the North and the West had a candidate. He was "the people's candidate," brought forth not by a convention of office-holders bowing to the dictates of King Andrew but by his unbossed fellow citizens. He was, moreover, a hero, standing only slightly behind Jackson in his claims on the nation's gratitude.[10]

Van Buren's second major opponent was equally improbable. Hugh Lawson White of Tennessee had long been one of Jackson's closest friends and political associates. As a member of the Senate he had warmly supported Jackson's policies. For reasons that may never be satisfactorily explained, he became disenchanted with Jackson in 1834 and amenable to suggestions that he challenge Van Buren. By his own lights, White was not a Whig—like Jackson he called himself a Republican—but he was strenuously opposed to the President's attempt to impose Van Buren as his successor.[11]

White's candidacy owed much to factional discord within the ranks of the Tennessee Jacksonians. John Bell, who had accepted opposition support in defeating James K. Polk for the speakership of the House of Representatives in June 1834, arranged late in 1834 with several members of the Tennessee delegation to secure White's consent to be a candidate. To avoid the appearance that White was merely a favorite-son candidate, he was first placed in nomination by Alabama legislators early in January 1835. Soon two newspapers were established in Washington to advance his cause, and several presses throughout the South declared their support. With the movement steadily gaining adherents, the Tennessee legislature, to

Jackson's everlasting dismay, unanimously re-elected White to the Senate and in October 1835 nominated him for President. At the same time, the legislators adopted resolutions approving generally the foreign and domestic policies of the Jackson administration and declaring that no candidate embodied so well as White the principles on which Jackson had been elevated to the presidency. Their sole criticism was directed against the Democratic National Convention, which they characterized as being as evil as the discredited congressional caucus.[12]

White's candidacy was deplored both by Whigs and Democrats. Webster observed that it "had disgusted deeply, the whole body of our friends in the North." Clay, noting that White held "no one principle (except in the matter of patronage) as to public measures in common with the Whigs," thought that "the election of either Mr. Van Buren or Judge White would be a great misfortune, although that of the Judge would be least." Senator Willie P. Mangum of North Carolina, soon to become one of the most respected Whig leaders, reflected the bewilderment of many southern politicians. Calhoun had been his first choice as a presidential candidate; then he had veered to Clay. Finally, as the least evil of the available choices he turned to White, whose Jacksonian principles he found offensive. His political associates in North Carolina, expressing their gratification that White was an opponent of a high tariff, internal improvements, and the Bank, emphasized their divergence from northern Whig views. In making their choice of White over Van Buren, they declared, "we deem it a safe rule in choosing a public servant, to take him who is identified with us in interest . . . rather than one who is not bound to us by such ties."[13] Unlike Van Buren, White was a slaveholder.

To the Jacksonians, White was a deluded apostate whose candidacy threatened to divide the party and result in that most deplorable of eventualities, a contingent election by the House. Denouncing the evil forces that had united behind "Judge White's sectional popularity" and fuming over his betrayal by his own state, the Old Hero blamed Bell, Calhoun, and Clay for what he described as a strategy of "divide and conquer." On the other hand, White's followers denied that what they termed the "Van Buren party" had an exclusive claim to the Republican designation and insisted that their man, rather than Van Buren, was the authentic successor to Jefferson and Jackson.[14]

With several opposition candidates in the field and with the party apparently crumbling in the South and West, the Jacksonians faced a dismal prospect early in 1835. In an effort to rally the party and hold it firmly together behind Van Buren, the National Convention met in Baltimore in May 1835, nearly a year and a half before the election. Van Buren was nominated unanimously, but there was a sharp and significant division over the vice-presidential nominee. One contender was Colonel Richard M. Johnson of Kentucky, famed as the slayer of Tecumseh and noted as well for his opposition to imprisonment for debt. A hero to the West and to eastern workingmen, his notorious domestic arrangements—he lived with his black mistress and their two daughters—were offensive to southerners. He was opposed by Senator William C. Rives of Virginia. With the backing of the White House, and especially of the erstwhile Kentuckians, Amos Kendall and Francis P. Blair, Johnson won the necessary two-thirds vote by a narrow and dubious margin. It was a remarkable decision, for it implied that the traditional New York-Virginia alliance was to be broken in favor of a North-West axis. The rupture was highlighted by the Virginia delegation's announcement that it would not support Johnson. Instead, that state was to give its electoral votes to William Smith of Alabama.[15]

Confronted for the first time by formidable, if diverse, opposition in every state, the Democrats solidified their organizations, appealed for party unity, and emphasized that were Van Buren not elected, the contest would undoubtedly be thrown into the House. Van Buren, in carefully worded statements, made special efforts to assure the South that he opposed any interference with slavery. Harrison broke with tradition by embarking on a three-month campaign tour through the West and the North, expressing in lengthy speeches his somewhat ambiguous views on economic issues but stressing his opposition to the excessive use of executive power. White's adherents portrayed their candidate as a man whose sound republican principles had not been corrupted by partisan considerations and as one who would always safeguard southern interests. Webster remained in the contest as the candidate of the Massachusetts Whigs, but his support was confined to that state. South Carolina, under Calhoun's potent influence, declined to identify with any of the candidates, eventually giving its electoral votes to Willie P. Mangum of North Carolina.

The results of this extraordinary contest were heartening to the Democrats and to the opposition. Van Buren, with slightly more than half of the popular total, secured an electoral majority of only twenty-three votes. Harrison ran well throughout the North and the West, carrying seven states, and White, although he was victorious only in Georgia and Tennessee, received more than 40 percent of the vote in six other southern states. Massachusetts went for Webster, but it had been prepared to shift its electoral votes to Harrison if such action would ensure his election. Similarly, South Carolina was ready to give its votes to White in the event that Van Buren did not get a majority in the electoral college.[16]

Harrison and White had been effective in rallying the opposition in the West and in the South, but Van Buren was able to improve on Jackson's showing in the North—carrying four New England states as well as New York and Pennsylvania—and his party strength in the West and in the South was sufficient to hold off his challengers in those regions. Johnson was less successful. Essentially because of Virginia's disaffection, he fell one vote short of an electoral majority. Consequently, the election of the Vice President had to be decided by the Senate, which chose the controversial Kentuckian over Harrison's running mate, Francis Granger of New York, whose presence on the ticket represented a bid for the support of the Anti-Masons.[17]

The presidential election of 1836 brought the Democratic party to maturity. No longer dependent on Jackson's charismatic and diffuse appeal, its thinned but disciplined ranks had closed behind Van Buren. Aided vastly by the direction and patronage that emanated from the White House, by a growing consensus on policy questions, by a host of leaders with a vested interest in its welfare, and by the voters who had come to identify with it, the party assumed the characteristic features it was to maintain with little change for the next twenty years. The election also demonstrated the potential strength of the opposition. By November 1836 opposition parties of various doctrinal hues and labels shared an antipathy to Van Buren, executive usurpation, and the iniquities of convention nominations. If they could be brought to extend the area of their agreement, adopt a common designation, and achieve unity behind a single candidate, the presidential contest would become a two-party game.

The trend of events, coupled with the determination of opposition leaders everywhere to ensure harmony, produced the desired results. When Van Buren called Congress into special session and asked for the establishment of an Independent Treasury, in order to divorce government funds from all banks, he provided an ideal issue to unite both his own and the opposition party. Devoid of sectional over-tones and less explosive than the issue of the Bank recharter, the Independent Treasury bill was battled over in Congress for more than two years before it was adopted by a partisan vote in June 1840.[18] In the meantime, Calhoun returned to the Democratic party, relieving the opposition of his discordant voice and influence. Several notable Democrats, styling themselves Conservatives, broke from the party ranks in New York and Virginia over the Inde-pendent Treasury issue, reinforcing the "hard money" image of the Democrats. Aiding the opposition cause was the Panic of 1837, a severe economic downturn that fostered discontent with the Van Buren administration.

What was to become the basic strategy of the opposition was set forth early by the Ohio Whigs. Meeting in convention on the Fourth of July, 1837, they adopted with enthusiasm the report of a committee on national affairs that castigated the Van Buren administration for its abuses and its usurpations.[19] The miscreants must be pulled down. "All sections of the country must unite—all minor divisions must be laid aside—all personal prejudices must be given up. . . ," declared the manifesto. "The advocates of *nullifica-tion* and the supporters of the *force bill* have a common interest in the matter . . . The slaveholder and the abolitionist, the mason and anti-mason, are alike its victims . . . The rally must be made upon the presidential election of 1840, and the *reform suffrage* concen-trated upon a single candidate. . . ." Such a concentration could be achieved, declared the committee, only through a national con-vention, and it respectfully proposed that one should be held as early as June 1838. The Ohio Whigs announced their decided preference for Harrison, but in the spirit of harmony they proclaimed their willingness to support any nominee of the national convention. Here, indeed, was a pragmatic and latitudinarian appeal, accompanied by an extremely practical plan of action.

The Ohio proposal met a cordial reception elsewhere, although not without some expression of embarrassment on the part of those who a year earlier had been so vehement in their condemnation of the convention system. Clay lent his sanction, and in May 1838 "the opposition members of Congress" authorized the announcement that a convention would meet in Harrisburg, Pennsylvania, on the first Wednesday in December 1839. Fearful that discord over the presidential question might shatter the fragile coalition, opposition leaders as well as party presses and meetings constantly urged that no state nominations be made and that all pledge to support whoever might be the convention choice.[20]

Clay expected that the choice would fall on him. He was, after all, the most conspicuous leader of the opposition and a senior statesman. He could count on the ardent support of southern foes of the administration, who were now prepared to overlook the centralizing tendencies of his American System and emphasize his commitment to slavery and his courageous resistance to executive usurpation. Exuding confidence, he announced in June 1838 that he would "remain in an attitude perfectly passive, doing nothing whatever with the intention of attracting the current public feeling to . . . [himself]."[21]

Harrison was not passive. A popular figure in the West and the North, as the result of his active and impressive campaign in 1836, he made a well-publicized speaking tour of Ohio and Indiana in the summer of 1838, acknowledging the great attainments of Clay and Webster but depicting himself as an "older statesman" who had always been "the ardent supporter of the rights of the people, in the councils of the nation, and in the field their faithful and devoted soldier." In November he received the nomination of the National Anti-Masonic Convention, and in accepting it, he set forth a seven-point platform that ignored economic issues and instead defined his narrow concept of the role of the President. Setting aside his earlier self-denying ordinance, Clay made a triumphal tour from New York to Washington in August in an effort to stem the rising Harrison tide. Webster was again brought forward by Massachusetts, and there was some sentiment in New York for General Winfield Scott, but what the opposition sought most of all was unity behind a candidate who could win.[22]

Pennsylvania well illustrates this determination. There the opposition was divided into a large and effective Anti-Masonic party and a weak Whig party. With a view to bringing these elements together, the "democratic anti-Van Buren" members of the legislature issued a call for a state convention to meet in Harrisburg in September 1839. The announced purpose was "to unite the anti-Van Buren party." The president of the convention, describing himself as "surrounded by Whigs, anti-masons, and conservatives," found in the assemblage a "spirit of determination to merge all minor differences of opinion in one grand and patriotic object of redeeming our beloved country from the grasp of the spoilers." After expressing its great esteem for Henry Clay, "who should one day have the highest evidence of the nation's affection," but whose candidacy now would be "unjust to him and fatal to the party," the convention then declared for Harrison as the only candidate who could produce "union and harmony."[23]

Similar sentiments prevailed when the "Democratic Whig National Convention" met in Harrisburg in December. The delegates were determined to nominate a winner, and Clay had too many enemies to fill that role. By an intricate process that was intended to prevent any discord over the nomination on the floor of the convention, Harrison was nominated. As a concession to the state-rights southern wing of the party, John Tyler of Virginia was named as his running mate. No semblance of a platform was adopted.[24] Although Clay and his warm advocates were keenly disappointed with the outcome, the prospect of victory inspired a euphoric spirit of harmony within the new-born party.

The Democrats, after twelve hectic years in power, were dispirited and divided. No one challenged Van Buren for the presidential nomination, but there were irreconcilable differences over the vice presidency. The Virginia Democrats were so hostile to Johnson that at their state convention they nominated James K. Polk as

Van Buren's running mate and then resolved not to attend the Democratic National Convention. When that body met in Baltimore in May 1840, several states were unrepresented and some others sent only a single delegate. After adopting a nine-point platform— the first by a national party convention—the delegates awaited with apprehension the report of a committee on nominations.

There was no dissent from the recommendation that Van Buren be renominated. But Johnson's supporters were disappointed when the committee reported that they deemed it expedient not to make any nomination for the second place on the ticket but to "leave the decision to their republican fellow citizens in the several states, trusting that before the election shall take place, their opinions shall become so concentrated as to secure the choice of a vice president by the electoral colleges." Johnson was unacceptable, but no agreement could be reached on an alternative. When this fact became apparent, the Johnson men yielded in the interest of party harmony, and the nomination committee's awkward solution was accepted. In addition to Polk, William R. King of Alabama and John Forsyth of Georgia received state nominations, but all three later announced their withdrawal, leaving Johnson as the sole Democratic candidate.[25] Thus, after some vicissitudes, did the forces of party regularity manifest themselves.

Now, for the first time, two parties that were national in scope and similarly organized contested vigorously for the presidential prize. Never before had the voters of the whole country been so closely aligned behind rival candidates, and the exertions made by the two parties to activate their followers and win new recruits vastly exceeded all previous efforts. The candidates themselves, and especially Harrison, were far more active than any of their predecessors in stating their views and overtly soliciting votes. Above all, the campaign was made memorable by its theatrical quality, with its log cabins, Tippecanoe Clubs, mass rallies, flamboyant rhetoric, stump speeches, and aggressive canvassing.[26] The combination of close party competition in almost every state and the interest aroused by the exciting campaign style produced an unprecedented outpouring of voters; four-fifths of the eligible electorate surged to the polls. The new party game demonstrated its popularity. The contest for the presidency, once of peripheral interest, had become the central, all-absorbing object of American politics.

Harrison won in an electoral landslide, carrying all but seven states. But Van Buren received nearly 47 percent of the popular vote and lost in several states by narrow margins. The Democrats attributed the Whig victory to "political buffoonery," to "the triumph of fraud and falsehood over truth and argument," to the evil influence exerted by the "monied power," but they were not disconsolate. "This discordant combination of the odds and ends of all parties cannot long continue," prophesied the Richmond *Enquirer*. For the Whigs, it was "a brilliant victory of men—high minded men—over corruption and power," an expression of national harmony that surmounted sectional divisions, a victory for liberty in a contest against executive power, a triumph for republican institutions over the forces of corruption; above all, "the people" had asserted their power over the politicians.[27]

The dynamics of the contest for the presidency, operating within the context of new conditions after 1824, had at last resulted in the formation of two nation-wide electoral parties. The party that had mobilized to elect Jackson in 1828, and which had assumed distinctive form by 1835, was now opposed by the Whig party, which had been stimulated to unite by the attractive prospect of overthrowing Van Buren in 1840. Subordinating sectional and doctrinal differences, refusing to permit a diversity of opinion regarding candidates to mar their quest for harmony, and appealing to the electorate to oust the spoilsmen and strike down executive usurpation, the Whigs had rallied behind an aged hero and carried the election.

The election of 1840 exhibited most of the attributes of a party game, but it remained to be determined whether the new format would persist, or whether, as so frequently had been the case in the past, it would veer off in some different direction. Could the Democrats survive the adversity of the loss of the White House, or would they wither away as the Adams party had done after 1828 or break up into squabbling factions? Could the Whigs, with their many discordant elements, retain their unity when confronted with the responsibilities of governing? Would the party system be viable as new issues arose to agitate the political scene? Would the primary agencies of party organization, notably the national conventions, be adequate to deal with genuine internal conflicts, or would they, like the old congressional caucus, prove unequal to the task? Would parties, themselves, retain their qualified acceptance, or would old republican anti-party ideology reassert its force and weaken or destroy what had so recently been created? Not until the party system had survived an extraordinary array of challenges between 1840 and 1844 could these questions be answered with any degree of confidence.

Important and potentially devastating as these challenges were, we must constrain ourselves to a bare enumeration of them. There was, first of all, the death of the Whig party's nominal leader a month after his inauguration and the accession of John Tyler, soon to be cast out of the party for his refusal to co-operate with the Clay-led Whig Congress. There was the real threat that Tyler would attempt to form a new party, oriented strongly toward southern interests. There was the disruptive influence of Calhoun within the Democratic party, manifesting itself in 1843 when he tied his presidential ambitions to an assault on the makeup and procedures of the national convention. There were the signs of mounting factionalism within the Democratic party, presaging a bitter contest over the presidential nomination. Most important of all, there was the sudden and dreadful emergence of a new issue—the annexation of Texas—which immediately became associated with the causes of slavery and expansionism and even raised the specter of war.[28]

Remarkably enough, partisan identification had acquired sufficient hold within the electorate and the necessity for party regularity had become such a paramount consideration for political leaders that all these crises were surmounted. By 1843 the Whigs had solidified their ranks behind Clay as their undisputed standard bearer and had even accepted a somewhat softened version of his American System.[29] Tyler's plans for a third party, which actually proceeded to the point of holding a national convention, were frustrated when the Democrats took over his main issue, Texas annexation, and he withdrew from the contest. Calhoun's divisive maneuvers, as usual, came to naught, and he again left the Democratic party to ally himself with Tyler. The most formidable problem was posed by the annexation issue, which exploded on the political scene in April 1844, when Tyler submitted to the Senate the treaty that had been secretly negotiated with Texas. It had dissimilar effects on the two parties.

Clay immediately announced his opposition to annexation, arguing that such an action would bring war with Mexico and introduce a serious element of discord in the nation at a time when "union, peace, and patience" were required. Four days after his statement was published he was nominated by acclamation by the Whig National Convention, which gave every indication of wishing to ignore entirely the Texas question. Although in subsequent statements during the campaign, Clay seemed to moderate his stand against annexation, and obviously preferred to bring other issues into focus, his party loyally fell into line behind him. Even in the South, where annexation sentiment was strong, the ranks scarcely wavered.[30]

The Democrats were less harmonious. Van Buren sought the party's nomination, and enough state conventions had declared for him to assure him a majority in the national convention. But there were powerful undercurrents of opposition, especially in the South and West. Late in April, Van Buren disclosed his position on annexation in his usual ponderous and lengthy style. He opposed immediate annexation because it would involve the nation in an unjust war with Mexico. But he left the door open by stating that if, after the issue had been discussed in the coming election, there was strong popular sentiment for the measure, and both houses of Congress supported it, he would bow to the popular will. His opponents within the party, who had already obtained a letter from Jackson favoring immediate annexation, declared that Van Buren's position made him unacceptable.[31]

Meeting late in May, the Democratic National Convention faced a grave crisis. The Van Buren forces lost a battle to repeal the two-thirds rule, which meant that a minority could block his nomination. He secured a majority of the votes on the first ballot, but by the seventh ballot his strength was fading, and the opposition was seeking to mobilize behind Lewis Cass of Michigan, who was loathed by the Van Burenites. They could, at this stage, deadlock the convention—preventing any nomination—or they could throw their support to a compromise candidate. They chose the latter course. After a night of feverish negotiations, it was decided to bring forth James K. Polk of Tennessee, who had always been a loyal adherent of Van Buren but whose announced stand in favor of immediate annexation made him acceptable to the South. Accordingly, with considerable anguish, Van Buren was dropped, and on the ninth ballot Polk won the nomination. Almost as an afterthought, a plank was inserted in the platform calling for "the reoccupation of Oregon and the reannexation of Texas, at the earliest practicable period . . . ." To appease the Van Buren faction, the vice-presidential nomination was offered to Silas Wright of New York, but when he refused to accept it, it went to George M. Dallas of Pennsylvania. The convention had been a success. Disruption had been averted. Harmony ostensibly reigned within the party. Jubilation was especially evident among southern Democrats; after having been saddled with Van Buren in the past two elections, they at last had a candidate who was one of their own.[32]

The election of 1844 was fought out by the unified and disciplined national parties, both of which had met and surmounted serious crises. Well organized in every state, they employed the campaign techniques that had been tested in 1840 to bring their partisans to the polls. No previous election had been so closely contested; not until 1880 would the presidency be decided by a narrower margin. How much effect the Texas issue had in the campaign is still debated by historians. It is ironical that the final outcome may well have been determined by a tiny third party—the Liberty party. First launched in 1840 by northern foes of slavery, it had garnered fewer than seven thousand votes. Now, in 1844, its strength increased nearly tenfold, giving its candidate, James G. Birney, 2.3 percent of the total popular vote. Had the Liberty party vote in New York gone to the Whigs, Clay would have carried that state, and the election. But Polk, with a popular plurality of under 40,000 in a total of over 2,704,000, got an electoral majority of thirty-two votes.

The election is best understood as a test of partisanship, as a manifestation of those partisan identities that had been forged in successive state and national contests for a decade or more. Seen in this context, the election of 1844 brought the party game to maturity. After more than half a century the contest for the presidency had assumed a format whose general outline was to persist into the twentieth century.

The transformation of the contest for the presidency into a game played by two contending parties required an acceptance of the idea of political parties. Such acceptance was achieved grudgingly, with considerable ambivalence, and subject to many qualifications. There were formidable ideological and institutional obstacles to be overcome or evaded; suffice it to say that Americans even now are confused and divided in their concepts of the proper roles and functions of parties. Jefferson and his associates had justified the organization of a party committed to large principles as a means of saving the republic from the extreme peril of subversion. Such an attitude could scarcely provide a rationale for a two-party system, for it accorded no legitimacy to an opposition party. This thinking persisted. Jackson, who saw himself as Jefferson's heir, and who almost invariably called himself a Republican, regarded partisanship as representing personal loyalty to himself and his policies. He viewed the opposition as embodying all the forces of evil, as something to be "crushed." He was largely indifferent to party as organization; he was not, in that sense, a party builder. Martin Van Buren represented a different breed. A product of the rough and tumble school of New York factional politics, he came to have a reverence for party regularity, for party as organization, and he could even recognize that in the absence of meaningful opposition a party could not be held together. It was Van Buren's rather than Jackson's view that prevailed by 1844.[33]

There were many variants of the Jackson and the Van Buren attitudes. Some political figures were prepared to accept only parties based on principles; parties formed to advance the interests of individuals were mere factions and therefore reprehensible. Others granted the inevitability, even the necessity of parties, but reacted negatively to party managers, conventions, patronage, and the sordid elements that seemed to accompany partisan politics. Many legislators and Congressmen were willing to accept a party label when they were running for election, but then they resisted "dictation," refused to be "collar men," and claimed to be responsible only to their own consciences and their constituency.

It remained a common complaint that parties represented not "the people," but rather the office-holders and office-seekers and were therefore unworthy of credence or support.

As has been commonly observed, the exceedingly complex character of the American electoral system posed problems for parties, and especially for party government. "The Fathers hoped to create not a system of party government under a constitution," concluded Richard Hofstadter, "but rather a constitutional government that would check and control parties."[34] Hence the varying terms and constituencies of Representatives, Senators, and the President; the division of governing authority between the states and the federal government; the complex of checks and balances and separation of powers. The election calendar made it difficult to integrate state, congressional, and presidential politics. Down to 1845, Congressmen were rarely elected at the same time as the President; they were chosen in most states in conjunction with the election of state officials. State elections were held at various times from March to November. Consequently, the "coattail" effect, that might have bound congressional candidates to the positions of their national parties and their presidential nominees, was lacking. The federalized nature of American electoral politics, which, as Michael Holt points out so vividly, encouraged candidates of the same party to espouse conflicting views in different sections of the country, hardly made for well-disciplined parties. Finally, the parties required such vast resources of personnel to staff their organizations and conduct the multiplicity of election campaigns for offices at all levels of government that "the hope of reward and the fear of punishment" loomed exceedingly large, often larger than the more exalted goals associated with parties. The wonder is not that parties in this era lacked cohesion, that they functioned best as electoral machines, but rather that they were able to operate as effectively as they did in the face of such ideological and institutional inhibitions.

The acceptance of parties was very much at issue between 1834 and 1840. In the South and West particularly, where there had been relatively little experience with two-party politics, anti-party sentiments were prevalent. The opposition, as it emerged in those years, could win popularity by denouncing the Jacksonians as rank partisans who bowed to the dictates of their leader, even to the point of accepting the man he designated as his successor. John Bell, in a well-publicized speech in 1835, put the case in terms that won widespread approval:

> It is now for the first time in the history of free states solemnly proposed and seriously attempted to give an organized and systematic party action to the government, under the plausible and delusive pretext that it is necessary, in order to preserve the great objects for which the government was formed. I regard this . . . as the most daring, and at the same time the most dangerous conception of the age.

Party, in his words, was "that eternal foe to the repose and stability of all free states"; it was "the only source whence destruction awaits our system." He and his associates were governed not by party, but by principle.[35]

Vice-presidential candidate Richard M. Johnson, in a public letter to the constituents of his old congressional district in 1836, was aware of the anti-party sentiment there. "I do not consider the principles of party politics involved in this election," he blandly declared, "but, even in such cases, my friends and fellow citizens will remember that, in serving them, I have never yielded to party feelings or party considerations." Members of Congress in 1834, under conflicting pressures to support or oppose Jackson's removal policy, declaimed in anguished tones against the influences of party. John C. Calhoun, always somewhat apart from the mainstream, devised an especially original criticism of national parties. Because, in his analysis, they were designed to prevent presidential elections from going to the House of Representatives, they vitiated that compromise in the Constitution that had been intended to give the smaller states an equal voice with the large in the final choice of the nation's chief executive.[36]

The assaults on parties in the 1830s were only thinly disguised attacks on the party of Jackson and Van Buren. In response, a committee appointed by the Democratic National Convention issued a "statement" in July 1835, defending and extolling their party.[37] It was, first of all, the Republican party, the party of Jefferson and of the "principles of '98" to which they belonged and gave their wholehearted allegiance. "Fellow citizens," read their appeal, "there have always been two great political parties in our country. Names have been changed, but the principle or grounds of difference between the two remain the same." The Republicans stood for limited and economical government, for non-intereference with the rights of the states, for intersectional harmony, and for obedience to the popular will. It was entirely appropriate for citizens to unite in defense of such principles. "An individual in the political world taking his own course without consulting those of the same principles and opinions with himself, would become insignificant." Parties, therefore, were essential in a free government. "Nor is the existence of such parties destitute of public utility . . . They excite a jealousy and vigilance which insures fidelity in public functionaries. They check attempts at the usurpation of power, and thereby preserve the rights of the People."

It was quite proper for a party to organize, whether through a congressional caucus or a national convention, to secure agreement on a candidate for the presidency, ran the argument. Otherwise, because of that "radical defect" in our Constitution, the election would be determined by the House of Representatives and the will of the people would be defeated, as it had been in 1825. By their insidious attacks on parties and their attempts to play upon sectional jealousies, the "evil men" in the discordant opposition were seeking to "divide and conquer." Only through such tactics could the anti-Republican forces, "whether called Federal or National Republican, Whig or Tory, Abolitionist or Nullifyer," hope to overthrow the party of the people. "We sincerely believe, that upon the preservation of the old Democratic Republican party the prosperity and happiness of our country greatly depend." To those who had become estranged from the Republican ranks because of their hostility to the party's candidate, thereby creating an unfortunate schism, the hand of forgiveness was extended. "Let them return, then, to the Republican fold of their fathers."

James K. Polk put the case more succinctly. "In all free governments parties must exist," he stated in obvious rebuttal to John Bell. "They are the natural and necessary consequences of freedom of opinion . . . So long as our system of Government is preserved, parties must and will continue to exist." He forcefully condemned those who sought to obliterate the lines that had for so long distinguished Republicans from Federalists but directed his most severe censure toward those, such as Bell and White, who were of "the 'No party' party."[38]

The Whigs, as they drew together for the election of 1840, relaxed their attacks on party, and even laid aside their opposition to the convention system. Fire must be fought with fire; the nation must be rescued from the spoilsmen. By 1845 the editor of the *American* [Whig] *Review* could write: "We regard the presence, activity and vigilance of great political *parties*, in this country, as alike essential to the permanence of liberty and the best security for the virtual and beneficent dominion of constitutional government." But were there two great parties? Party was defined as "an organized union upon the basis of principle or a system of principles," and which "proposes the good of the country." A faction, by contrast, "confines its aims and objects within itself; 'its be all and end all' is self-aggrandisement." The Whigs were a party in 1844; the Democrats were a faction.[39]

Both Whigs and Democrats accepted the idea of parties, but they were reluctant to concede the legitimacy of their opponents. The Democrats continued to insist that the Whigs were the lineal descendants of the old Federalists, still aiming to destroy republicanism. To the Whigs, the principles of the Democrats could be reduced to two: " 'regular nominations'—and that 'to the victor belong the spoils of the enemy.' "[40] Much of this rhetoric may be discounted as mere campaign verbiage, but it would not have been so commonly employed if it had not produced resonant responses. In the same vein, each party tended to employ epithets, rather than accepted designations, when referring to the other. To the Democrats, their opponents were the Federalists, the Bank party, the "coons," or the Opposition, while the Whigs used such terms as the Locos, the Van Buren party, or Office Holders. These parties were not mutually respecting rivals; they were enemies.

The party game resembled a kind of bloodless warfare. "The spirit of the party, like that of fetishistic patriotism," observed M. Ostrogorski, "is made up of sectarian contempt and dislike for those who are outside the fold, and of mechanical attachment to those who are inside." Henry Sumner Maine was more explicit. "Party feeling is probably far more a survival of the primitive combativeness of mankind than a consequence of intellectual differences between man and man. It is essentially the same sentiment which in certain states of society leads to civil, intertribal, or international war; and it is as universal as humanity." Bryce said of party that "even if intellectual conviction had much to do with its creation, emotion has more to do with its vitality and continued power. Men enjoy combat for its own sake, loving to outstrip others and carry their flag to victory . . . ."[41] Once American parties had formed and acquired the intense loyalties of their adherents, they contended not only for principle, but also for victory. Adopting the military term, they waged campaigns. The greatest token of their triumph was the presidency.

Closely associated with the question of the acceptability of parties was that of the acceptability of conventions. The most essential attribute of an electoral party is some arrangement for securing agreement on a single candidate, or slate of candidates. By the 1830s the delegate convention system was being adopted for this purpose in most of the states, and national conventions had been held for the first time to nominate candidates for the 1832 presidential elections. They represented an innovation, and—like the old congressional caucus—they were controversial. Their legitimacy and their effectiveness as party agencies remained very much in doubt down to 1844, when at last they became accepted features of the presidential game.

Condemnation of the national convention figured prominently in the attacks by the opposition on Van Buren's candidacy, especially by the supporters of Hugh L. White. The commonest charge was that the convention was made up of office-holders and office-seekers who served their own interests, rather than the interests of the people, and were subservient to the dictates of the White House. If the Republican party was truly the party of the people, then the people should choose their candidate, not the party managers and politicians. "The multitude cannot go to caucuses and conventions; they are necessarily made up of office-holders and their agents," was an often repeated criticism, "and when they once agree upon their man, he is put forward as the 'regular nomination,' and the people are told it would be high treason to go against 'regular nominations'."[42]

These attacks were addressed at length in the statement issued by the 1835 Democratic National Convention. Unless some means were employed to unite the votes of a majority of the people behind a single candidate, ran the argument, the "radical defect" in the Constitution would result in having the choice of the President devolve upon the House of Representatives. A national convention "springing immediately from the People, and representing the various parts of the Union" was the best way to "unite the Democracy of the country" and ensure that the President would be chosen by a popular vote. "Is it not a thousand times better that the evils even of a Convention, whatever they may be, should be borne, than that we should be exposed to the calamities of an election by the House of Representatives, the Pandora Box of our whole system?" Moreover, in the absence of a convention, the party of Jefferson and Jackson, upon which the safety of the nation depended, would be divided and fall prey to the enemies of true republicanism.[43]

After the election, as the opposition sought to unite its forces for the 1840 contest, antipathy to the national convention soon subsided. By 1837 Henry Clay was urging that there was no better means of collecting the general sense of those opposed to the Van Buren administration than a national convention. In the same year the Ohio Whigs issued their call for a convention. In the South, Whig newspaper editors set about the task of educating their readers on the merits of the convention system. By 1838 the conversions had taken place, and the opposition members of Congress could announce plans for the Harrisburg convention. Evidencing the new conviction, the Tippecanoe Club of Philadelphia issued an address "recognizing the national whig convention as the only legitimate body for the nomination of the whig candidate for the presidency."[44] Thus by 1840, both major parties had accepted the national convention as the best expedient for promoting unity in support of candidates for the presidency.

But how should a convention be constituted and what should be its procedures? This awkward question was raised by John C. Calhoun and his zealous adherents in 1843. Although practices varied from state to state, there was a trend for delegates to Democratic national conventions to be chosen *en bloc* by state conventions and to be instructed to cast their votes as a unit. The Calhoun faction insisted that each state's number of delegates to the 1844 national convention should be limited to the number of electors to which the state was entitled, that they should be chosen by district meetings, and that they should cast their votes individually. It contended that the appointment of an entire delegation by a state convention resulted in undue political management, the unfair exclusion of delegates who might favor a candidate who was opposed by the state party leaders, and a perversion of the notion that the convention should emanate from the people. Furthermore, the unit rule, in its view, meant that a few large states could dominate the decisions of the convention. District delegates voting *per capita* would better represent the preferences of the rank-and-file of the party. Such an arrangement, Calhoun argued, would be more in accord with the theory of the Constitution, which was to equalize the power of the large and the small states in the election of the President.[45]

Spokesmen for Virginia and New York took the lead in defending the existing arrangements. Because electors in all states (except South Carolina) were chosen by the general-ticket method, they pointed out, a state's delegation should support the candidate who had the best prospect of securing a majority of the popular votes in their state. It was not important how districts within a state voted; what really counted was the state-wide plurality. The Calhoun plan would threaten party harmony within a state and violate the principle of majority rule. It would destroy the advantage possessed by the large states without giving them anything by way of compensation. Finally, in line with the party's traditional regard for state rights, each state party should be free to determine how its delegates should be chosen and what procedure they should follow in voting.[46]

The debate went on furiously for several months, until it became apparent that the Calhoun plan, like his candidacy, was unacceptable. In February 1844, Calhoun announced that he would not permit his name to go before the national convention because it would be so wrongly constituted. He charged that such conventions tended "irresistibly to centralization—centralization of the control over the presidential election in the hands of a few of the central, large states, at first, and finally in political managers, office holders, and office seekers . . ."[47] There was more merit to his accusation than his opponents were disposed to recognize, but by their lights their position was justifiable on much the same ground as the general-ticket system.

The acceptance of the national convention by both Whigs and Democrats added a large and significant new dimension to the presidential game. The convention became the arena where contests were to be fought out among factions of the parties in support of rival candidates, and, in the course of time, over the positions that the parties were to espouse on campaign issues. The contest for the convention nomination, staged in vigorous pre-convention campaigns, assumed an importance within the parties nearly equaling that of the presidential contest. In this context, the process of presidential selection became vastly more complicated, subject to many more influences, than had previously been the case. From another perspective, the adoption of the convention device finally provided the national parties with an institution that could be used for conflict resolution, thereby enhancing their ability to remain united. Conventions became essential to the party game.

Although a detailed examination of the development of the national convention as an institution would be beyond the scope of this study, some cursory observations are relevant. The Whig conventions of 1840 and 1844 are best characterized as ad hoc assemblies, each reflecting the exigencies of the party's condition at the time. They varied widely from each other in organization, procedure, and function. The purpose of the first was to find an expedient way to set aside Clay in order to name a candidate who held greater promise of success. The second met to name Clay by acclamation. In institutional terms, the two Whig conventions had yet to become regularized.

The Democrats, with longer experience and a sturdier party base, made greater progress. By 1844 it had become established that the national convention would meet in May of the presidential year in Baltimore; that while a state might send any number of delegates, its voting strength would be equal to the number of its electoral votes; that the credentials of delegates were subject to examination; that the two-thirds vote was required for a nomination; that a platform—or statement of principles—would be adopted; and that the candidates would in due course make a formal acceptance of their nominations. The manner in which the delegates were to be chosen, the extent to which they were pledged, and whether their votes would be cast as a unit was determined by the state parties. As yet no settled mode had been adopted for placing the names of candidates in nomination, there was no regularized procedure for issuing the call for the convention, and no provision had been made for constituting a national committee. With these exceptions—and the absence of any floor fights over the platform—the 1844 Democratic convention very much resembled those that were to be held quadrennially for the next century.

As the national convention acquired legitimacy, prospective candidates devised and implemented strategies to acquire the coveted party nominations. This new facet of the presidential game involved both pre-convention activities and elaborate maneuvers within the convention. The process can best be illustrated by looking at Harrison's successful quest in 1840 and Van Buren's frustrated effort in 1844.

Although Harrison had run well against Van Buren in those states where the two were in competition in 1836, he had not demonstrated any strength in the South—where White was favored —nor did he hold an office that might keep him prominently before the public. Clay, on the other hand, was soon recognized as the leader of the Whigs in Congress, effectively championed the holding of a national convention, and gained southern support. As the foremost Whig statesman, he expected to receive the party's nomination. So confident was he that he said he would make no "personal exertions" in his own behalf. "In announcing this course of conduct for myself," he declared, in an obvious reference to Harrison, "it is foreign from my intention to mark out any course for others, or to intimate any dissatisfaction with whatever line they may consider it proper to pursue."[48] By the summer of 1839, however, leading Whig politicians were saying that while Clay was an admirable figure, he could not be elected. He was decidedly unpopular among the Anti-Masons, whose backing in New York and Pennsylvania was deemed to be essential, and his pronounced stands on major issues had made him offensive to other elements. Thurlow

Weed of New York sought to persuade him to withdraw, judging that he could not carry New York, but Clay decided to remain in the race. In an effort to bolster his declining fortunes, he made what amounted to a campaign trip in August, delivering major addresses in New York City and Baltimore and giving shorter speeches wherever else crowds assembled along his route.[49]

Harrison, meanwhile, kept his candidacy alive by occasional public appearances and judicious statements. In a tour through Ohio and Indiana in the summer of 1838, he described himself modestly as the people's candidate, recalled his civil and military services to the nation, and eagerly solicited support. His success in securing the nomination of the Anti-Masonic party greatly enhanced his "availability," as did a mounting number of endorsements by Whig meetings in the West and the North. But Clay's adherents were singularly zealous in their devotion to the Kentuckian, and the nomination was still very much in doubt when the Whig National Convention assembled in Harrisburg in December 1839. Anticipating that the Clay and Harrison forces might produce a deadlocked convention, the astute Weed planned to bring forth General Winfield Scott as a compromise candidate.[50]

Determined not to have Clay as their candidate, Whig leaders from New York and Pennsylvania were instrumental in devising an ingenious plan to secure their ends. Over the objections of Clay's followers, the convention agreed that a committee composed of representatives from each delegation should be appointed to confer on the nomination. In the negotiations, the representatives of each state were to give the electoral vote of their state under the unit rule. The committee was instructed to continue to take ballots until some candidate had a majority; only then was it to report to the full convention. On the morning of the second day of the convention, the nominating committee met in the basement of the Lutheran Church, while the delegates marked time in the pews on the main floor. At nine o'clock that evening, it reported that after repeated balloting it had failed to produce a majority for any candidate. A motion by one of Clay's lieutenants that the committee be discharged and that the full convention vote on the nomination was laid on the table, and the committee continued its labors. An hour later it reported. Harrison had 148 votes to 90 for Clay and 16 for

Winfield Scott. The decisive break had come when New York abandoned Scott and, at Weed's direction, shifted its large vote to Old Tippecanoe.

At this point the convention prudently adjourned to let tempers cool and to prepare the way for graceful concessions by those who had been committed to Clay. On the following day, after the reading of a letter from Clay pledging his cordial support to whomever the convention might nominate and several effusive speeches laudatory of the great statesman, Harrison's nomination was made unanimous. In the meantime, on the recommendation of the nominating committee, John Tyler was unanimously accorded the vice-presidential spot on the ticket. Although, as Weed later recalled, "the unanimity was anything but cordial," the convention adjourned with every appearance of harmony.[51]

The Whigs had been determined to name a winner, and that meant someone who might carry New York and Pennsylvania. Harrison met those specifications. Clay and his adherents were cleverly outmaneuvered in the convention. The unique procedure that was employed to contrive the nomination of Harrison muted dissension on the convention floor and facilitated the prompt restoration of unity within the party. In the long tradition of "smoke filled rooms," the negotiations at Harrisburg must rank not only first in time but also first in brilliance of conception and execution.

The nomination of Polk in 1844 was a product of the intricate game of convention politics. In 1843 Van Buren had no formidable competitors. He had the strong backing of the most influential party newspapers—the Washington *Globe*, the Richmond *Enquirer*, the *Ohio Stateman*—and of nearly all the stalwart party leaders. Calhoun's bid posed only minor problems in the South; elsewhere modest efforts were put forth in behalf of Richard M. Johnson, James Buchanan, and Lewis Cass. Johnson, alone, engaged in a vigorous public campaign, embarking on a three-month speaking tour through the Middle States and New England late in 1843. With charming candor, he advertised his willingness to accept either the presidential or the vice-presidential nomination. Calhoun disdained such tactics, proclaiming in classic terms that the presidency "should be the exclusive reward of merit and services such as may be well known to the whole country . . . ."[52] In response to an interrogatory from the Indiana State Democratic Committee, all five candidates set forth their views on the Bank, the tariff, distribution, and the veto power, as well as on their disposition to abide by the decision of the national convention. They also responded with appropriate restraint to inquiries put to them by other questioners.[53]

The pre-convention campaign was enlivened by a controversy over the date the Democrats should convene. Aware of their overwhelming strength, and properly fearful that it might later erode, the Van Buren forces sought to have the national convention held in November 1843, but the Calhoun faction insisted on May 1844 and won the support of enough states so that its will prevailed. The maneuver to delay the date of the convention was crucial to the developing plot to deny Van Buren the nomination, for plans were already under way to exploit the Texas issue.[54]

By early in April 1844 the convention delegates had been appointed. Delegations from fourteen states were pledged or instructed to vote for Van Buren's nomination; those from the other eleven states were unpledged. Calhoun and Buchanan had announced their withdrawals, Johnson was quite prepared to accept the second place on the ticket, and Cass could not even count on the Michigan delegates, who were instructed for Van Buren. Then, with the revelation of the Texas treaty, the aspect altered. Van Buren's qualified stand against immediate annexation caused many of his erstwhile allies to denounce him, especially in the South, and suddenly a severe contest loomed.

How that contest was resolved has already been reported. The central point is that the convention proved to be an effective instrument for resolving intra-party conflict. In the process, it produced the first "dark horse" among presidential candidates—James K. Polk. Polk was not an inconspicuous figure—he had been a steadfast Jacksonian Congressman and had served as Speaker of the House and as governor of Tennessee—but he had been mentioned only as a possible vice-presidential candidate. He had, however, promptly declared himself in favor of the "immediate re-annexation of Texas,"[55] and he had cordial and effective friends both in the Van Buren faction and among the southern delegates. With a deadlock threatening, he was "available," and frantic behind-the-scenes negotiations led to his unexpected selection as the party's standard bearer. More clearly than on any previous occasion, party took precedence over the candidate. Polk was chosen not because of his stature as a statesman or because of his personal popularity but because he met the needs of a divided party.

The main function of the national convention was to nominate candidates. But it was instrumental as well in preparing the party for the ensuing campaign. The gathering together of delegates from all the state parties, in itself, generated a sense of unity and engendered enthusiasm for the common cause. Spirits were raised by bombastic speeches foretelling a glorious victory and making extravagant predictions of the margins by which the orator's state would be carried. Bitter disappointments were buried under effusive hymns to harmony. Hortatory diatribes aroused passions against the enemy with whom the battle was to be joined. It was also common to name a committee to organize the party for the campaign, but such agencies scarcely functioned. Not until 1848 did the Democrats take the forward step of appointing a national committee, finally giving the party some semblance of a permanent organization.

Almost incidentally, as an element in the campaign preparations, the practice developed of setting forth the party's creed, ultimately in the form of a platform. Such declarations had a long history. As early as 1800, state party agencies formulated and published "Addresses to the People," setting forth and lauding their accomplishments and decrying the misdeeds of the opposition. It became customary for both state conventions and legislative caucuses to issue such addresses.[56] Interestingly enough, the congressional caucus did not adopt the practice, and the closest approximation to a national party platform prior to 1832 was the address published by the New York Committee of Correspondence in behalf of DeWitt Clinton in 1812.

In conformity with these precedents, the national conventions that met in preparation for the 1832 election all appointed committees to draft addresses. Without debate or division, those drafted for the Anti-Masonic and National Republican conventions were adopted unanimously and published. The committee of the Democratic convention, however, reported that it would not be expedient to issue an address, recommending instead that each state delegation should make such report as it wished to its constituents. Four years later the Democrats named a six-member committee "to draft an address to the people of the United States, or resolutions, to be submitted to the convention, or both, as the committee shall think most advisable."[57] Perhaps for reasons of prudence, the committee did not make any report to the convention. Instead, its lengthy and eloquent statement was published nearly three months after the convention had adjourned.

A significant advance was made in 1840. The Whigs, fully pre-occupied with the difficult task of naming their candidates, ignored a resolution proposed by one delegate that called for the appoint-ment of a committee to prepare an address to the people. The Democrats, by contrast, named two committees; one "to draft resolutions declaratory of the principles of the republican party of the union" and the other to write an address supportive of those principles. The first committee proposed nine succinct resolutions, setting forth in clear language the position of the party on major economic and Constitutional issues. Each resolution was voted on separately and adopted unanimously. After having been read to the delegates, the address was approved with similar unanimity.[58]

A pattern had been established. At their hectic 1844 convention the Democrats deferred the appointment of a committee on resolu-tions until after the presidential nomination had been determined. The committee speedily recommended a platform that incorporated the nine resolutions that had been adopted four years earlier and added three planks, including that calling for the "reoccupation of Oregon and the re-annexation of Texas." Without discussion, and possibly without consideration by the weary delegates, the platform was adopted unanimously. No address was published. The Whigs, as in 1840, were negligent. No committees were constituted to frame a platform or address. Instead, Reverdy Johnson, a Maryland delegate, proposed a series of resolutions as the convention ap-proached adjournment, one of which summarized in a brief and vague paragraph the principles of the party. It contained no refer-ence to Texas.[59]

Like the two-party system itself, the convention had become an accepted feature of the presidential game. Convention politics deter-mined the designation of candidates. The classic view that aspirants for the presidency should be so conspicuously eminent for their talents and so visible through their attainments as to commend them almost automatically to their countrymen no longer held. The nomination of Harrison—instead of Clay—in 1840 and of Polk—instead of Van Buren—in 1844 demonstrated that new rules were operative. Three considerations shaped the actions of state delegations. They wanted a candidate who could aid the fortunes of the party in their states, one on whom the party could unite in harmony, and who could win. For the Whigs this meant Clay or a military hero. For the Democrats after 1840 it meant a "dark horse." Until the schism that destroyed the Democratic party in 1860, the convention was an adequate instrument for mobilizing the parties, nominating their candidates, and framing the platforms on which they would base their appeals to the electorate. A peculiarly American invention, it represented the crowning achievement of party-as-organization. With minor exceptions, the legitimacy that it acquired was sufficient to ensure that most essential of party virtues—regularity. Thus it became the rule that in selecting a President, the American voter would be constrained to making a choice between candidates nominated by the major parties at their national conventions.

With their candidates before the people, the parties employed every resource to arouse and persuade the mass electorate. Like the parties and the conventions, the presidential campaign assumed a pattern; it became a predictable ritual. Combining the elements of a quadrennial national folk festival, a gigantic enterprise in political socalization and education, and a bloodless war between mobilized rival hosts, it provided Americans with a cathartic experience even exceeding that of the occasional religious revival. Foreign observers were struck by the resemblance between political campaigns and the great religious festivals of Catholic Europe.[60] Each had its processions; its ikons, banners, and vestments; its creeds; its sacred texts; its hymns; its pantheon of saints or heroes; its exhorters; its apocalyptic visions; its ecstatic exclamations of faith and identification. Political campaigns met and fulfilled deep-seated needs for emotional expression on the part of the American people at the same time that they produced acceptable verdicts on the question of who should govern the nation. Their significance as cultural manifestations—too little appreciated or investigated—must be placed alongside their importance as political phenomena.

The "log cabin and hard cider" extravaganza of 1840 is deservedly recognized as the epitome of the new, popular-style campaign. "There can never again be a campaign of such enthusiasm and hurra [*sic*] as that of '40," wrote its wistful chronicler nearly a half-century after he had experienced its excitement.[61] The Whigs, rallying behind "Tippecanoe and Tyler too," set the pattern. With their thousands of Tippecanoe Clubs, their log cabin raisings, their "monster rallies," their song books, and their hard cider, they succeeded in reaching and activating segments of the electorate that had never before been drawn into the presidential contest. Loosely directed by an "executive committee" in Washington which distributed tons of documents and pamphlets and issued directives to campaign units, and by a "Committee of 76" and a "Committee of 41" which stimulated the formation of Tippecanoe Clubs, the campaign gathered momentum as state and local party organizations vied with one another in arousing enthusiasm. Harrison was aided by a personal staff, which the Democrats erroneously charged "kept him in a cage." Party notables—among them Clay, Webster, Tyler, and Harrison himself—took to the stump to denounce the iniquities of the Van Buren regime. Horace Greeley's *Log Cabin* attained a circulation of eighty thousand, carrying the Whig message throughout the nation in a far livelier fashion than the *Rough Hewer*, the vehicle for Democratic propaganda.

The Whig line was that Harrison, the venerated Cincinnatus from North Bend, was the people's candidate. The symbolism of the log cabin and hard cider, the accidental result of the attempt by an obscure Democrat journalist to ridicule the Whig candidate, exerted immediate appeal. Van Buren, the "office holder candidate," was a "wily magician" who lived in splendor in the presidential palace, oblivious to the distress brought upon the people by his ruinous policies. This theme was sounded by John Bear, the unlearned but entertaining "Buckeye Blacksmith," in over three hundred speeches, and by countless other Whig orators. Even women were brought into the political arena, joining their husbands and brothers at the Whig rallies, making the banners and transparencies that enlivened the processions, and assisting with the feeding of the multitudes. So notable was their contribution that Webster graciously agreed to address a special evening meeting of the Whig ladies of Richmond in the course of his campaign tour.

The Democrats were at first shocked by the theatrical and demagogic tactics of their opponents. Rational political discourse, in their view, had been replaced by slogans, songs, irrelevant stunts, and humbuggery, all abundantly financed by the bankers and speculators. When they perceived the effectiveness of the Whig tactics and sought to emulate them, they were unsuccessful. The party establishment—including men like Kendall, Blair, Benton, Ritchie, and Van Buren—was the product of another era; it had yet to adjust to the sudden onslaught of the newer breed of politician —like Thurlow Weed, Thad Stevens, and Tom Corwin—which exploited so expertly the popular taste for participation and excitement. Years afterwards, Van Buren still believed that his defeat was accomplished "almost without reference to the soundness or unsoundness of . . . [his] principles but thro' the instrumentalities and debaucheries of a political Saturnalia, in which reason and justice had been derided . . . ."[62]

Memorable and stirring though it was, the 1840 campaign brought forth little that was entirely novel. Almost all the techniques that were employed—the Washington committees, the array of party presses, the conventions of "young men," the songs, slogans, and banners, the mass rallies, and the political clubs—had been used prior to 1840. In place of Old Hickory there was Old Tip; the Tippecanoe Clubs were modeled on the Hickory Clubs; stump speaking had acquired vogue in the South and West in the 1830s in state campaigns, as had the generous use of money. What most set the "log cabin and hard cider" campaign apart from its predecessors was the close competition between two nation-wide parties, lending excitement to the contest in virtually every state, and the imaginative adoption everywhere by the well-organized Whigs of tested methods for recruiting and stimulating their supporters. The result was an unprecedented outpouring of voters, far exceeding that in any previous presidential election. The contest for the presidency had been thoroughly democratized, or at least popularized.

The fervor was not entirely recaptured in 1844, although now both parties demonstrated their expertise in activating the electorate. Perhaps because the Democrats won in 1844, Thomas Hart Benton reflected that the campaign had been conducted "without those appeals to 'hard cider, log-cabins, and coonskins' which had been so freely used by the Whig party" in 1840.[63] But with "Young Hickory" confronting the "Mill Boy of the Slashes," there were the same mass rallies, marching clubs, special campaign newspapers, stump speeches, and intense canvassing efforts that had created such a furor four years earlier, and continued to be part of the ritual fifty years later.

What still remained ambiguous was the proper role of the candidates. Jackson in 1824 had marked out a new course with his "rule" that candidates, in response to legitimate inquiries, should disclose their views on public questions. Although in later campaigns he bowed prudently to the insistence of his friends that he remain silent, a precedent had been created that others were to follow. The formalities of the convention afforded another opportunity for candidates to express themselves, through the dignified medium of their letters accepting the nomination. Beyond these statements, it remained unclear how far a candidate might go without offending republican sensibilities or, no less hazardous, rendering himself vulnerable to misinterpretation or attack.

New boundaries of candidate behavior were explored during the preliminaries to the 1836 election. White, Harrison, and especially Van Buren wrote numerous letters for publication. In his acceptance letter, Van Buren stated that although his views on public issues were well known, he would comply with requests for his opinions "on all suitable occasions."[69] In at least nine statements he addressed at some length the matter of the Constitutional authority of Congress with respect to slavery; the staple issues of banking and currency, the tariff, internal improvements, and the distribution of the land-sale revenues; as well as giving his views on the appointment of Masons to office. Harrison was equally voluble, though less precise, and White also made his positions known.

Far more daring was Harrison's three-month campaign tour through Virginia, Maryland, Delaware, New Jersey, New York,

Pennsylvania, and Ohio. All along the route he attended public dinners in his honor and made innumerable impromptu speeches. Richard M. Johnson was no less energetic. An extremely popular if somewhat preposterous figure, he traveled extensively in the year before the election, usually reciting his valorous deeds and avoiding serious political discourse. Even Judge White, with his strict principles, had the temerity to make a lengthy address at a public dinner arranged by his admirers in Nashville. Strangely enough, these unprecedented actions aroused little adverse comment, even though such old-fashioned republicans as Calhoun and Clay regarded them with distaste.[65]

The trend toward increased candidate visibility continued in 1840. Van Buren's code of behavior did not permit him to take the stump in the brazen manner of Harrison or Johnson, but he traveled in an open barouche from Washington to Kinderhook in June 1839, making numerous stops in Pennsylvania to receive the plaudits of his admirers in that critical state and climaxing his tour with a forceful political address in New York City.[66] Subsequently he expounded his positions on all the lively issues of the day in a dozen published letters to citizens in Pennsylvania, Georgia, Virginia, Kentucky, Illinois, North Carolina, and New York. Harrison traveled almost constantly throughout Ohio during the summer of 1840, addressing enormous throngs in more than twenty communities. At Dayton, on September 10, according to Whig reports, 100,000 people assembled to hear him give his equivocal views on the need for a "correct banking system" and announce that if elected he would serve only one term. He had declared early in the campaign that he would not respond to any inquiries, both because he had previously made his views known and because he did not believe that the President should interfere with Congress, and he adhered to that strategy.[67] The irrepressible Richard M. Johnson was on the stump for four months, and even John Tyler essayed a brief campaign tour of Virginia, Pennsylvania, and Ohio. Old inhibitions, it seemed, had been relaxed; even candidates for the nation's highest offices might engage in the once-forbidden practice of personal canvassing.

No less shocking to old republican purists was the behavior of ex-President Andrew Jackson. Not only did he publish a strong endorsement of Van Buren—at the same time condemning Harrison's "federal principles" and denigrating his military reputation—but he even overcame his extreme reluctance to speak in public and addressed a meeting in West Tennessee in behalf of his successor. This action drew from John Quincy Adams the acerbic statement that from the beginning of the republic "a sense of decorum universally prevailing, has forbidden a president of the United States from active or even indirect canvassing of votes for himself and has alike interdicted the exercise of influence by any preceding president, upon the election of his successor."[68]

During the campaign of 1844, Clay and Polk pursued different strategies. After having made an extensive pre-convention speaking tour of the South, Clay announced immediately after his nomination that he would not make any public appearances as a candidate. The people should be "free, impartial, and wholly unbiased by the conduct of the candidate himself," he declared. "Not only, in my opinion, is it his duty to abstain from all solicitation, direct or indirect, of their suffrages," he explained, "but he should avoid being voluntarily placed in situations to seek, or in which might be supposed to seek, to influence their judgment." He even decided, on the advice of Thurlow Weed, to write no letters for publication. This resolve weakened, and he was soon issuing statements on the tariff, the Cumberland Road, dueling, abolition, and—most clumsily —on Texas. Finally, sensing that his pronouncements were involving him in difficulties, he announced in September that he would decline to answer any further inquiries, at the same time endeavoring to correct the "misinterpretations" that had been placed on some of his utterances.[69]

Polk was more prudent. His only statement, released after much anguish, was his "Kane Letter" to a Pennsylvania supporter on the tariff. He would favor, he said, "such moderate discriminatory duties, as would produce the amount of revenue needed, and at the same time afford reasonable incidental protection to our home industry." Other insistent efforts to draw him out were resisted adamantly, bringing forth the condemnation from the Whigs that he was a "mum candidate."[70] Jackson once again entered the fray, giving his strong endorsement to Polk and Dallas and attacking Clay and all his policies. Van Buren, despite his bitterness, also played the role of a party regular by urging his followers to give their full support to the Democratic candidates.[71]

By 1844, presidential candidates were inhibited in their public actions less by the old republican code than by their estimates of what was to be lost or gained by remaining silent. Following the example of Polk, later Democratic candidates—except Stephen A. Douglas in 1860—remained quietly at home and rarely put pen to paper. The Whig candidates were more active; Zachary Taylor published numerous letters in 1848 and Winfield Scott in 1852 made a tour of prospective sites for military hospitals. The strategy of having candidates maintain a low profile was a significant aspect of the party game. The presidential contest, especially as it was conceived by the Democrats, was to be a contest between electoral parties, rather than between candidates. The fact that the Democrats were inclined to run "dark horses" while the Whigs exhibited a preference for generals is an indicator of differences between the two parties. The Whigs throughout their brief history remained a kind of pseudo-party, never quite attaining the cohesion or the ideological clarity of the Democrats.

With the presidency now the chief prize of the party game, the very nature of the office underwent important changes. Jackson's broad assertions of executive authority, his claim that the President represented the whole people of the United States, and even his unprecedented use of the veto power derived more from his own personality and from the circumstances of his election than from the influence of an emerging party system. The Whigs, of course, made a partisan issue of "executive usurpation" and proposed such measures as a single presidential term and restrictions on the veto power. They did so with genuine concern about what they perceived as a radical alteration of the presidential role. But experience was to demonstrate that personal qualities, more than institutional factors, were to determine whether a President was "weak" or "strong."[72]

More directly associated with the operation of the party game was the President's new role as a dispenser of patronage to reward partisan services. During his first year in office Jackson had ejected more than nine hundred federal office-holders and replaced them with his own appointees. Although their number was but a small fraction of the total corps of federal employees, the scale of the removals was unprecedented. With the principle established that office-holders could be dismissed without cause and replaced by loyal partisans, the spoils system, as it was soon called, became a controversial feature of national politics. Not surprisingly, party workers were now inspired with a new avidity for office, and the executive was placed under incessant pressure to gratify their desires. Once initiated, the practice of punishing enemies and rewarding friends could scarcely be reversed.

Needless to say, the opponents of the Jacksonians were especially ardent in denouncing the practice, arguing effectively that it constituted a radical innovation and one that threatened the constitutionally contrived balance among the branches of government. Through the use of his patronage powers, the executive could gain an overweening ascendency over Congress and even dictate the choice of his successor. A Select Committee on the Extent of the Executive Patronage, chaired by Calhoun, exposed the evils of the spoils system in 1835. Noting that it was "only within the last few years, that removals from office have been introduced, as a system," the committee found that "the entire character and structure of the Government itself, is undergoing a great and fearful change . . . ."[73] It recommended several measures to address the evil, but they came to naught. During the 1836 campaign both White and Harrison attacked the spoils system, pledging not to use the executive patronage for partisan ends, but when the Whigs came to power in 1841, Harrison was overwhelmed by demands that Van Buren's "corrupt crew" be thrown out and replaced by his own supporters. Tyler, in turn, used the patronage in his vain efforts to build a party that would advance his presidential aspirations. Despite all the protestations, the spoils system had become attached to the presidency.

The extent to which patronage had become involved with the presidential game was examined in Congress by a Select Committee on Retrenchment in 1842. After acknowledging that presidential candidates must be identified with political parties and describing the enormous patronage at the disposal of the victor, the committee's report pointed out the consequences of the new system.

The election ceases to be a fair and calm expression of the popular judgment on the principles and policy of Government, and becomes a tumultuous scramble for place and power. It is not merely a contest between the candidates for the highest prize in the lottery, but between the incumbent of each subordinate office in the Government and all those who have fixed their eyes on his place. . . . Who shall dispense the patronage? is the absorbing question, not only with those who expect favors themselves, but with those who, in the various relations of society, are connected and interested with them. When the election has ended, nothing is decided more than when it commenced, except that one set of men are to go out and another set are to come in. . . . The responsibility of the President is transferred from the Constitution and laws to cliques and juntos, who combine to increase his power and gratify their ambitions. Fidelity on his part to these influences excuses, if it does not justify, infidelity to everything else.[74]

Dreadful as this system was, the committee could devise no acceptable remedy.

Henry Clay in 1843 reluctantly conceded the inevitability of the abhorrent innovation. "No man felt more profoundly than he did," read the report of an address he made in Lexington, "the evils which were likely to grow out of the struggles for the prize of government, with the distribution of all its honors and offices exclusively confined to the successful party." But, he declared, if a Whig President was elected in 1844, "it would be his imperative duty to do ample justice, in the administration of the public patronage, to the great whig party of the country."[75] "To the victor belong the spoils" had become an accepted rule of the presidential game.

By 1844 the presidential game had become the party game. Its basic rules were that pledged electors would be chosen by popular vote on general tickets, that the contest would be waged by two major political parties, that the selection of candidates would be arranged by national conventions, that campaigns would be designed to arouse committed partisans, that candidates would play decidedly subordinate roles, and that the spoils of office would constitute the rewards of the victorious party. Every element of this game was at variance with the republican ideology that had shaped the actions of the Framers when they contrived their process of presidential selection.

Although every element acquired acceptance, and the rules of the game persisted, the disparity between ideal and practice was profoundly disturbing. Active politicians, no less than ordinary citizens, were often appalled by what they had created. They had voiced their dismay at various times over the adoption of the general-ticket system, over the formation of parties, over the national conventions. They had deplored the debasement of rational political discourse resulting from the resort to demagogic campaign appeals. They denounced the pernicious effects of the spoils system. They could take little pride in their handiwork. But their occasional and half-hearted efforts to devise an alternative were unavailing. They had no option but to play the party game.

Epilogue

After more than a half century and many vicissitudes, the presidential selection process had assumed the form of the party game. It was now governed by rules that were to remain broadly applicable as late as the 1960s, when an accumulation of long- and short-term influences worked profound changes. This is not to say, of course, that precisely the same format persisted, but it is to suggest that there were strong continuities. "Over the long term," Stephen Hess has observed, "the presidential selection system appears far more notable in its stability than in its tendency to change."[1] However much the term may be qualified, this "stability" provides the justification for bringing this study of the *origins* of the presidential game to a close in 1844.

Yet in order to appreciate the persistence of the rules that shaped the party game, and also to identify those modifications that came with time, it seems appropriate to add this epilogue, bringing the story of the presidential game down to the present. Without any pretensions to definitiveness, such a cursory survey can touch upon only the most relevant developments. Particular attention will be paid to elements of continuity and change in the Constitutional and legal environment, in the character of political parties, in the processes affecting candidate selection, and in the conduct of campaigns. Finally, to indicate how the long-familiar party game has been transformed in recent years, some notice must be taken of the extraordinary innovations associated with the reformist influences that burst forth late in the 1960s.[2]

In point of time, the first important change in the legal sphere was made in 1845, when Congress decreed that thereafter the electors should be chosen on the same day throughout the Union. The date specified was "the Tuesday next after the first Monday in the month of November." Previously states had voted on various days; in 1840 the interval had extended from October 30 to November 10. The chief reason for establishing a uniform election day was to lessen fraud. It was notorious that in 1840 hordes of voters, having cast ballots in their home states, crossed into neighboring states with later election days and voted a second time.[3] In 1872, Congress fixed the same date for the election of members of the House of Representatives, thereby consolidating federal elections and bringing into full force the "coattail" effect that was to tie the political fate of congressional candidates to that of the presidential nominees.

The general-ticket system became the uniform mode of choosing electors when South Carolina—the lone holdout after 1836—capitulated for the 1868 election. Except for anomalous situations in Florida in 1868, Colorado in 1876, and Michigan in 1892, the general ticket prevailed until Maine in 1972 opted for a modified version of the district arrangement. Still without the sanction either of Constitutional amendment or congressional enactment, and almost continually the subject of contention, the winner-take-all method has remained the dominant influence in shaping the electoral strategies of contenders for the presidency.[4]

The dimensions of the electorate have been greatly extended over the past century by Constitutional amendments. Racial barriers were ostensibly eliminated by the Fifteenth Amendment (1870), and women were enfranchised by the Nineteenth Amendment (1920). With the Twenty-fourth Amendment (1964), citizens could not be denied the vote for failing to pay a poll tax, or any other tax. By the Twenty-sixth Amendment (1971), the voting age was lowered to eighteen years. In theory, then, the potential electorate has come to include all citizens above the age of eighteen. In reality, because of exacting requirements governing the registration of voters, the stringency of residency qualifications, impediments to absentee voting, and similar factors affecting access to the ballot, the actual electorate is considerably smaller than the theoretical maximum.

Proposals for sweeping reforms of the process for electing the President were rarely absent from the congressional agenda, but effective action in the form of Constitutional change was confined to relatively minor modifications in the established format. In order to lessen the interval between the election of the President and his assumption of the office—and also to eliminate the so-called "lame duck" session of the Congress—the Twentieth Amendment (1933) was ratified. Now the presidential term would begin on January 20, rather than March 4, following the official count of the electoral vote on January 6. By the terms of this amendment, Congress was authorized to provide for a contingency where neither the President-elect nor a Vice President-elect had qualified by January 20, as well as for the eventuality of the death of any of the persons from whom the House of Representatives was to choose a President when such a choice devolved upon that body.

Of great contemporary interest was the Twenty-second Amendment (1951), limiting any President to two terms. This proposition had been considered and rejected by the Constitutional Convention and had been raised frequently over the years in congressional discussions of proposed amendments. It acquired cogency after the long-standing "two-term tradition" had been breached by Franklin D. Roosevelt's four successive elections to the presidency. Because, in effect, it gave explicit sanction to what had come to be regarded as accepted practice, the amendment confirmed rather than altered one of the basic rules of the game. In a quite different vein, the Twenty-third Amendment (1961) gave the citizens of the District of Columbia a voice in the election of the President; they were to cast an electoral vote equal to that of the least populous state.

The Twenty-fifth Amendment (1967) was designed to deal with the matter of presidential disability. Prompted by the serious illnesses that had afflicted President Dwight D. Eisenhower, the amendment specified that in the event of the death, resignation, or removal from office of the President, the Vice President should become President. Procedures were defined for determining when a President was unable to discharge his duties, in which case the Vice President would serve as Acting President. In addition, whenever the vice presidency became vacant, the President would nominate a person for that office, who would assume the position after being confirmed by majority votes of both houses of Congress. It was through this process that Gerald R. Ford replaced Spiro T. Agnew in 1973, and Nelson A. Rockefeller succeeded Ford in 1974.

These four amendments dealt with peripheral matters; they did not alter basically the major features of the presidential game. In the meantime, however, there continued to be widespread dissatisfaction with the existing arrangements, especially with the general-ticket system, and Congress often debated alternative modes.[5] Four plans, each with intricate variations, commanded most attention. The district plan, generally favored by conservatives and those from the smaller states, was periodically brought forth and defeated. The automatic plan, which would merely eliminate the electors and award a state's electoral vote to the candidate receiving a popular plurality, was a modest proposal that failed to satisfy those who sought more fundamental reform. The proportional plan, which would divide a state's electoral vote among the candidates in proportion to the popular votes they received, was approved by the Senate in 1950 in the form of the Lodge-Gossett Amendment, but failed in the House. Recently, enthusiasm has focused on plans for a direct election by the voters of the nation at large, with provisions for a run-off between the two highest finishers in the event that no candidate received 40 percent of the total vote. This quite radical change has received endorsement in public-opinion polls and was approved by the House of Representatives in 1969. As in the years between 1813 and 1827, when the issue first received extensive consideration, the general-ticket system has been subjected to severe criticism, but its opponents have been divided over alternatives, with the result that no change has been effected.

Aside from these efforts at comprehensive reform, there has been periodic concern about what may be termed technical problems inherent in the present system. One is the matter of the "faithless elector." In six elections since 1948 there have been instances of electors who voted contrary to the expectations of the party on whose ticket they ran. In no case did such aberrant behavior affect the outcome. But a special version of the problem created serious alarm in 1968. George C. Wallace, candidate of the American Independent party, planning to secure the decisive influence if neither Richard M. Nixon (Republican) nor Hubert H. Humphrey

(Democrat) could secure an electoral majority, required his own electors to pledge that they would vote for him, "or whomever he may direct." Wallace obtained forty-six electoral votes, but he could not use them for bargaining purposes because Nixon had a clear majority. It was the problem of the "faithless elector" that was in part responsible for the proposal of the automatic plan of allocating electoral votes, but the hazard still remains.

Another troublesome area, which had been recognized as early as 1800, involved the question of how contests were to be resolved in counting the electoral votes. There had been minor difficulties prior to 1876, but in that year a serious crisis arose, when the outcome of the election hinged on decisions regarding conflicting returns from three southern states and the eligibility of a single Oregon elector. Some years earlier, before counting the 1864 electoral vote, Congress had adopted the "Twenty Second Joint Rule" to apply to such contingencies. This rule stated that at the joint session convened to receive the electoral votes, no vote to which objection was made could be counted except with the concurrent approval of both the Senate and the House. Under this rule, Congress in 1873 refused to accept electoral votes from three southern states. But the rule lapsed, with the result that Congress had no accepted procedure to govern its deliberations in 1877. As an expedient, it created a fifteen-member Electoral Commission, to which all disputes were referred. The Commission, in each case by an eight-to-seven vote, awarded all the disputed votes—and thereby the election—to Rutherford B. Hayes. Later, in 1887, a durable law governing the electoral count was enacted. In essence, responsibility was vested in each state to determine which electors had been chosen legally. A concurrent majority of both houses was required to reject any electoral vote. The act was applied only in 1969, when objection was made to the vote cast by a Nixon elector from North Carolina for George C. Wallace. Neither house sustained the objection, however, creating at least the presumption that electors could be "faithless."

Two important innovations with respect to electoral mechanisms can be singled out for their bearing on presidential elections. One was the so-called Australian ballot, adopted by most states between 1888 and 1892 and subsequently by the remaining states. Printed at public expense, available only at the polling place, and containing the names of all candidates for each office, this ballot replaced the former party tickets, which had been prepared by party agencies and distributed by poll workers even before the day of the election, and which contained the names of the candidates of only a single party. This device reduced fraud, facilitated split-ticket voting, and initiated the trend toward public regulation of political parties, which heretofore had been treated as private organizations. It may also have contributed to some decline in voter turnout because it was more difficult to use the Australian ballot than the old party ticket, which did not have to be marked by the voter.

The new ballot form was soon followed by a far more striking innovation, the direct primary.[6] Reflecting a distrust of party-as-organization, and especially of the convention system, this novel plan for enabling party voters to nominate candidates directly through primary elections was widely adopted during the Progressive Era. By 1912, twelve states had enacted presidential primary legislation, providing either for the choice of national convention delegates in primaries or the expression of a candidate preference, or both. In his first annual message to Congress in December 1913, President Wilson urged "prompt enactment of legislation which will provide for primary elections throughout the country at which the voters of the several parties may choose the nominees for the Presidency without the intervention of nomination conventions." Although this recommendation was not adopted, the movement spread to over half the states by 1916, but then it waned as eight states abandoned presidential primaries between 1917 and 1945. Except in 1912, when Theodore Roosevelt battled William H. Taft in several contests, the primaries had little effect on the eventual nominations. Until after World War II prominent candidates, as well as dark horses, showed little inclination to enter primaries and campaign personally.

Signs of a revival of interest in presidential primaries came in 1948 when Harold E. Stassen, lacking support from Republican party regulars, sought to advance his candidacy by scoring victories in primaries. A similar tactic was adopted by Estes Kefauver in 1952 and 1956 in his efforts to win the Democratic nomination. Of even greater public interest were the fierce Republican primary contests in 1952 between the rival forces of Dwight D. Eisenhower and Robert A. Taft. The trend continued in 1960, when John F. Kennedy projected himself to the position of the leading Democratic candidate by his successes in the primaries, chiefly at the expense of Hubert H. Humphrey. After 1952 candidates could no longer avoid primaries, and by 1968 this route to the nomination, rather than the old method of relying on the support of influential state and national party leaders, had become fully accepted. By 1976 there were presidential primaries in twenty-six states and the District of Columbia; four years later the movement embraced thirty-seven states. No single innovation, as will be made apparent subsequently, has had a greater impact on the presidential game than the recent wide acceptance of the primary as the chief means for determining the presidential nominees of the political parties.

Finally, the context of presidential politics has been affected by legislation designed to curb the extent of executive patronage and to lessen the influence of government employees in political affairs. Starting with the Pendleton Act (1883), which introduced the principles of the merit system in the federal civil service, and represented even more conspicuously by the Hatch Act (1939), the movement to end the old "spoils system" has achieved a large measure of success. At the state level, so-called Little Hatch Acts have imposed restraints on political activities by state workers. Altogether, the resources of party leaders at all levels—in terms of jobs awarded for party services—have been greatly curtailed, though not eliminated. Much less than formerly are presidential contests waged for control over patronage, and by the same token, incentives other than the spoils of office must be offered to enlist recruits to work actively in presidential campaigns.

Over the broad sweep of a century—or from Polk to Truman— changes in the Constitutional and legal environment modified but did not alter radically the rules of the presidential game. The electorate became more diversified, election procedures were refined, the two-term tradition was given Constitutional status, and the importance attached to patronage was reduced. But the general-ticket system readily survived every assault, electors continued to perform their customary rituals, and the two major parties maintained their dominance of the contest.

The two-party system, so integral to the party game, retained familiar features well into the second half of this century, although it was not immune to occasional realignments and to behavioral alterations.[7] Party-as-organization in the United States had assumed its distinctive forms by the 1840s. Conditioned by the complexities of the American electoral system—which required the parties to operate at several levels of government, nominate an incredible number of candidates, and engage in frequent contests—the parties were more heavily burdened with electoral tasks than those of any other democracy. In addition, they were constrained by an ideological environment that embodied persistent anti-party attitudes, along with generalized suspicion of rationalized authority in any form. Consequently, these American parties were to be very loosely organized as national entities, they were to be preoccupied with managing election contests, and they were to impose little discipline on elected officials.

Their most conspicuous organizational feature was the delegate convention, which designated party nominees, formulated platforms, engendered feelings of unity, and appointed the members of official party agencies. Their greatest resource was the intense loyalty of their partisans in the electorate, who were disposed to respond strongly to party appeals not only in presidential contests but in elections at every level of government. They were vulnerable, however, to internal factionalism, occasioned by their unstable coalitional bases. When issues of unusual salience—such as free-soilism, monetary policy, prohibition, or economic reform—came to the fore, third parties might be formed to champion new causes. Or substantial shifts of voters from one major party to another—coupled with the abstention of some voters and the reactivation of others—might produce a realignment of the parties. Over the long term, the survival of the two-party system would depend on the ability of the major parties to fend off the threats posed by third parties, to counter the forces that were hostile to party-as-organization, and to retain at least the appearance of viability in the eyes of most of the electorate. With diminishing success, especially after 1900, the two-party system struggled against these challenges.

A severe crisis developed in the 1850s as a consequence of aggravated sectional differences that were reflected most acutely in issues related to slavery. The Whig party disintegrated, the Democrats in 1860 divided along sectional lines, and the Republican party—oriented to northern interests—was formed. The second American party system, which had taken shape during the Jacksonian era, had been utterly disrupted. Then came the Civil War, deferring any possibility of national party formation. In the North, a new two-party alignment of Republicans and Democrats was speedily established, but in the Confederacy there was no semblance of a national two-party structure. With the end of the war in 1865, abnormal conditions associated with Reconstruction fostered short-lived Republican dominance in the former Confederate states, which gave way to lopsided Democratic control when military forces were gradually withdrawn.

By 1876, the shape of the third American party system was clearly defined. The South was solidly Democratic, although pockets of Republican strength survived. In the North and the West, the Republican party was in control in most states; only New Jersey showed consistent Democratic tendencies. Connecticut, New York, Indiana, and California were swing states, where Democrats and Republicans were so closely balanced that there were frequent shifts in dominance, while in Ohio, Michigan, and Illinois the Republican margin was so thin as to make those states major battlegrounds in presidential years. Nationally, the two major parties were almost equal in voting strength from 1876 through 1892. During that period, the only presidential candidate to secure a majority of the popular vote was Samuel J. Tilden in 1876, yet he lost the election to Rutherford B. Hayes. In 1888 Grover Cleveland ran slightly ahead of Benjamin Harrison in popular votes, but Harrison obtained a decisive electoral majority.

In part because of the close balance nationally between Republicans and Democrats, there was a succession of one-term Presidents between Ulysses S. Grant and William McKinley. The Democrats were victorious behind Grover Cleveland in 1884 and 1892 and were deprived of their triumph in 1876 only by the decisions of the Electoral Commission. No incumbent President succeeded in winning re-election; both Cleveland in 1888 and Benjamin Harrison in 1892 tried and failed. In this respect, too, conditions were similar to those that had maintained between 1836 and 1860.

With the parties so evenly arrayed, and with most of the states predictably in one party's column, strategy dictated that candidates should be selected from the doubtful states. The South was so assuredly Democratic, for example, that neither party looked to that region for candidates. On the other hand, New York, with its large electoral vote and exceedingly close party balance, was represented by at least one candidate on the electoral ticket of the major parties in every election from 1864 to 1920, except in 1896. Of the sixty candidates of the major parties for President and Vice President between 1864 and 1920, eighteen were from New York, ten from Ohio, eleven from Indiana, and six from Illinois. It is to be doubted that these states were more singularly endowed with men of presidential caliber than were Pennsylvania, Massachusetts, or Virginia, but the realities of the presidential game dictated that nominees be selected above all on the basis of their presumed ability to carry one or more of the small number of states where the outcome was in doubt and where large numbers of electoral votes were at stake.

Although the third party system, with its decided sectional orientation, differed markedly from the second American party system in its coalition alignment, it functioned in much the same way as its predecessor.[8] National party agencies, except for the quadrennial conventions, remained weak. National party committees, created first by the Democrats in 1848 and subsequently instituted by the Whigs in 1852, became a regular feature of both major party organizations, but their functions were largely restricted to making preparations for the national conventions. As in the past, power rested chiefly in the hands of influential state party leaders, and the national conventions were the arenas where these potent figures negotiated the selection of candidates and the drafting of platforms. Because party loyalties forged in the excitement of the period of the Civil War and Reconstruction were intense and durable, presidential contests were determined less by the charisma of the candidates or the salience of the issues than by insistent appeals to "stand by the party." Reinforcing such appeals were spectacular campaigns, superb canvassing techniques, and extravagant expenditures of money to bribe voters. One index of the effectiveness of these efforts was the heavy turnout of voters. It was common for more than three-quarters of the potential electorate to go to the polls in presidential elections, and in 1896 the proportion exceeded four-fifths.

Somewhat paradoxically, third parties flourished in this era when the two major parties were so competitive and well mobilized.[9] The Liberal Republicans in 1872, the Greenbackers in 1880, the Prohibitionists in 1888, and the Populists in 1892 all polled popular votes that were often greater than the margin between the two major party candidates. It was, in effect, these third-party votes that deprived the victorious presidential candidates of popular majorities and constituted a factor of uncertainty in the elections. On the other hand, the force of traditional party loyalties was so strong that the third parties remained on the fringe of politics and tended to be short-lived and to succumb to fusion arrangements with one or another of the major parties.

The "political universe," to use Walter Dean Burnham's apt phrase, showed many signs of change in the 1890s.[10] The inability of the Cleveland administration to cope with the economic crisis that hit the nation in 1893, the unsettling influences of Populism and the "free silver" issue, the mounting dissatisfaction with the hollowness and corruption of Gilded Age politics, and the growing sophistication of important segments of the electorate, all contributed to important changes in the shape and conduct of American politics in the succeeding decades. The most obvious was a significant increase in Republican strength outside the South; a shift occurred within the electorate of such magnitude as to give that party dominance in national elections down to 1932, except for the Wilson interlude between 1913 and 1921. This realignment, although it was less drastic than that which followed the upheaval of the 1850s, produced what is now commonly referred to as the fourth American party system.

Along with this realignment there were other developments of no less consequence. Between 1890 and 1920 a host of innovations exerted important effects on parties and on voter behavior. These included the Australian ballot, corrupt practices legislation, personal registration laws, direct primaries, popular election of United States Senators, direct legislation through the initiative and the referendum, non-partisan municipal elections, woman suffrage, and black disfranchisement. The motivation behind these so-called reforms was varied. Some were designed to curb participation by "undesirables," thereby lessening fraud and corruption in the election process. Others were aimed at reducing the influence of party-as-organization, or, more specifically, weakening the power of "bosses" and "machines." Many were intended to place authority directly in the hands of the people, at the expense of both parties and elected officials. Taken altogether, they represented a drastic overhauling of electoral procedures.

At the same time there were occurring observable, if less readily explainable, attitudinal changes in the American electorate. Voters were less disposed than formerly to adhere rigidly to their traditional party allegiances, or to vote straight party tickets. Perhaps because there were now many competing forms of involvement, entertainment, and identification, party politics lost some of the captivating attractiveness it once had. For some segments of the electorate, elections ceased to be important, and they simply dropped out. Other groups, notably those comprising the rapidly expanding class of managerial, technical, and professional personnel, entered more zestfully than ever into political affairs, often through special-interest groups or non-partisan organizations.

The combination of electoral reforms and attitudinal changes weakened somewhat the role of parties and altered the behavior of voters. Although the Australian ballot and the direct primary had less effect in undermining the party bosses and machines than had been forecast, there was a rise in split-ticket voting and, on occasion, successful revolts by insurgents over regulars. Less able than in the past to rely merely on appeals to partisan loyalty, the parties now had to place greater emphasis on the attractiveness of their candidates—Roosevelt and Wilson representing conspicuous examples—and on popular issues. With Republican preponderance greater than ever outside the South, and with that region even more solidly Democratic as a consequence of the demise of the Populists and the disfranchisement of blacks, there were now fewer "doubtful" states and, except in the event of a schism in the Republican ranks, only remote prospects for a Democratic victory.

Such a contingency arose in 1912, when the unusual ferment of the Progressive movement bred dissension among the Republicans. Dissatisfied with the performance of his designated successor, William Howard Taft, Theodore Roosevelt launched a belated but vigorous effort to secure the party's nomination, including challenges in the newly instituted presidential primaries. When the convention nominated Taft, Roosevelt's disgruntled followers bolted, organized the Progressive party, and rallied behind their colorful leader. Meanwhile the Democrats, having thrice suffered crushing defeats with William Jennings Bryan, chose the former Princeton University president and New Jersey governor, Woodrow Wilson, to head their ticket. With only 42 percent of the popular vote, Wilson triumphed easily over Roosevelt, with Taft running third. Although the Republican schism had been healed by 1916, Wilson edged out a narrow victory over Charles Evans Hughes. But by 1920, the normal Republican ascendancy was re-established, not to be broken until discontent produced by the Depression brought Franklin D. Roosevelt to power in 1933.

Roosevelt succeeded in putting together a new Democratic coalition that was to endure for over thirty years. So pronounced was the realignment within the electorate as to produce the fifth American party system. Fortified by the addition of organized workers, new ethnic constituencies, blacks, lower-class urban dwellers, and liberal elements of the upper middle class, the Democrats now became the majority party. Roosevelt went on to win an unprecedented four elections, and the New Deal coalition held together behind his successor, Harry S Truman. Then extraordinary personal popularity carried General Dwight D. Eisenhower to victory twice, even though far more voters continued to identify themselves as Democrats than Republicans. The Democratic majority reasserted itself in the election of John F. Kennedy in 1960, despite the issue of Kennedy's Roman Catholic faith, and the tide continued with Lyndon Johnson's easy win over Barry Goldwater in 1964.

With the formation of the fifth party system, there was some lessening of the trends that had been evident since early in the century toward greater independence of partisan ties, split-ticket voting, and declining turnout. In 1937, fewer than 20 percent of the voters described themselves as independents, and that proportion increased only slightly down to 1964. Participation in presidential elections, which had fallen from a high around 80 percent of the potential electorate in the 1890s to below 50 percent in 1920, mounted above the 60 percent mark by 1936, and—except for a post-World War II slump—remained around that level through the 1960s. The two-party system, it seemed, was still quite viable, capable of enlisting the loyalties of the overwhelming majority of American voters and effective as well in stimulating respectable—if not spectacular—voter participation. Third-party threats continued to arise, but even in 1948 the separate candidacies of Henry A. Wallace and of J. Strom Thurmond attracted less than 5 percent of the total popular vote.

Despite the apparent vigor of the two-party system, some disquieting symptoms could be detected by the 1950s.[11] The lopsided Eisenhower victories, coming at a time when Democratic identifiers greatly outnumbered Republicans, implied that influences other than partisanship were swaying voters. Then in 1964, the anomalous candidacy of the conservative ideologue, Barry Goldwater, gave the Democratic candidate, Lyndon B. Johnson, a victory of unprecedented proportions. These were signs, to say the least, of increasing volatility within the electorate. Moreover, as interest in presidential primaries revived after 1944, and aspiring candidates made increasing use of them to win delegates, the decision-making role of the national conventions was undermined. After 1952, no more than a single ballot was required in the conventions of either party to nominate the candidates. Noticeable, too, was the increased activity of "amateurs" in presidential campaigns, along with campaign organizations that were separate from the party apparatus and relied heavily on media experts, pollsters, professional advertising firms, and even on non-partisan appeals to independent voters. The control by the parties over their traditional resources was eroding; functions once performed exclusively by party-as-organization were now falling into other hands.

Parties were eroding, and the old party game seemed likely to give way to a different format. Perhaps the turbulent election of 1968 represented the end of a long era that had its origins in the 1840s and the beginning of a new era whose characteristic features have yet to assume clear definition. Richard M. Nixon and Hubert H. Humphrey were entirely plausible candidates; they were recognizable types in the traditional party game. But ahead were George McGovern, Jimmy Carter, and Ronald Reagan, products of a new kind of politics that scarcely conformed to standard patterns. The wonder is not that such basic elements of the American political system as the traditional electoral parties were succumbing to the forces of change; rather the wonder is that forms and practices dating from the 1840s persisted for more than a century.

Fundamental to the party game was the utilization of the national convention for the purpose of nominating a party's candidates, drafting a platform, and exercising some control over party affairs. The American-style nominating convention, it might be noted, is a unique mechanism, having no exact counterpart in other Western democracies. It reflects both the distinctive character of the American presidency and the peculiar nature of American party politics. Its survival for more than a century is suggestive of its central role in the party game. By the same token, the drastic changes it has undergone since 1948, and more especially since 1968, may be regarded as symptomatic of a larger transformation in the American political universe.[12]

In format and function, the national convention remained much the same from 1844 to 1944, although its procedures were refined, regularized, and in some instances elaborated. In response to the calls issued by the national party committees, the Republicans usually convened in the latter part of June, followed two weeks later by the Democrats. After 1860, sites in the Midwest were favored, with the Republicans showing a special partiality for Chicago. Customarily each state was allotted delegates equal in number to twice its electoral vote, with nominal representation for the territories and the District of Columbia authorized by both parties after 1868. In order to take account of actual party voting strength, a bonus plan was instituted by the Republicans after the 1912 convention, which had the effect of diluting the influence of the southern delegations, and the Democrats in 1944 introduced a similar arrangement. The addition of women to the convention ranks after 1920 swelled the size of the delegations, and other changes in apportionment formulas ultimately increased the size of the conventions from around a thousand delegates early in the twentieth century to 2622 members of the 1968 Democratic Con-

vention and half that number for the Republicans. How the delegates were selected was left very much to the discretion of the state
parties, which followed divergent practices. After the 1912 debacle,
the Republicans adopted rules to guide the process, but the Democrats took no definitive action in this important area until 1968.
Because of laxity in the selection process, fights over the seating of
delegates with questionable, or conflicting, credentials were not
uncommon.

The ritualistic aspects of the conventions, which made them ever
more colorful over the years, developed slowly. By the post-Civil
War era the temporary chairman was expected to deliver a rousing
address, which became known as the "keynote speech." Formal
speeches placing presidential candidates in nomination were excep-
tional before 1876; it was assumed that delegates would be cognizant
of the manifold virtues of any individual of presidential stature. In
1876 such reticence was abandoned, and thereafter there were not
only florid nominating speeches but several seconding speeches as
well. Now, too, elaborately staged demonstrations in behalf of the
favorites enlivened the scene, and protracted the proceedings.
Except in the cases of some early vice-presidential nominees, who
happened to be present on the occasion, there were no acceptance
speeches. Instead, in the time-honored custom extending back to
the era of the congressional caucus, the candidates were expected
to signify acceptance of their party's designation in a public letter,
usually issued several weeks after the convention had adjourned.
Grover Cleveland departed from this tradition in 1892, by accepting
his nomination at a public ceremony in Madison Square Garden,
and Bryan followed suit four years later. Franklin Delano Roosevelt
set a new pattern in 1932 by flying to Chicago to deliver his
acceptance in person, at the same time addressing his fellow citizens
throughout the nation by radio. Not until 1948, by which time
television covered the proceedings, did personally delivered acceptance speeches by both candidates—followed by symbolic appearances of party notables—become an invariable part of the ritual.

Convention procedures were governed more by custom than by
formal rules. It was customary, for example, to adopt the platform
before proceeding to the business of nominating candidates, but
this sequence was not always observed. Similarly, formal ballots

were supposedly required in voting on nominations, but on some occasions this rule was ignored and candidates were named by acclamation. Two rules that were of considerable consequence, however, were long adhered to by the Democratic National Convention. One was the ancient "two-thirds rule," requiring that a candidate receive two-thirds of the delegate vote for nomination. A source of controversy at many conventions, it was finally dropped in 1936. The unit rule, by which state party authorities could require a delegation to vote as a unit, lingered on until 1968.

The high point of each convention was, of course, balloting for the presidential nominee. Very commonly this drama pitted rival factions of the party against each other and brought into play intricate tactical maneuvers, including the use of stalking horses and favorite sons, as state leaders sought to gauge how best to wield their influence. Occasionally, as with the choice by the Democrats of Horatio Seymour (1868) or John W. Davis (1924) and by the Republicans of James A. Garfield (1880) or Warren G. Harding (1920), stalemates between prominent aspirants were resolved only by the choice of a dark horse. But such contingencies were relatively rare. Between 1860 and 1948, the Republicans chose their standard bearer on the first ballot in fourteen of twenty-four conventions; in only two instances were ten or more ballots required. The Democrats were more contentious. Although in the same period they achieved thirteen first-ballot nominations, there were four occasions when more than twenty ballots were required. Most notable was the imbroglio in 1924, with 103 ballots taken over the course of two weeks in the longest of all national conventions.

The nomination of the vice-presidential candidate was always anticlimatic. Until recent decades, when it has acquired importance as a possible stepping stone to the first office, the position was neither highly regarded nor much sought after. It was commonly used to "balance the ticket," either geographically or ideologically. On some occasions the presidential nominee, especially if he was an incumbent, dictated the choice. Since World War II it has become the practice for the head of the ticket to signify his preference for a running mate, and for the convention merely to ratify the selection. The adoption of party platforms was nearly as perfunctory as the nomination of the Vice President. Serious controversy over platform planks arose in the Democratic conventions of 1860, 1896, 1924, and 1948, and the Republicans experienced milder difficulties in 1908 and 1932. Ordinarily, however, disputes were resolved—often by the use of bland language—within the Committee on Resolutions.

The national conventions were very much dominated by party notables: experienced congressional figures, governors, and state or large-city party bosses. The dynamics of convention politics made it an "insiders'" game, with the crucial decisions being made in the fabled "smoke filled rooms" by factional chieftains. Delegates were expected to follow the dictates of their leaders. The ultimate objective was to negotiate the selection of a candidate who could win and who, at the same time, could add strength to the party's ticket in critical states. It was a game conducted by skilled professionals; "outsiders," amateurs, and ideologues were not encouraged to participate, nor was close public scrutiny invited. Aspiring candidates entrusted their fate to managers who sought to build coalitions of state delegations, offering in turn the prospect of party victory, as well as more tangible promises of patronage and influence. The system had the virtue of fostering accommodation within the parties in most instances—1896 and 1912 being conspicuous exceptions—and producing candidates around whom all factions could unite.

The men who emerged from the process as presidential nominees conformed to no single type. The Democrats tended to select governors, especially those from the swing state of New York. The Republicans were more apt to look to the Midwest for their candidates, many of whom had congressional experience. Men who had acquired large reputations during years of service in Washington were rarely chosen; James G. Blaine (1884) was a conspicuous exception, and he went down to defeat. Until the twentieth century, when new campaign styles began to develop, the personal popularity —or charisma—of the candidates was of minor importance; appeals to party loyalty were relied on more than appeals in behalf of a personality.

In the post-World War II decades several new influences came into operation and began to undermine and alter the old convention system. One such factor was the revival of interest in presidential primaries. As they acquired acceptance, the process of transforming the selection of candidates from a closed system controlled by "insiders" to one that favored "outsiders" who could demonstrate vote-getting ability was under way. After 1960, the candidates who dominated in the primary contests won their parties' nominations, except for the unusual circumstances that produced the choice of Hubert H. Humphrey in 1968. Consequently, the conventions were decreasingly decision-making bodies; they followed the edicts of the primaries. Delegates selected in primaries, and pledged to specific candidates, were no longer the pawns of brokers meeting in "smoke filled rooms"; in many cases they had been elected in opposition to slates supported by state party organizations.

After 1948 the format of the conventions was altered to conform to the requirements of television. Rigorous limits were imposed on nominating and seconding speeches, demonstrations were curtailed, important events were carefully scheduled for evening prime time, and features such as film clips and appearances by show business personalities were added to attract and hold viewers. "Favorite son" nominations were all but prohibited in the interest of streamlining and expediting the proceedings. Assiduous television reporters mingled with delegates on the floor and behind the scenes, bringing virtually every episode in the unfolding drama immediately before the public. Instead of "smoke filled rooms," there was now a public spectacle, complete with producers, directors, and Walter Cronkite. Hopeful candidates, and members of their families, were scrutinized for their telegenic qualities. Delegates were cautioned against behavior that would create negative impressions on home viewers. In short, the old style convention fell victim to the new medium.

In evaluating elements of persistence and change in the traditional party game, some reference must be made to campaign styles, and most particularly to the role of the presidential candidate in the campaign. Here again, the patterns established in the 1840s tended to persist well into the present century and did not change radically until after World War II, when the declining influence of parties, the development of new technologies in transportation and communication, and the importance attaching to presidential primaries revolutionized this aspect of the presidential game.[13]

So long as partisan loyalties remained fervent among the mass of the electorate, campaigns were designed mainly to reinforce and activate those loyalties. The standard ingredients of the campaign were the hundreds of highly partisan presses, the tons of party pamphlets, the spectacular rallies and parades, the stump speeches delivered by hosts of party notables, and the intensive canvassing efforts of local party organizations. Indoctrination was combined with entertainment, and both were provided in abundance. Although vital issues, especially those of local relevance, were not ignored, and the personalities of the candidates were the object of both adulation and abuse, the greatest emphasis was placed on the elemental appeal to partisanship. To employ Richard Jensen's terminology, these were "army-style" campaigns, featuring "rally-type" activities to mobilize the troops of party voters. The basic techniques had been introduced by 1840, and they continued in vogue for generations.

The role of the presidential candidate in the campaign long remained surprisingly ambiguous and varied. For other than incumbents seeking re-election, where aloof silence remained the rule until 1912, three generalized strategies were followed. Down to 1880 most candidates of both parties chose to make no public utterances, aside from their acceptance statements. Some, especially those whose prospects were poor, played active parts in the campaign. Winfield Scott in 1852 made a well-publicized tour of potential sites for military hospitals, addressing throngs along the way. In 1860 Stephen A. Douglas boldly spent several months on campaign tours that even took him into the deep South. Horatio Seymour, nominated over his strenuous objections by the Democrats in 1868, reluctantly undertook a speaking tour from Syracuse to Chicago and back, and the ill-fated Horace Greeley made two hundred speeches during the 1872 campaign. The first Republican candidate to break with precedent was James G. Blaine, who tried to bolster his faltering cause with a six-week personal campaign in 1884. William Jennings Bryan's extraordinary exertions in 1896, when he traveled 18,000 miles and gave more than six hundred speeches in twenty-seven states, was merely the most ambitious of the ventures into personal campaigning before 1900.

The third alternative, favored most by Republican candidates, was the "front porch" campaign. This technique acquired classic form with James A. Garfield in 1880. Serving as his own campaign manager, he received innumerable visiting delegations at his home in Mentor, Ohio, delivering to them bland but encouraging homilies and avoiding any statements that could lead to controversy or criticism. Harrison (1888) and McKinley (1896) followed Garfield's example, as did Wilson in 1916 and Harding in 1920. This format enabled the candidates to bring themselves to public attention under carefully controlled conditions without appearing to be engaged in an "undignified" quest for office and was well adapted to those with good prospects for victory.

After 1900, extensive campaign tours, especially by the Democratic candidates, became common. Wilson in 1912 was the first to employ this tactic and win. James Cox in 1920 stumped in thirty-six states, with sufficient effect to induce Harding to leave his front porch in October 1920 for a series of speeches. By 1928 both major party candidates were touring the nation, focusing their efforts on major addresses devoted to the leading issues and expanding their audiences through the medium of the radio. Thereafter the campaign tour in its modern form was a "must" for all candidates.

Subtle alterations were also made in campaign organization and techniques. Harrison's managers in 1888 refined fund-raising practices, securing over $3,000,000 to finance his successful race. Mark Hanna went even farther in managing McKinley's 1896 campaign, raising unprecedented sums, allocating them carefully to maximize their impact, and overseeing their expenditure in accordance with approved business methods. By 1920 the Republicans were utilizing the services of a professional advertising specialist, and Alfred E. Landon's campaign in 1936 was the first to enlist a public-relations firm to guide the candidate's efforts against Roosevelt. With the advent of radio, candidates continued to make extensive tours, but their speeches were broadcast nationwide and there was soon considerable use of spot advertisements as well.

Steadily after 1900 campaigns became more candidate-oriented. The nominees' personalities, promises, and potential for leadership, rather than the old emphasis on party loyalty, engaged public attention. The man, no less than the party and its platform, had to be "sold" to the electorate. With this new orientation, the traditional "entertainment" features of the campaign—the pageantry, the rallies, the torchlight processions, the marching clubs, and even the colorful stump speakers—receded into the past.

Change in campaign style proceeded even more rapidly after 1948. Now, with the electorate more volatile, less bound by partisan ties, appeals were couched in non-partisan terms to the growing host of independent voters. Auxiliary campaign organizations—"Citizens for Eisenhower," "Independents for Stevenson," "Labor for Kennedy"—often staffed by amateur volunteers and eschewing party labels, shared campaign responsibilities with regular party agencies. Air travel extended enormously the ability of candidates to meet face-to-face with voters in every part of the nation; in 1960 Richard M. Nixon somewhat desperately kept his pledge to campaign personally in every one of the fifty states. Television both increased the cost of conducting campaigns and gave every voter who cared to look an intimate close-up of the presidential contenders. Televised debates between the major candidates—originated by Kennedy and Nixon in 1960—introduced a new element of drama into the campaigns. On the other hand, the insatiable appetite of the television medium for spot news—measured in seconds of precious air time—tended to trivialize the campaigns by rendering the major speeches of the radio era obsolete and by focusing on visual events of negligible significance.

The duration of the campaigns became enormously extended. No longer was the political season confined to the period between Labor Day and the November election. Aspiring candidates must now tour the country months, or even years, in advance of the first presidential primaries. Then, starting off in the snows of New Hampshire, with its over-publicized February primary, they must proceed with their caravan of media specialists, pollsters, organizers, and speech writers to thirty or more states, usually ending up in California in June. Next came the party conventions, followed soon by the resumption of even more strenuous campaigning up to the eve of election. Nothing more graphically illustrates the change that had taken place in the presidential game than the contrast between Coolidge remaining silent in the White House in 1924 and Richard M. Nixon doggedly visiting fifty states in 1960. The party game had been replaced by a national popularity contest in which parties-as-organizations played a declining role.

For roughly a century the party game had adapted surprisingly well to the forces of change and had retained familiar lineaments. Despite alterations in the Constitutional and legal environment, despite successive party realignments, despite the slow erosion of partisan fervor, despite technological innovation, the closely fought contest between Harry S Truman and Thomas E. Dewey in 1948 was strongly reminiscent of twenty-five earlier presidential elections. But over the next two decades, the old rules became increasingly outmoded. The pace of what Walter Dean Burnham has termed "electoral disaggregation" accelerated; more voters classified themselves as independents, split-ticket voting increased, the electorate became more volatile. The spread of presidential primaries dealt a blow to the convention system. The airplane and television, along with the media experts and the pollsters, transformed campaign styles. Ideological influences, as evidenced by the nomination of Barry Goldwater in 1964 and the independent candidacy of George Wallace in 1968, became more potent. Functions that were once the exclusive preserve of regular party agencies were now shared with others. The candidates and their vast personal staffs, rather than the parties, dominated the election scene.

But these developments were but a prelude to the greater upheaval that was to occur in 1968. Stemming from the general turbulence of the 1960s, which brought a heightened emphasis on "openness" and "participation" at the expense of confidence in traditional authorities, as well as from the culmination of trends that in some instances extended back as far as the Progressive Era, an irresistible reform impulse wrought tremendous changes in parties, political mechanisms, and voter behavior. Only the most striking of the innovations need be mentioned in order to convey some sense of the magnitude of the transformation that resulted.[14]

As a consequence of mounting dissatisfaction with the process of delegate selection, which had been brought into focus at their 1964 convention, the Democrats in 1968 created the McGovern-Fraser Commission to restructure the national convention. The major criticisms of existing arrangements were that they failed to provide adequately for the representation of women, young people, and minorities; that they gave undue influence to party bosses at the expense of the rank-and-file; and that the winner-take-all rules that applied in many states did not fairly represent diverse views within the party. Accordingly, detailed guidelines were adopted in 1971 to govern the process of delegate selection, and they were subjected to later refinements. The most salient features were that delegates were to be selected in a fair and open manner in small districts within the same year that the convention met. Affirmative action goals were set to encourage appropriate representation of youth and minorities, and men and women were to have equal numbers of delegates. Instead of the winner-take-all principle, there were complex rules to ensure that each candidate's support was represented proportionally. Delegates would be apportioned among the states in accordance with a formula that combined population and a standard measure of Democratic party voting strength. In what some regarded as a retrogressive move, provisions were made in 1978 to increase the number of delegates by 10 percent to afford representation to designated state party and elected officials.

The new rules had both intended and unintended consequences. Not anticipated, or even favored, was the rapid increase in the number of presidential primaries: from seventeen states in 1968 to thirty-seven in 1980, including the District of Columbia and Puerto Rico. The proportion of delegates chosen in this manner by both parties rose from 40 percent to 75 percent. The characteristics of the delegates changed markedly after 1968 in response to the affirmative action mandate. At the same time, old-line party professionals were vastly outnumbered by new activists, many of them committed to special issues or interest groups. Because fewer than 30 percent of the eligibles participated in primary elections—and a much smaller number in the redesigned caucuses—the representativeness of the convention remained open to question. In any event, with most of the delegates legally committed to vote for particular candidates, they had little discretion in the matter; their function was to ratify the verdict of the primaries. As Gerald M. Pomper succinctly phrased it, "The purpose of the . . . [national convention] is no longer to select a nominee, but to legitimize the individual who has proved his mettle and his popularity in the long pre-convention period."[15]

The Republicans were less caught up in the reform enthusiasm than the Democrats. They continued to permit wide latitude to the state parties in regulating the selection of delegates, although they were not indifferent to affirmative action goals. They did not outlaw winner-take-all primaries or require proportional representation of candidate strength. However, they were affected by the spread of the presidential primaries, with the result that their national convention, too, lost its deliberative function.

A second innovation of portentous significance was federal financing of presidential campaigns.[16] Because campaign costs escalated markedly after 1960 and because of concerns about the sources of campaign funds—raised to prominence by the Watergate investigation—Congress enacted legislation between 1971 and 1979 under which candidates could qualify for generous public funding, both for the primary contests and for the general election. In 1976, Carter and Ford each received $21.8 million for campaign expenses, in addition to lesser sums for pre-convention campaigns.

This new departure revolutionized campaign financing, and it had other consequences as well. Because the funds went to the candidates, not to the party organizations, the dependence of candidates on parties was all but ended. Indeed, party sources were virtually prohibited from contributing financially to the election of their candidates. Along with federal funding came federal control. Elaborate regulations, enforced by the Federal Elections Commission, required minute accounting for receipts and expenditures, limited certain categories of expenditures, and necessitated the addition of large staffs of lawyers and accountants to presidential campaign organizations. What had once been an enterprise conducted by autonomous "private" associations had now become thoroughly enmeshed in legal and bureaucratic controls. In the process, the role of parties was further attenuated and confused.

As the cumulative effects of the post-1968 reforms became increasingly evident, authoritative observers offered pessimistic appraisals of the future of American political parties. Gerald M. Pomper, noting that parties had lost control over their basic resources, concluded: "The process has now reached the point at which the American political party is little more than one of many groups, not greatly disparate in their influence, which participate in elections." He attributed the condition to a failure of theory. "Parties can be both hierarchical and participatory only if they are also irrelevant," was his summary judgment.[17] From a different perspective, Everett Carll Ladd, Jr., saw the end of the old "accommodationist" parties, which had operated to de-emphasize conflict, and their replacement by unstable parties-in-the-electorate shaped by new "purist" activists who were disposed to emphasize issues and ideology at the expense of consensus, or even victory. "The electorate," as he analyzes it, "has become, for the long run, more issue oriented and more candidate oriented, and necessarily, then, less party oriented. As such, it is up for grabs."[18] Nelson W. Polsby and Aaron Wildavsky, who have examined the changing character of presidential elections closely since 1960 in five editions of their authoritative text, are equally convinced that we have entered a new political era. "When we wrote the first edition of *Presidential Elections*, in the early 1960s," they reminisced, "the rules and practices of the presidential nomination and election process had not changed for thirty years. Since then, they have done nothing but change." The consequences were now apparent. "Today," they note, "the influence of parties on government is extremely weak as a result of successful efforts to centralize national parties and spread participation toward candidate activists and away from party regulars."[19] Stephen Hess shared these appraisals. "It is doubtful," he surmised, "that American political parties can ever regain the influence they had in the nineteenth century."[20]

Many indicators substantiated the insights of these experts. It was estimated that by 1974 more than one-third of the electorate acknowledged no partisan ties, and this phenomenon was especially characteristic of younger voters. Split-ticket voting rose sharply after 1964. More citizens adopted the position that the appeal of the candidates took precedence over party affiliation. Voter turnout declined from around 62 percent of the potential electorate in 1960 to about 52 percent in 1980. In another context, the nomination by the Democrats of George McGovern in 1972 and Jimmy Carter in 1976, without the endorsement or support of most party regulars, provide convincing demonstrations that the game was being played according to new rules.

Somewhat paradoxically, as the influence of parties in presidential elections declined, the national party organizations—especially that of the Democrats—acquired added authority and expanded structures. The most remarkable evidence of this enhanced vitality was the ability of the national organization to impose stringent new rules for the selection of convention delegates after 1968. Nothing of this sort had ever been attempted before. The party adopted a formal charter for the first time in 1974, which provided for, among other things, mid-term conventions to chart party policy. The permanent staff of the national committee was enlarged, and other measures were taken to institutionalize the party apparatus. Less spectacular but perhaps more effective steps were taken to improve the Republican organization, especially during the chairmanship of William Brock. But requirements for party membership remained vague, mechanisms for enforcing party discipline on candidates were non-existent, ties with state party organizations were weak, and even the connection between presidential campaign staffs and national party agencies was loose. In a sense, the parties had been nationalized, but the form was more apparent than the substance.

The post-1968 reforms had shaken, if not quite disrupted, the familiar party game. But there was the possibility that even more revolutionary changes in the rules were in prospect. Proposals to eliminate the electoral college in favor of a direct election of the President by a nation-wide popular vote gained support. A Constitutional amendment to this effect was passed by the House of Representatives overwhelmingly in 1969, only to be blocked in the Senate by a filibuster. President Carter recommended a similar measure in 1977, and although it received the approval of the Senate Judiciary Committee, it was never brought to the floor. Meanwhile, opinion polls consistently showed strong public support for direct, popular elections. In a closely related area, there was evident sentiment to replace the hodge-podge of presidential primaries—conducted at various times under diverse and changing rules— with a single national primary. Whatever the merits of these proposals, and here opinions differ widely, they would surely change the presidential game quite beyond recognition.

In summary, then, the party version of the presidential game took form in the Age of Jackson and survived amid changing conditions for more than a century. Integral to the game were two major electoral parties making similar use of national conventions to select their candidates, mobilizing their resources for the ensuing campaign, and competing for each state's bloc of electoral votes. Slowly after 1900, then more rapidly after 1948, changes in the rules, in the larger context of politics, and in political behavior operated to alter the game. Between 1968 and 1980 a host of major innovations revised the rules of the presidential game so drastically as to create a new game. Few continuities lingered from the past, except in the realm of symbol and myth.

In bringing this study to an end we add a coda, recurring to themes sounded earlier. We recall the exultation of one of the Framers, William R. Davie, as he described the electoral college: "It is impossible for human ingenuity to devise any mode of election better calculated to exclude undue influence." Then, after the near-catastrophe in 1800, Albert Gallatin voiced his despair about the unpredictable consequences of the dual-vote arrangement. "I see the danger," he confessed, "but cannot discover the remedy." The remedy was the Twelfth Amendment. However, other problems arose. We are struck by Senator Dickerson's anguished charge in 1817 that no official was "elected or appointed by a rule so undefined, so vague, so subject to abuse, as that by which we elect the Chief Magistrate of the Union." In the same vein there was Congressman McDuffie's lament that "we have no constitutional provision at all" to govern the election of the President. We envision Andrew Jackson declaiming in his singular fashion against the inequity of the process that deprived him of the presidency in 1824 and calling in the name of the people for a popular election. We hear Andrew Stevenson, while championing the general-ticket system, lauding political parties. "They enable the views and wishes of the People to be carried into effect, and not scattered and broken . . . . Without such parties, what should we have been, or what shall we become?" In rejoinder, there was John Bell's denunciation of such a line of thought "as the most daring, and at the same time the most dangerous conception of the age." Out of this background of illusion and reality, of discord and confusion, of experimentation and change, there emerged at last the version of the presidential game that we have termed "the party game."

For half a century after 1787, the rules governing the election of the President remained vague, unstable, and transitory. The "hazardous game" was succeeded by "the Virginia game," which in turn gave way to "the game of faction." Then, between 1832 and 1844, new rules shaped "the party game." For the ensuing century, the rules of that game remained in effect, though not without refinements, modifications, and elaborations.

What is of most compelling interest with respect to the party-game era is the reciprocal relationship between parties and the election of the President. The Constitutional requirement of a majority of the electoral votes for election operated powerfully to limit competition for the presidency to two contenders, especially if a contingent election was to be avoided. Parties formed in the 1830s behind rival candidates. The contest for the presidency in turn shaped the characteristics of those parties. It was the contest for the presidency that most defined the national goals of parties; it provided, indeed, the clearest reason for the existence of national parties. The quadrennial mobilization for the presidential election, epitomized in the national party conventions and manifested in the ensuing fervor of the campaign, called forth the greatest of partisan exertions. Recurrent campaign appeals in these elections established and maintained the basis for distinctive partisan identities at all levels of government and politics.

But even while this party game flourished, its foundations were flawed. The formal method of electing the President was constantly subjected to questioning. So was the institution of political parties. Neither enjoyed full acceptance. In broad terms, there was never a consensus on a rationale for a process of presidential selection or for political parties. The vaguely defined republican ideology of the Framers led to an unrealistic prescription for presidential selection; it made no place for parties. Therefore that ideology, though it long continued to inspire reverence and exert influence, was largely irrelevant. It was irrelevant to the practices that developed in choosing the President. It was irrelevant to parties.

The aura of that ideology lingered on through the years of the

Virginia dynasty, and it even found expression later in the utterances of Jackson and his contemporaries. But it is best understood as being productive of tension between remote ideals and torturous actualities. The Jeffersonians could rationalize their deviant practices on the grounds that the very existence of the republic was at stake. Later generations were denied the comforts of such apocalyptic visions in assuaging their consciences. Somewhat awkwardly, and with a lack of concern for ideological consistency, they came to terms with a system of politics that appeared to meet their needs.

They accepted the general-ticket system, the popular election of electors, and the continued possibility of contingent elections by the House not because they agreed it was the best system, or because it was thought to be consistent with some underlying principles, but rather because—through the vagaries of politics—matters had turned out that way. Meanwhile, some of them continued to agitate for Constitutional changes in the selection process. As the years passed, even confidence in the "federative principle"—the notion that the role of the states in the selection process was best effectuated through the general-ticket plan—began to wane. The retention of electors, with their vestigal functions, seemed anachronistic, if not a source of potential hazard. Employing the rhetoric of democracy and nationalism, reformers now called for the direct popular election of "the people's president." "What good reason is there to continue such an irrational voting system in an advanced democratic nation, where the ideal of popular choice is the most deeply ingrained of governmental principles?" queried one such advocate.[21] Indeed, when no other rationale for the selection process was forthcoming, who could withstand the force of such a simplistic appeal to place all decisions in the hands of the people?

Parties were also vulnerable, especially party-as-organization, or electoral parties. Identifying the crux of the problem, Stephen Hess has observed: "We are an antiparty people and an antiparty society whose government is organized around a party system."[22] In the republican ideology, parties were abhorrent. The strain of antiparty sentiment remained in evidence throughout the period of the party game. Now the argument was less that parties promoted discord within the republic than that they were managed by "bosses" and converted into "machines" that deprived the people of their political efficacy and served venal interests. There were such outcries from segments of the Whigs in the 1840s, from Liberal Republicans in the 1870s, from Mugwumps in the 1880s, and the Populists in the 1890s. During the Progressive Era, active efforts to weaken party-as-organization produced the direct primary, corrupt practices laws, civil service reform, the initiative and referendum, and similar measures. The assaults were renewed in the 1960s, culminating in the extension of presidential primaries, the emasculation of the national conventions, and federal financing of campaigns. Here, again, the point is that Americans were unable to define a secure role for parties in the political process, including the process of selecting the President.

Lacking either explicit Constitutional sanction or firm consensual acceptance, the party version of the presidential game was nevertheless sustained by the forces of tradition and by the ability of the electoral parties to produce tangible rewards for their leaders and diverse gratifications to their adherents. It was sustained, as well, by the lack of any acceptable alternative. As it began to deteriorate, theorists came forth to explain its virtues. A two-party system was essential to the maintenance of political stability and to the formulation of moderate alternative courses of public policy. Some yearned for the restoration of the "accommodationist" parties of the nineteenth century; others wished to make the parties "responsible," able to govern when in power. Both schools of thought viewed with alarm the rise in the proportion of "independents," the decline in turnout, the erosion of party functions, the emergence of "single interest" groups, the new emphasis on ideology, and the trend toward "plebiscitary democracy." But neither their exhortations nor their prescriptions seemed capable of reversing the forces that were destroying the old party game.[23]

How should the President of the United States be selected? What relation, if any, should political parties have to that process? These two questions have been before the American people since 1789. They were especially vexing in the years between Washington and Jackson, the period of the origins of the presidential game. They were never answered satisfactorily then. They were muted, but not entirely ignored, while the party game held sway. Now they are before us again with renewed urgency. It is increasingly doubtful that we can address them, as we did in the past, within a limited context of electoral politics. We may not be able longer to postpone a reconsideration of a theory of American politics. There may be limits to the durability of a political system that rests on ambiguous attitudes toward basic values. Such, at least, are the concerns aroused by this study of the origins of the presidential game.

Notes

Chapter I

1. Charles Francis Adams, ed., *Memoirs of John Quincy Adams, Comprising Portions of His Diary from 1795 to 1848* (12 vols.: Philadelphia, 1874–77), X, 468.
2. *Annals of the Congress of the United States* [1789–1824] (Washington, 1834–56), 15th Cong., 1st Ses., 179 (hereafter cited as *Annals of Congress*).
3. *Ibid.*, 18th Cong., 1st Ses., 851.
4. Although I must accept responsibility for this attempt to summarize the principles and beliefs that constituted what I term the "republican ideal," my understanding has been influenced by Bernard Bailyn, *Ideological Origins of the American Revolution* (Cambridge, Mass., 1967); Lance Banning, *The Jeffersonian Persuasion: Evolution of a Party Ideology* (Ithaca, 1978); Richard Buel, *Securing the Revolution: Ideology in American Politics, 1789–1815* (Ithaca, 1972); and especially Gordon Wood, *The Creation of the American Republic, 1776–1787* (Chapel Hill, 1969).
5. The Framers anticipated that parties, or factions, would arise, but—as Madison explained so lucidly in *Federalist* No. 10—they could and must be controlled if the republic was to avoid the fate of earlier democracies. The device of representation, especially when the representatives were drawn from the diverse constituencies of a republic vast in area, was one safeguard against the establishment of the tyranny of a majority faction. Another was the indirect election of Senators by the state legislatures. A third was the division of authority between the central government and the states.

In addition, there were the safeguards of staggered elections and checks and balances. Taken altogether, these contrivances would control the operation of factions in the legislative branch. The exceedingly intricate arrangements for choosing the President, it was hoped, would not merely control but virtually eliminate the influence of faction, although it was expected that there would be rivalry between large and small states. On Madison's theory of politics, see Douglass Adair, "That Politics May Be Reduced to a Science: David Hume, James Madison, and the Tenth Federalist," *Huntington Library Quarterly*, XX (1957), 343–60.

Chapter II

1. Standard studies that are still reliable are Max Farrand, *The Framing of the Constitution of the United States* (New Haven, 1913) and Charles Warren, *The Making of the Constitution* (Boston, 1937). The most stimulating recent work is Gordon Wood, *The Creation of the American Republic, 1776–1787* (Chapel Hill, 1969). Although I differ with his interpretation, I have been aided greatly by Charles Thach, Jr., *The Creation of the Presidency, 1775–1789* (Baltimore, 1926), in tracing discussions of the presidency in the Constitutional Convention.

2. My treatment of the work of the Constitutional Convention is based on a thorough study of Max Farrand, ed., *The Records of the Federal Convention of 1787* (4 vols.: New Haven, 1911, 1937). Because this source is accessible and familiar, my citations are minimal.

3. Farrand, *Records*, III, 397–404.

4. William T. Hutchinson and William M. E. Rachal, *The Papers of James Madison* (12 vols.: [to 1790] Chicago, 1962–79), X, 115–16 (hereafter cited as *Papers . . . Madison*).

5. Farrand, *Records*, II, 30.

6. *Ibid.*, 114.

7. *Ibid.*, 113.

8. *Ibid.*, 30.

9. *Ibid.*, 493–94.

10. *Ibid.*, 537.

11. *Ibid.*, 522–23.

12. *Ibid.*, 527.
13. These objectives were summarized most effectively by Gouverneur Morris on September 4 (*ibid.*, 500).
14. Jonathan Elliott, ed., *The Debates of the Several State Conventions on the Adoption of the Federal Constitution* (2nd ed., 5 vols.: Philadelphia, 1863), IV, 105.
15. Farrand, *Records*, III, 459.
16. Farrand, *Records*, II, 500, 512.
17. Elliott, ed., *Debates*, IV, 304–5.
18. *Ibid.*, 112.
19. Elliott, ed., *Debates,* II, 511.
20. Julian P. Boyd, ed., *The Papers of Thomas Jefferson* (19 vols.: [to 1791] Princeton, 1950–74), XII, 440–41.
21. Paul L. Ford, ed., *Pamphlets on the Constitution of the United States . . . 1787–1788* (Brooklyn, 1888), 263.
22. Among 124 amendments proposed by state ratifying conventions, the only ones touching on the presidency dealt with the issue of re-eligibility. New York, Virginia, and North Carolina offered amendments limiting the number of terms a President might serve. Only one of these amendments came before the Congress, where it met defeat in both houses. Herman V. Ames, "The Proposed Amendments to the Constitution of the United States during the First Century of Its History," *Annual Report of the American Historical Association . . . 1896*, II, (Washington, 1897), 307–10; *Annals of Congress*, 1st Cong., 1st Ses., 76, 762–63.
23. My discussion of the legal arrangements that were made for the first presidential election is based largely on Merrill Jensen and Robert A. Becker, eds., *The Documentary History of the First Federal Elections, 1788–1790*, I (Madison, 1976) (hereafter cited as *First Federal Elections*). Also useful is Charles O. Paullin, "The First Elections Under the Constitution," *Iowa Journal of History and Politics*, II (1904), 3–33.
24. *First Federal Elections*, I, 229–302.
25. *Ibid.*, 437–538.
26. *Ibid.*, 767–832.
27. Lynn W. Turner, *William Plumer of New Hampshire, 1759–1850* (Chapel Hill, 1962), 37–38.
28. Paullin, "First Elections," 21–23; Charles A. O'Neil, *The American Electoral System* (New York, 1887), 34–35.
29. *First Federal Elections*, I, 156–211.

30. Richard P. McCormick, *Experiment in Independence: New Jersey in the Critical Period, 1781–1789* (New Brunswick, 1950), 288.
31. Paullin, "First Elections," *passim.*
32. Norman Risjord, *Chesapeake Politics, 1781–1800* (New York, 1978), 324; *Papers . . . Madison*, XI, 336–38.
33. New York and North Carolina both had dual suffrage requirements —that is, higher property qualifications were required to vote for governor than for members of the lower house. It is conceivable that the Framers may have had such discrepancies in mind in according discretion to state legislatures.
34. *First Federal Elections*, I, 480.
35. *Ibid.*, 289.
36. There is a vast literature relevant to the first election, but a convenient summary is Marcus Cunliffe, "Elections of 1789 and 1792" in Arthur M. Schlesinger, Jr., ed., *History of American Presidential Elections, 1789–1968* (4 vols.: New York, 1971), I, 3–19. Although the essays in this useful compendium are uneven in quality, I have consulted them discriminatingly and have drawn upon them extensively. The illustrative documents appended to the accounts of each election were especially convenient and helpful.
37. John C. Fitzpatrick, ed., *The Writings of George Washington* (39 vols.: Washington, 1931–44), XXX, 66–67, 95–98, 109–12 (hereafter cited as *Writings . . . Washington*). *Papers . . . Jefferson*, XIV, 17–18, 339–40.
38. *First Federal Elections*, I, 16; Kate Mason Rowland, *The Life of George Mason, 1725–1792* (2 vols.: New York, 1892), II, 233–81.
39. Hamilton's role in the election is fully documented in Harold C. Syrett, ed., *The Papers of Alexander Hamilton* (26 vols.: New York, 1961–79), especially Vol. V (hereafter cited as *Papers . . . Hamilton*).
40. *Writings . . . Washington*, XXX, 66–67, 109–12; *Papers . . . Hamilton*, V, 231, 248.
41. *Papers . . . Madison*, XI, 296–97, 335, 367, 381; *Papers . . . Hamilton*, V, 236.
42. *Papers . . . Hamilton*, V, 248–49, 249–50.
43. *Writings . . . Washington*, XXX, 117–20, 189–90.
44. *Papers . . . Hamilton*, V, 252, 252n; *First Federal Elections*, I, 401.
45. *First Federal Elections*, I, 296–324, 372–81.
46. Risjord, *Chesapeake Politics*, 330–37.
47. *Ibid.*, 326–30; *Papers . . . Madison*, XI, 401–4.
48. *First Federal Elections*, I, 390–91, 531–34, 609–23, 800–801.

49. One of the Framers, Charles Pinckney of South Carolina, stated in a Senate speech in 1800 that it had been intended that the votes of the electors "should be secret and unknown, until opened in the presence of both Houses" (Farrand, *Records*, III, 390). But it was immediately the practice to make public the votes cast by the electors. In Massachusetts, for example, newspapers promptly reported that the electors "gave in their votes unanimously, for His Excellency Geo. Washington, Esq., and the Hon. John Adams, Esq., as President and Vice President of the United States" (*First Federal Elections*, I, 542). Although, strictly speaking, the electors cast both of their votes *for President*, it had already come to be understood that the "second vote" was, in fact, intended to be for the Vice President.

50. Page Smith, *John Adams* (2 vols.: New York, 1962), II, 739–40, 760, 763–69; Charles Francis Adams, *The Works of John Adams* (10 vols.: Boston, 1856), IX, 485n, 567.

51. For a recent interpretation of the Framers' intentions, see James W. Ceaser, *Presidential Selection: Theory and Development* (Princton, 1979), ch. 1. Although there is considerable merit in Ceaser's analysis, his zeal to attack the recent trend toward a "plebiscitary" presidency gives a polemical tone to his work.

Chapter III

1. Paul L. Ford, ed., *Pamphlets on the Constitution* . . . , (Brooklyn, 1888), 65.

2. For useful summaries of presidential politics, 1792–1801, see the essays by Marcus Cunliffe, Page Smith, and Noble E. Cunningham, Jr., in Schlesinger, Jr., ed., *History of American Presidential Elections,* I. There are concise but authoritative histories of the Federalist and Republican parties by Linda K. Kerber and Cunningham in Arthur M. Schlesinger, Jr., *History of U.S. Political Parties* (4 vols.: New York, 1973), I. A standard political history of the period is John C. Miller, *The Federalist Era, 1789–1801* (New York, 1960). Among the host of special studies that I found most helpful are James M. Banner, Jr., *To the Hartford Convention: The Federalists and the Origins of Party Politics in Massachusetts, 1789–1815* (New York, 1970); Lance Banning, *The Jefferson Persuasion: Evolution of a Party Ideology* (Ithaca, 1978); Noble E. Cunningham, Jr., *The Jeffersonian Republicans: The Formation of Party*

Organization, 1789–1801 (Chapel Hill, 1957); Stephen G. Kurtz, *The Presidency of John Adams: The Collapse of Federalism, 1795–1800* (Philadelphia, 1957); Dumas Malone, *Jefferson and the Ordeal of Liberty* (Boston, 1962); and Norman Risjord, *Chesapeake Politics, 1781–1800* (New York, 1978). My own understanding of the period has been enhanced by studying the published correspondence of all the major political figures.

3. Gaillard Hunt, ed., *The Writings of James Madison* (9 vols.: New York, 1900–1910), VI, 106–19 (hereafter cited as *Writings . . . Madison*).

4. Paul Leicester Ford, ed., *The Writings of Thomas Jefferson* (10 vols.: New York, 1892–99), VI, 1–6 (hereafter cited as *Writings . . . Jefferson*).

5. *Papers . . . Hamilton*, XI, 426–45.

6. *Writings . . . Jefferson*, VI, 116.

7. *Ibid.*, 5.

8. *Writings . . . Washington*, XXXII, 32, 136n.

9. *Ibid.*, 46; *Papers . . . Hamilton*, XII, 137–39; *Writings . . . Jefferson*, VI, 114.

10. *Writings . . . Washington*, XXXII, 32, 131, 133, 186.

11. The debate can be traced in *Annals of Congress*, 2nd Cong., 1st Ses., 220, 278–82, 302–3, 401–18, 1341–43.

12. *Writings . . . Madison*, VI, 95–96; *Papers . . . Hamilton*, XI, 426–45.

13. *Writings . . . Jefferson*, VI, 144; Stanislas Murray Hamilton, ed., *The Writings of James Monroe* (7 vols.: New York, 1898–1903), I, 241–42 (hereafter cited as *Writings . . . Monroe*).

14. *Writings . . . Jefferson*, VI, 90; *Writings . . . Monroe*, I, 237.

15. *Papers . . . Hamilton*, XII, 384, 408, 544, 548. On Federalist uncertainty about Republican plans, see George Gibbs, *Memoirs of the Administrations of Washington and John Adams* (2 vols.: New York, 1846), I, 80–81, 83.

16. *Writings . . . Monroe*, I, 242–45.

17. Edmund Berkeley and Dorothy Smith Berkeley, *John Beckley: Zealous Partisan in a Nation Divided* (Philadelphia, 1973), 72–73; Alfred F. Young, *The Democratic Republicans of New York: The Origins, 1763–1797* (Chapel Hill, 1967), 324–32.

18. Cunningham, *Jeffersonian Republicans*, 11–12, 46–48; Young, *Democratic Republicans*, 324–32; *Writings . . . Jefferson*, VI, 73–74, 89–90, 93–94.

19. *Papers . . . Hamilton*, XX, 177, 239.

20. That leading Federalists opposed to Adams did not consider the

rule absolutely binding is evident from their attempt in 1799 to persuade Washington to seek a third term (Kurtz, *Presidency of John Adams*, 387–88). Similarly, Republican political leaders in 1807 put pressure on Jefferson to run again (Cunningham, *Jeffersonian Republicans*, 109). Much later, the Stalwart faction of the Republican party made a determined effort to nominate Grant in 1880. On the other hand, what amounted to a "one-term tradition" developed after 1840. Harrison declared he would serve only one term, and except for Franklin Pierce, no President between 1840 and 1860 sought a second term. Theodore Roosevelt, Calvin Coolidge, and Harry S Truman—Vice Presidents who succeeded to the presidency on the death of the incumbent President and then were elected to the presidency—all declined to seek renomination for what would have approximated a third term. In 1940 Franklin D. Roosevelt successfully challenged the two-term rule. By the Twenty-second Amendment (1951), Presidents were limited to two full terms.

21. *Writings . . . Jefferson*, VII, 10; *Writings . . . Madison*, VI, 301; Malone, *Ordeal*, ch. 18.

22. Charles R. King, ed., *The Life and Correspondence of Rufus King* (6 vols.: New York, 1894–1900), II, 46–48 (hereafter cited as *Correspondence . . . King*). *Writings . . . Jefferson*, VII, 89–90.

23. Berkeley and Berkeley, *John Beckley*, 132–51.

24. *Papers . . . Hamilton*, XX, 376; Gibbs, *Memoirs*, I, 397, 401–2.

25. *Papers . . . Hamilton*, XX, 371–72; Ulrich B. Phillips, ed., "Southern Federalist Correspondence, 1789–1797," *American Historical Review*, XIV (1909), 782–83.

26. *Papers . . . Hamilton*, XX, 376–77, 418–19.

27. Seth Ames, *Works of Fisher Ames* (2 vols.: Boston, 1854), I, 205.

28. *Papers . . . Hamilton*, XX, 403–6, 418–19.

29. Gibbs, *Memoirs*, I, 408–9.

30. *Writings . . . Jefferson*, VII, 91–92.

31. Gibbs, *Memoirs*, I, 412.

32. O'Neil, *American Electoral System*, 56–63, 65–66.

33. *Correspondence . . . King*, II, 135; Gibbs, *Memoirs*, I, 413.

34. *Works of John Adams*, VIII, 525, 535.

35. The most concise information on how electors were chosen in each state is in Charles O. Paullin, *Atlas of the Historical Geography of the United States* (Washington, 1932), 89.

36. See, for example, *Papers . . . Hamilton*, XXIV, 444–52, on this point.

37. Banner, *To the Hartford Convention*, 226–27; *Writings* . . . *Jefferson*, VII, 401; Risjord, *Chesapeake Politics*, 555–56; O'Neil, *American Electoral System*, 72–73.

38. O'Neil, *American Electoral System*, 71; *Writings* . . . *Jefferson*, VII, 402; *Papers* . . . *Hamilton*, XXIV, 464–66.

39. O'Neil, *American Electoral System*, 77–83; *Correspondence* . . . *King*, III, 237–38; *Annals of Congress*, 6th Cong., 2nd Ses., 126–46; *Writings* . . . *Madison*, VI, 40.

40. For examples of such political calculations, see *Writings* . . . *Jefferson*, VII, 401–3; *Writings* . . . *Madison*, VI, 408; *Correspondence* . . . *King*, III, 155–56.

41. Jared Sparks, *The Life of Gouverneur Morris, with Selections from His Correspondence* (3 vols.: Boston, 1832), III, 123–25; *Works* . . . *Adams*, IX, 45n; J. Franklin Jameson, ed., "Letters of Stephen Higginson," *Annual Report of the American Historical Association* . . . *1896*, I (Washington, 1897), 833–35; *Papers* . . . *Hamilton*, XXIV, 168.

42. *Papers* . . . *Hamilton*, XXIV, 509–10; *Correspondence* . . . *King*, III, 238.

43. Marvin R. Zahniser, *Charles Cotesworth Pinckney* (Chapel Hill, 1967), 200–218; *Correspondence* . . . *King*, III, 238; *Papers* . . . *Hamilton*, XXIV, 451n, 452–53, 467–68, 475, 569.

44. *Papers* . . . *Hamilton*, XXIV, 475.

45. *Correspondence* . . . *King*, III, 277–80, 298; *Works of Fisher Ames*, I, 279, 281–82; Samuel Eliot Morison, *The Life and Letters of Harrison Gray Otis* (2 vols.: Boston, 1913), I, 193–95.

46. Cunningham, *Jeffersonian Republicans*, 162–64; *Writings* . . . *Madison*, VI, 410.

47. *Writings* . . . *Jefferson*, VII, 327–29, 344.

48. For representative selections see the Appendix to Cunningham's essay on the election of 1800 in Schlesinger, Jr., *History of American Presidential Elections*, I.

49. "Jefferson and the Election of 1800: A Case Study of the Political Smear," *William and Mary Quarterly*, 3rd Ser., V (1948), 467–91.

50. *Papers* . . . *Hamilton*, XXIV, 574–85n; *Correspondence* . . . *King*, III, 430–31; *Works of Fisher Ames*, I, 286–87.

51. *Writings* . . . *Jefferson*, VII, 466–71. The question of why "arrangements" were not made to have at least one Republican elector throw a vote away from Burr, in order to prevent a tie, remains a mystery. In 1824 Madison revealed to Jefferson that the tie "was the result of false assurances despatched at the critical moment to the Electors

of one State, that the votes of another would be different from what they proved to be" (*Writings . . . Madison*, IX, 175). He was probably referring to a report from David Gelston, one of Burr's intimates, that the electors in at least two states would give Jefferson more votes than Burr (Douglass Adair, ed., "James Madison's Autobiography," *William and Mary Quarterly*, 3rd Ser., II, (1945), 206; John S. Pancake, "Aaron Burr: Would-Be Usurper," *William and Mary Quarterly*, 3rd Ser., VII (1951), 204–13; Daniel Sisson, *The American Revolution of 1800* (New York: 1974), 408n; Cunningham, *Jeffersonian Republicans*, 239–40).

52. *Writings . . . Jefferson*, VII, 490–91, 494; *Writings . . . Monroe*, III, 253–74; Henry Adams, ed., *The Writings of Albert Gallatin* (3 vols.: Philadelphia, 1879), I, 18–23 (hereafter cited as *Writings . . . Gallatin*).

53. *Writings . . . Jefferson*, VII, 494–95.

54. Sisson, *Revolution of 1800*, 436.

55. A convenient source of election data is J. R. Pole, *Political Representation in England and the Origins of the American Republic* (London, 1966), 544–64.

Chapter IV

1. Accounts of the successive elections from 1800 through 1820 will be found in the essays by Manning Dauer, Irving Brant, Norman K. Risjord, and Lynn W. Turner in Schlesinger, Jr., *History of American Presidential Elections*, I. Important special studies from which much of the material in this chapter has been derived are Harry Ammon, *James Monroe: The Quest for National Identity* (New York, 1971); James H. Broussard, *The Southern Federalists, 1800–1816* (Baton Rouge, 1978); James S. Chase, *Emergence of the Presidential Nominating Convention, 1789–1832* (Urbana, 1973); Noble E. Cunningham, Jr., *The Jeffersonian Republicans in Power, 1801–1809* (Chapel Hill, 1963); David Hackett Fischer, *The Revolution of American Conservatism: The Federalist Party in the Era of Jeffersonian Democracy* (New York, 1965); Louis C. Hatch, *A History of the Vice Presidency of the United States* (New York, 1934); Richard Hofstadter, *The Idea of a Party System: The Rise of a Legitimate Opposition in the United States, 1780–1840* (Berkeley, 1969); Ralph Ketcham, *James Madison* (New York, 1971); Dumas Malone, *Jefferson the President: First Term, 1801–*

1805 (New York, 1974); Roy F. Nichols, *The Invention of American Political Parties* (New York, 1967); Leonard White, *The Jeffersonians* (New York, 1951); and Lucius Wilmerding, Jr., *The Electoral College* (New Brunswick, 1958). I have also made extensive use of published correspondence, contemporary newspapers, the *Annals of Congress*, and of that incredible treasury of political information, Hezekiah Niles's *Weekly Register*, published by Niles in Baltimore from 1811 to 1836 and continued by various successors till 1848 (hereafter cited as *Niles' Register*).

2. Harry Ammon, "The Republican Party in Virginia, 1799 to 1824" (Ph.D. dissertation, University of Virginia, 1948) and "The Richmond Junto," *Virginia Magazine of History and Biography*, LXI (1953), 395–418.

3. On New York's subordination to Virginia, see especially Jabez D. Hammond, *The History of Political Parties in the State of New York* (2 vols.: Albany, 1842), I, 405–6, and the series of essays, "Sovereignty of the People" in *Niles' Register*, XXVII, Sept.-Oct. 1824.

4. *Writings . . . Gallatin*, I, 51–52.

5. Hofstadter, *Idea of a Party System, passim.*; Michael Wallace, "Changing Concepts of Party in the United States: New York, 1815–1828," *American Historical Review*, LXXIV (1968), 453–91.

6. On the isolation of the southern Federalist, see especially Broussard, *Southern Federalists*, 260.

7. *Writings . . . Gallatin*, I, 51–52.

8. The only substantial, though inadequate, treatment of the Twelfth Amendment is Lolabel House, *A Study of the 12th Amendment of the Constitution of the United States* (Philadelphia, 1901). On congressional action in 1802, see *Annals of Congress*, 7th Cong., 1st Ses., 472, 509, 602–3, 629, 1289–96, 304.

9. Sparks, *Morris,* III, 174–75.

10. *Annals of Congress*, 7th Cong., 2nd Ses., 304, 483–93.

11. Sparks, *Morris*, III, 194–96; Farrand, *Records*, III, 400–403.

12. Everett S. Brown, ed., *William Plumer's Memorandum of Proceedings in the United States Senate, 1803–1807* (New York, 1923), 63, 68.

13. *Annals of Congress*, 8th Cong., 1st Ses., 761, 182, 178.

14. *Ibid.*, 98, 158, 741, 87.

15. *Ibid.*, 209, 775; O'Neil, *American Electoral System*, 95.

16. Brown, ed., *Plumer's Memorandum*, 64.

17. *Ibid.*, 450.

18. Hatch, *Vice Presidency*, 138; Cunningham, *Jeffersonian Republicans in Power*, 103–4; *Correspondence . . . King*, IV, 357.
19. Cunningham, *Jeffersonian Republicans in Power*, 104–5.
20. *Papers . . . Hamilton*, XXVI, 79–81; *Correspondence . . . King*, IV, 350; Turner, *Plumer*, 133–50.
21. Brown, ed., *Plumer's Memorandum*, 199.
22. Ammon, *Monroe*, 264–70; *Writings . . . Gallatin*, I, 311; *Writings . . . Jefferson*, VIII, 448.
23. (Richmond) *Enquirer*, Jan. 23, 26, 30, 1804.
24. Cunningham, *Jeffersonian Republicans in Power*, 114–15.
25. Schlesinger, Jr., *History of American Presidential Elections,* I, 185–221, 228, 236.
26. Samuel Eliot Morison, "The First Nominating Convention, 1808," *American Historical Review*, XVII (1912), 744–63; *Correspondence . . . King*, V, 101; Morison, *Otis*, I, 307.
27. Schlesinger, Jr., *History of American Presidential Elections*, I, 241–242; (Richmond) *Enquirer*, Oct. 18, Nov. 1, 1808.
28. *Writings . . . Monroe*, V, 74–81.
29. Cunningham, *Jeffersonian Republicans in Power*, 121–23.
30. The political background is sketched admirably in Roger H. Brown, *The Republic in Peril: 1812* (New York, 1964).
31. *Niles' Register*, II, 192–93, 276, 321–22; *ibid.*, III, 133; *Writings . . . Gallatin*, I, 518.
32. *Niles' Register*, II, 235.
33. Hammond, *New York*, I, 298.
34. *Correspondence . . . King*, V, 264–72.
35. *New York Evening Post*, Aug. 18, 1812; *Correspondence . . . King*, V, 275; Sparks, *Morris*, III, 273–74.
36. Morison, *Otis*, I, 309–10, 316–20; *Correspondence . . . King*, V, 276–80.
37. *Boston Patriot*, Sept. 23, 1812; *National Intelligencer*, Oct. 15, 24, 27, Nov. 10, 1812.
38. *Niles' Register*, III, 17–19.
39. Schlesinger, Jr., *History of U.S. Political Parties*, I, 310–20.
40. Schlesinger, Jr., *History of American Presidential Elections*, I, 258, 260.
41. (Boston) *Columbian Centinel*, Oct. 28, 31, 1812; (Philadelphia) *U.S. Gazette*, Oct. 1–31, 1812; (Raleigh) *Star*, Oct. 9, 1812.
42. *Boston Patriot*, Oct. 17, 1812; O'Neil, *American Electoral System*, 105; *Correspondence . . . King*, V, 285; Richard P. McCormick, *The History of Voting in New Jersey, 1664–1911* (New Brunswick,

1950), 109; Delbert H. Gilpatrick, *Jeffersonian Democracy in North Carolina, 1789–1816* (New York, 1931).

43. Ammon, *Monroe*, 286–88; *Writings . . . Jefferson*, IX, 266.

44. Robert V. Remini, "New York and the Presidential Election of 1816," *New York History*, XXXI (1950), 308–23.

45. *Niles' Register*, X, 16; *National Intelligencer*, Feb. 16-March 28, 1816.

46. *National Intelligencer*, March 18, 1816; *Niles' Register*, X, 54–60, 162–63.

47. *Writings . . . Gallatin*, I, 702. The incident is ably described in Chase Mooney, *William H. Crawford, 1772–1834* (Lexington, Ky., 1974), 213–20.

48. *Niles' Register*, XI, 314–15, 347; *ibid.*, XXVII, 51.

49. *Correspondence . . . King*, V, 535.

50. Sparks, *Morris*, III, 360–61.

51. *Writings . . . Monroe*, VI, 2–4, 5; Ammon, *Monroe*, 357–65.

52. *Writings . . . Monroe*, V, 342–48; *ibid.*, 289–91; *Writings . . . Gallatin*, II, 2, 36.

53. Charles Francis Adams, ed., *Memoirs of John Quincy Adams, Comprising Portions of His Diary from 1795 to 1848* (12 vols.: Philadelphia, 1874–77), V, 58, 61; John Spencer Bassett, ed., *Correspondence of Andrew Jackson* (7 vols.: Washington, 1926–1935), III, 23; *Niles' Register*, XVIII, 97, 113.

54. The details are to be found in Paullin, *Atlas*, 89, and O'Neil, *American Electoral System*, chs. IX–XI.

55. *Annals of Congress*, 15th Cong., 1st Ses., 179.

56. Ames, *Proposed Amendments*, 75–115.

57. *Annals of Congress*, 13th Cong., 1st Ses., 830, 836; *ibid.*, 14th Cong., 2nd Ses., 308–10; *ibid.*, 15th Cong., 1st Ses., 180–81.

58. *Ibid.*, 14th Cong., 2nd Ses., 310.

59. *Ibid.*, 15th Cong., 1st Ses., 180.

60. *Ibid.*, 13th Cong., 2nd Ses., 830.

61. *Ibid.*, 14th Cong., 2nd Ses., 324–26, 350; *Niles' Register*, IX, 349.

62. *Annals of Congress*, 13th Cong., 2nd Ses., 827–35, 841, *ibid.*, 14th Cong., 2nd Ses., 346.

63. *Ibid.*, 14th Cong., 2nd Ses., 324, 330–33; *ibid.*, 14th Cong., 1st Ses., 213, 218; *ibid.*, 17th Cong., 1st Ses., 119; *ibid.*, 16th Cong., 2nd Ses., 964–67.

64. *Ibid.*, 13th Cong., 2nd Ses., 841–44.

65. *Ibid.*, 13th Cong., 2nd Ses., 843; *ibid.*, 16th Cong., 2nd Ses., 962.

66. *Ibid.*, 16th Cong., 2nd Ses., 967.
67. Richard P. McCormick, "New Perspectives on Jacksonian Politics," *American Historical Review*, LXV (1960), 288–301.

Chapter V

1. The elections of 1824, 1828, and 1832 are described in the essays by James F. Hopkins and Robert V. Remini in Schlesinger, Jr., *History of American Presidential Elections*, I. I have dealt with the period from another perspective in my *Second American Party System: Party Formation in the Jacksonian Era* (Chapel Hill, 1966). In addition to the works previously cited by James S. Chase, Louis C. Hatch, Roy F. Nichols, and Charles A. O'Neil, I have drawn to my advantage on Charles H. Ambler, *Thomas Ritchie: A Study in Virginia Parties* (Richmond, 1913); William J. Cooper, Jr., *The South and the Politics of Slavery, 1828–1856* (Baton Rouge, 1978); William Freehling, *Prelude to Civil War: The Nullification Controversy in South Carolina* (New York, 1965); Samuel R. Gammon, *The Presidential Election of 1832* (Baltimore, 1922); Richard B. Latner, *The Presidency of Andrew Jackson: White House Politics 1829–1837* (Athens, Ga., 1979); Robert V. Remini, *Martin Van Buren and the Making of the Democratic Party* (New York, 1959) and *The Election of Andrew Jackson* (Philadelphia, 1963); Charles G. Sellers, Jr., *James K. Polk, Jacksonian, 1795–1843* (Princeton, 1957); and Florence Weston, *The Presidential Election of 1828* (Washington, 1938). I have used intensively the published writings of John Quincy Adams, John C. Calhoun, Henry Clay, Andrew Jackson, James K. Polk, Martin Van Buren, and Daniel Webster and have mined thoroughly *Niles' Register* and the *Annals of Congress*.
2. *Niles' Register*, XXI, 338.
3. *Correspondence . . . Jackson*, III, 276.
4. The intrigues in which Monroe's Cabinet members were engaged are described in Ammon, *Monroe*, chs. 27 and 29.
5. John C. Fitzpatrick, ed., "The Autobiography of Martin Van Buren," *Annual Report of the American Historical Association . . . 1918* (Washington, 1920), 666; *Memoirs of John Quincy Adams*, VI, 237–44, 253; *Correspondence . . . Jackson*, III, 255.
6. *Memoirs of John Quincy Adams*, VI, 507.

7. Fitzpatrick, ed., "Autobiography . . . Van Buren," 514.
8. Robert L. Merwether, W. Edward Hemphill, and Clyde N. Wilson, eds., *The Papers of John C. Calhoun* (13 vols.: [to 1837] Columbia, S.C., 1959–80), X, xiii–xlvi, 308–9, 337–39 (hereafter cited as *Papers . . . Calhoun*).
9. Fitzpatrick, ed., "Autobiography . . . Van Buren," 366–84, 389.
10. Thomas Hart Benton, *Thirty Years' View* (2 vols.: New York, 1854–56), I, 219; *Correspondence . . . Jackson*, IV, 402.
11. Fitzpatrick, ed., "Autobiography . . . Van Buren," 399, 505–7; *Correspondence . . . Jackson*, IV, 260–61.
12. *Writings . . . Gallatin*, II, 259; *Correspondence . . . King*, VI, 507; James F. Hopkins, ed., *The Papers of Henry Clay* (5 vols.: [to 1826] Lexington, Ky., 1959–73), III, 363; *Correspondence . . . Jackson*, III, 192.
13. *Memoirs of John Quincy Adams*, VI, 506; *Papers . . . Calhoun*, X, 40, 28–29, 129, 252–53, 292.
14. *Niles' Register*, XXXI, 66.
15. *Papers . . . Calhoun*, XI, 215–17, 369–71, 394–95, 612–13; Freehling, *Prelude to Civil War*, 219–27.
16. *Niles' Register*, XXII, 135–36; *ibid.*, XXIV, 131–32; *ibid.*, XXV, 390–91.
17. *Ibid.*, XXV, 37.
18. *Ibid.*, XXV, 405–6, 390–91. Gallatin was later induced to withdraw from the contest (*Writings . . . Gallatin*, II, 292–300).
19. *Niles' Register*, XXVI, 19–20, 39–42.
20. On the adoption of the convention system, see my *Second American Party System, passim.*, and Chase, *Emergence of the Presidential Nominating Convention*, 93, 118.
21. Fitzpatrick, ed., "Autobiography . . . Van Buren," 514; Remini, *Martin Van Buren*, 129–33. It was the opinion of Rufus King in 1824 that national conventions, held for the purpose of nominating presidential candidates, were unconstitutional. "Because Conventions may be, and are, held to nominate State officers," he wrote, "it does not follow that they may be held in order to concentrate the opinion, of the States, relative to any officer of the U.S." (*Correspondence . . . King*, VI, 538, 557).
22. *Niles' Register*, XXXVIII, 169–72, 392–93; *ibid.*, XXXIX, 341.
23. (Lexington) *Kentucky Reporter*, Dec. 15, 1830; *Niles' Register*, XL, 28–29.
24. Reports of the proceedings of the National Republican convention, as well as the Anti-Masonic and Jackson conventions, will be found

in Schlesinger, Jr., *History of American Presidential Elections*, I, 515–73.

25. (Concord) *New Hampshire Patriot*, July 11, 1831.
26. Fitzpatrick, ed., "Autobiography . . . Van Buren," 506–9.
27. Chase, *Emergence of the Presidential Nominating Convention*, 265–66.
28. *Niles' Register*, XLII, 455–56.
29. *Ibid.*, 303, 339; *ibid.*, XLIII, 272–75.
30. *Correspondence . . . Jackson*, III, 184, 170, 173–74, 189–90, 238, 210–11.
31. *Correspondence . . . Jackson*, III, 242, 173–74, 203–4, 238, 269, 273, 246–47, 223–24; *Niles' Register*, XXVI, 161–68.
32. *Correspondence . . . Jackson*, III, 249–51, 253, 259–61; *Niles' Register*, XXVI, 245. See also Robert P. Hay, "The Presidential Question: Letters to Southern Editors, 1823–24," *Tennessee Historical Quarterly*, XXXI (1972), 170–86.
33. *Correspondence . . . Jackson*, III, 242, 390; Herbert Weaver, ed., *Correspondence of James K. Polk* (4 vols.: [to 1838] Nashville, 1969–77), I, 197 (hereafter cited as *Correspondence . . . Polk*).
34. *Correspondence . . . Polk*, I, 171, 176–77; *Niles' Register*, XXXIV, 158.
35. (Washington) *Telegraph Extra*, 360–68.
36. *Correspondence . . . Jackson*, III, 246–47.
37. *Ibid.*, IV, 110–11n, 329, 348, 379, 385, 418, 467; *Niles' Register*, XLII, 37–40.
38. *Niles' Register*, XXXIV, 326–27, 330, 396; *ibid.*, XXXV, 5.
39. *Ibid.*, XLII, 387.
40. *Ibid.*, XLIII, 124, 139.
41. On Johnston's activities, see *Papers . . . Clay*, III, 816–51.
42. John Henry Eaton, *The Life of Andrew Jackson . . .* (Philadelphia, 1824). Jackson's character is dealt with in pages 432–42. A second edition was published in 1828. On the subject of campaign biographies generally, see W. Burlie Brown, *The People's Choice: The Presidential Image in the Campaign Biography* (Baton Rouge, 1960) and William Miles, *The Image Makers: A Bibliography of American Presidential Campaign Biographies* (Metuchen, N.J., 1979).
43. *The Letters of Wyoming to the People of the United States on the Presidential Election, and in Favour of Andrew Jackson; Originally Published in the Columbian Observer* (Philadelphia, 1824). For Eaton's authorship, see *Correspondence . . . Jackson*, III, 244. See

also Robert P. Hay, "The Case for Andrew Jackson in 1824; Eaton's *Wyoming Letters*," *Tennessee Historical Quarterly*, XXIX (1970), 139–51.

44. *Correspondence . . . Jackson*, III, 293–96.

45. The organization of the Jackson campaign is described in Remini, *Election of Andrew Jackson* and Weston, *Election of 1828*. There is a wealth of detailed information in the (Washington) *Telegraph Extra*, the official campaign organ, published by Duff Green. See also Gabriel L. Lowe, Jr., "John H. Eaton, Jackson's Campaign Manager," *Tennessee Historical Quarterly*, XI (1952), 99–147.

46. Erik M. Eriksson, "Official Newspaper Organs and the Campaign of 1828," *Tennessee Historical Magazine*, VIII (1925), 231–47; Culver H. Smith, "Propaganda Technique in the Jackson Campaign of 1828," *East Tennessee Historical Society Publications*, VI (1934), 44–66.

47. *Correspondence . . . Jackson*, III, 426.

48. (Washington) *Telegraph Extra*, March 28, May 10–13, Oct. 11, 1828.

49. Erik M. Eriksson, "Official Newspaper Organs and Jackson's Re-election," *Tennessee Historical Magazine*, IX (1925), 37–58.

50. *Niles' Register*, XLII, 206, 218–19, 236–38; *ibid.*, XXXIV, 411; *New-York Enquirer*, Aug. 5, 1828; Dixon Ryan Fox, *The Decline of Aristocracy in the Politics of New York, 1801–1840* (New York, 1919), 297.

51. On the role of issues in the campaign, see Lee Benson, *The Concept of Jacksonian Democracy: New York as a Test Case* (Princeton, 1960), 59–62, and Robert V. Remini, "Election of 1832," in Schlesinger, Jr., *History of American Presidential Elections*, I, 513–16.

52. McCormick, "New Perspectives on Jacksonian Politics," 288–301.

53. *Annals of Congress*, 17th Cong., 2nd Ses., 101.

54. *Ibid.*, 177–78, 209–23.

55. *Ibid.*, 18th Cong., 1st Ses., 167–204, 417.

56. *Ibid.*, 851–66.

57. Farrand, *Records*, III, 459; *Writings . . . Madison*, IX, 174; *Annals of Congress*, 18th Cong., 1st Ses., 355–56, 370.

58. *Register of Debates in Congress* (Washington, 1825–37) 18th Cong., 2nd Ses., 1492–1504, 1521–32 (hereafter cited as *Register of Debates.*)

59. *Ibid.*, 1400–1416, 1559–97, 1438–82, 1534–40.

60. *Ibid.*, 1653–1857, 1931–59, 2004–5. The House voted 138–52 in

favor of amending the Constitution to prevent the presidential election from devolving on the House, but a select committee soon reported that it was unable to agree on any plan to implement this proposal (*ibid.*, 2659; *Niles' Register*, XXX, 233).

61. *Ibid.*, 16–19, 51–52, 692–94.
62. *Correspondence . . . Jackson*, IV, 98–99, 134.
63. *Register of Debates*, 19th Cong., 1st Ses., 1678.

Chapter VI

1. There are succinct accounts of the elections of 1836, 1840, and 1844 by Joel H. Silbey, William Nisbet Chambers, and Charles G. Sellers, Jr., in Schlesinger, Jr., *History of American Presidential Elections*, I. Also relevant are the brief histories of the Whig and Democratic parties by Glyndon G. Van Deusen and Michael F. Holt, buttressed by selected illustrative documents, in Schlesinger, Jr., *History of U.S. Political Parties*, I. The richness and the extent of the historical literature dealing with this period are best glimpsed in the admirable Bibliographical Essay in Edward Pessen's *Jacksonian America: Society, Personality, and Politics* (rev. ed., Homewood, Ill., 1978), especially 349–67. On many points I have drawn unashamedly on my *Second American Party System* and my "New Perspectives on Jacksonian Politics," both cited previously. Among the host of studies that have contributed to my understanding, I would single out for special notice Lee Benson, *The Concept of Jacksonian Democracy: New York as a Test Case* (Princeton, 1960); William R. Brock, *Parties and Political Conscience: American Dilemmas, 1840–1850* (New York, 1979); William J. Cooper, Jr., *The South and the Politics of Slavery, 1828–1856* (Baton Rouge, 1978); Matthew A. Crenson, *The Federal Machine: The Beginnings of Bureaucracy in Jacksonian America* (Baltimore, 1975); Ronald P. Formisano, "Political Character, Antipartyism, and the Second Party System," *American Quarterly*, XXI (1969), 683–709; Robert G. Gunderson, *The Log Cabin Campaign* (Lexington, Ky., 1957); O. D. Lambert, *Presidential Politics in the United States, 1841–1844* (Durham, 1936); Richard B. Latner, *The Presidency of Andrew Jackson: White House Politics, 1829–1837* (Athens, Ga., 1979); David J. Russo, "The Major Political Issues of the Jacksonian Period and the Development of

Party Loyalty in Congress, 1830–1840," *Transactions of the American Philosophical Society, New Series,* LXII, Part 5 (1972); Charles G. Sellers, Jr., *James K. Polk: Continentalist, 1843–1846* (Princeton, 1966); Culver H. Smith, *The Press, Politics, and Patronage* (Athens, Ga., 1977); and Leonard White, *The Jacksonians: A Study in Administrative History, 1829–1861* (New York, 1954). As in previous chapters, I have used the published writings of the prominent political figures, together with standard biographies. My heaviest debt by far is to *Niles' Register,* which missed little of consequence in its coverage of presidential politics in these years.

2. I have explored party formation in my *Second American Party System.*

3. *Niles' Register,* XLVI, 115, 131.

4. On party formation in the South, see Cooper, *Politics of Slavery,* chs. 1–3.

5. Here my understanding would be at variance with that of Silbey in Schlesinger, Jr., *History of American Presidential Elections,* I, 587–588, and numerous other authorities.

6. *Papers . . . Calhoun,* XII, 242, 348–49, 359, 534–38.

7. *Niles' Register,* XLVII, 47, 313, 378; Calvin Colton, ed., *The Works of Henry Clay* (6 vols.: New York, 1857), IV, 392–95.

8. *Niles' Register,* XLVII, 379; *ibid.,* XLVIII, 243–44; *ibid.,* XLIX, 201, 294; *ibid.,* LI, 242–43.

9. Freeman Cleaves, *Old Tippecanoe: William Henry Harrison and His Times* (New York, 1939) is the standard biography.

10. The origins of Harrison's candidacy are noted in *Niles' Register,* XLVII, 173–75, and subsequent developments can be traced in *ibid.,* XLIX, *passim.*

11. L. Paul Gresham, "The Public Career of Hugh Lawson White," *Tennessee Historical Quarterly,* III (1944), 291–318; Benton, *Thirty Years' View,* II, 185–86; Fitzpatrick, ed., "Autobiography . . . Van Buren," 226n; *Niles' Register,* LI, 59–61. Considerable testimony bearing on Jackson's attitude toward White's candidacy was presented to a House committee in 1837, and it is fully reported in *Niles' Register,* LII, 294–303.

12. On the relationship of White's candidacy to factional politics in Tennessee, see Sellers, *Polk: Jacksonian,* chs. 8 and 9; *Correspondence . . . Polk,* III, 41–52; *Niles' Register,* XLVIII, 39. The Alabama nomination was rescinded December 9, 1835, because of the concern that White's candidacy would throw the election into the House of Representatives, *ibid.,* XLIX, 328.

13. Cooper, *Politics of Slavery*, 82; *Works . . . Clay*, IV, 394–95; Henry Thomas Shanks, ed., *The Papers of Willie Persons Mangum* (5 vols.: Raleigh, 1950–56), II, 51–56, 75, 212–19, 247; J. G. De Roulhac Hamilton, ed., *The Papers of William Alexander Graham* (6 vols.: Raleigh, 1957–76), I, 415, 442–48.

14. *Correspondence . . . Jackson*, V, 322, 328, 338–40; *Correspondence . . . Polk*, III, 184, 251–52; *Niles' Register*, XLIX, 384.

15. *Niles' Register*, XLVIII, 226–29; *Correspondence . . . Jackson,* V, 349. Johnson obtained the requisite two-thirds vote only because he received fifteen votes from Tennessee. That disaffected state had sent no delegates to Baltimore, but the Convention seated one Edward Rucker, a Tennessean who happened to be present, and authorized him to cast the vote of that state. This incident prompted much adverse comment and was seized upon by the opposition as evidence that the Convention was a farce (*Niles' Register*, XLVIII, 273).

16. *Niles' Register*, LI, 242, 243; *Papers . . . Calhoun*, XII, 540.

17. *Niles' Register*, LI, 379, 404.

18. Russo, "Major Political Issues," 32–47.

19. *Niles' Register*, LII, 328–29.

20. *Papers . . . Mangum*, II, 513–14, 525–26; *Niles' Register*, LIV, 78, 240, 277; *ibid.*, LVI, 275–76, 306.

21. *Papers . . . Mangum*, II, 525–26; Cooper, *Politics of Slavery*, 121; *Niles' Register*, LIV, 277.

22. *Niles' Register*, LIV, 398; *ibid.*, LV, 177, 220, 360–61; *ibid.*, LVII, 8–10; Harriet A. Weed and Thurlow Weed Barnes, eds., *Life of Thurlow Weed, Including His Autobiography and a Memoir* (2 vols.: Boston, 1883–84), I, 480–82; Benton, *Thirty Years' View*, II, 204.

23. *Niles' Register*, LVII, 46–47, 190–91.

24. *Ibid.*, 248–52.

25. *Ibid.*, LVIII, 3, 147–52, 227, 336, 346.

26. Gunderson, *Log Cabin Campaign, passim.*

27. Excerpts of editorial opinions from more than a score of newspapers were compiled in *Niles' Register*, LIX, 163, 201–6.

28. These events are ably reviewed in Brock, *Parties and Political Conscience, passim.*

29. For illustrations of how the southern Whigs accommodated to Clay, see *Papers . . . Graham*, II, 283, 284.

30. *Niles' Register*, LXVI, 146–48, 152–53.

31. *Ibid.*, 153–57, 228.

32. *Ibid.*, 213–18; Sellers, *Polk: Continentalist*, ch. 3.
33. Michael Wallace, "Changing Concepts of Party in the United States: New York, 1815–1828," *American Historical Review*, LXXIV (1968), 453–91; Ceaser, *Presidential Selection*, ch. 3; K. Kolson, "Party, Opposition, and Political Development," *The Review of Politics*, XL (1978), 163–82; Formisano, "Political Character," 683–709.
34. *Idea of a Party System*, 53.
35. *Niles' Register*, XLVIII, 330–36. For the similar views of Hugh Lawson White, see *ibid.*, LV, 8–9.
36. *Niles' Register*, LI, 151; Richard K. Crallé, ed., *The Works of John C. Calhoun* (6 vols.: New York, 1854–61), I, 224. For numerous anti-party statements by members of Congress, see Alvin K. Lynn, "Party Formation and Operation in the House of Representatives, 1824–1837" (Ph.D. dissertation, Rutgers University, 1972), 125–34.
37. Schlesinger, Jr., *History of American Presidential Elections*, I, 616–38. For similar sentiments, see the "Address of the Republican Members of Congress," July 1838, in *Niles' Register*, LV, 4–8.
38. *Correspondence . . . Polk*, III, 313.
39. *American [Whig] Review*, I, 115.
40. *Ibid.*, 18.
41. M. I. Ostrogorski, *Democracy and the Party System in the United States* (New York, 1910), 409; Henry J. S. Maine, *Popular Government* (New York, 1886), 31; James Bryce, *Modern Democracies* (2 vols.: New York, 1921), I, 112.
42. *Niles' Register*, XLV, 19; *ibid.*, XLVII, 434; XLVIII, 39, 58, 364. See also C. M. Thompson, "Attitude of the Western Whigs Toward the Convention System," *Proceedings of the Mississippi Valley Historical Association*, V (1911–12), 167–89.
43. Schlesinger, Jr., *History of American Presidential Elections*, I, 618–21.
44. *Works . . . Clay*, IV, 416–17; *Papers . . . Mangum*, II, 513–14; *Niles' Register*, LVI, 128.
45. *Niles' Register*, LXIV, 219, 248–52, 349.
46. *Ibid.*, LXV, 24–27, 41–42.
47. *Ibid.*, 372–74; Benton, *Thirty Years' View*, II, 596–99.
48. *Niles' Register*, LIV, 277.
49. *Papers . . . Graham*, II, 24–27, 69–70; *Life of Thurlow Weed*, I, 480; *Niles' Register*, LVII, 8–10.
50. *Niles' Register*, LIV, 398; *ibid.*, LV, 221, 360–61.

51. The proceedings are reported in *Niles' Register*, LVII, 248–52. See also *Life of Thurlow Weed*, I, 280–82.

52. *Niles' Register*, LXV, 392–93, 11.

53. *Ibid.*, LXIV, 137–38, 167–68, 183–88.

54. *Ibid.*, 137, 349–51; Benton, *Thirty Years' View*, II, 581–90.

55. *Niles' Register*, LXVI, 228.

56. See Schlesinger, Jr., *History of American Presidential Elections*, I, 135–50, for examples.

57. *Niles' Register*, XLVIII, 228.

58. *Ibid.*, LVIII, 147–52, 182–86.

59. For the reports of both conventions, see *Niles' Register*, LXVI, 146–48, 213–18. Although Johnson's resolutions are commonly cited as the first Whig platform, it is doubtful that they should be accorded such a status.

60. See, for example, the comments of Michael Chevalier, *Society, Manners, and Politics in the United States* (Boston, 1839), 316–19.

61. A. B. Norton, *The Great Revolution of 1840: Reminiscences of the Log Cabin and Hard Cider Campaign* (Mt. Vernon, Ohio, 1888), 15. In addition to this source, I have relied on Gunderson, *Log Cabin Campaign* and *Niles' Register*, LVIII and LIX, for details of the campaign.

62. Fitzpatrick, ed., "Autobiography . . . Van Buren," 394.

63. Benton, *Thirty Years' View*, II, 625.

64. *Niles' Register*, XLVIII, 257–58. Van Buren's public statements, and those of the other candidates, were faithfully reported by Niles.

65. These activities are reported in *Niles' Register*, XLVIII–LI, *passim*.

66. *Ibid.*, LVI, 297–98, 299, 309–10, 366–67.

67. *Ibid.*, LVIII, 281, 294.

68. *Ibid.*, LVIII, 293; *ibid.*, LIX, 155–56, 175.

69. *Life of Thurlow Weed*, II, 119. Clay's statements are in *Niles' Register*, LXVI, 161, 255, 295–300, 402, 403, 439; *ibid.*, LXVII, 24, 30, 74, 75.

70. *Ibid.*, LXVI, 295; *ibid.*, LXVII, 24–25.

71. *Ibid.*, LXVI, 233, 372; *ibid.*, LXVII, 75–77.

72. The nature of the presidency in this era is explored in White, *Jacksonians*, *passim*. On the influence of personality, see James David Barber, *The Presidential Character: Predicting Performance in the White House* (Englewood Cliffs, N.J., 1972).

73. *Papers . . . Calhoun*, XII, 415–47, contains the committee's report.

74. *House Report* No. 741, 27th Cong., 2nd Ses., 4.

75. *Niles' Register*, LXIV, 136.

Epilogue

1. Stephen Hess, *The Presidential Campaign: The Leadership Selection Process After Watergate* (Washington, 1978), 102.
2. The sources for this chapter are vast but familiar. I have drawn heavily on the essays in Schlesinger, Jr., *History of American Presidential Elections*, II, III, and IV for information on elections from 1848 to 1968. A standard survey is Eugene H. Roseboom, *A History of Presidential Elections* (New York, 1957). The most valuable single compendium of information on the subject is Congressional Quarterly's *Guide to U.S. Elections* (Washington, 1975), which can be supplemented by the same organization's *Elections '80* (Washington, 1980). The best narrative of political developments is James L. Sundquist, *Dynamics of the Party System: Alignment and Realignment of Political Parties in the United States* (Washington, 1973). For the national conventions, Richard C. Bain and Judith H. Parris, *Convention Decisions and Voting Records* (2nd ed., Washington, 1973) provides splendid coverage, which can be supplemented by Paul T. David *et al.*, *The Politics of National Party Conventions* (Washington, 1960): Malcolm Moos, "New Light on the Nominating Process," *Research Frontiers in Politics and Government* (Washington, 1955); and Gerald M. Pomper, *Nominating the President: The Politics of Convention Choice* (Evanston, 1963). Useful for tracing changes in campaign styles and techniques are Richard Jensen, "Armies, Admen and Crusaders: Types of Presidential Election Campaigns," *The History Teacher*, II (1960), 33–50; Sidney Warren, *The Battle for the Presidency* (Philadelphia, 1968); and Marvin R. Weisbord, *Campaigning for President* (Washington, 1964). Special studies of unusual importance are Walter Dean Burnham, *Critical Elections and the Mainsprings of American Politics* (New York, 1970); James W. Ceaser, *Presidential Selection: Theory and Development* (Princeton, 1979); William B. Hesseltine, *Third Party Movements in the United States* (Princeton, 1962); Michael F. Holt, *The Political Crisis of the 1850s* (New York, 1978); Robert L. Marcus, *Grand Old Party: Political Structure in the Gilded Age, 1800–1896* (New York, 1971); and Richard L. McCormick, "The Party Period and Public Policy: An Exploratory Hypothesis," *Journal of American History*, LXVI (1979), 279–98.
3. *Congressional Globe* (Washington, 1835–73), 28th Cong., 2nd Ses., 9–143.

4. Constitutional and legal changes affecting presidential elections are ably summarized in *Guide to U.S. Elections*, 200–213.
5. The best brief analysis of the proposals to change the method of election is Wallace S. Sayre and Judith H. Parris, *Voting for President: The Electoral College and the American Political System* (Washington, 1970).
6. On the presidential primary, see *Guide to U.S. Elections*, 309–11, and James W. Davis, *Presidential Primaries: Road to the White House* (New York, 1967).
7. The literature on parties and their successive realignments is enormous, but a useful guide is Sundquist, *Dynamics of the Party System*.
8. Marcus, *Grand Old Party* gives a vivid description of party structure and activity in this period.
9. Hesseltine, *Third Party Movements* is a convenient survey.
10. "The Changing Shape of the American Political Universe," *American Political Science Review*, LIX (1965), 7–28.
11. Recent political changes are analyzed in Everett Carll Ladd, Jr., with Charles D. Hadley, *Transformations of the American Party System: Political Coalitions from the New Deal to the 1970s* (2nd ed., New York, 1978).
12. See works previously cited by Bain and Parris; David *et al.*; Moos; and Pomper.
13. For this summary of changes in campaign styles, I have relied heavily on the works previously cited by Schlesinger, Jr., Warren, and Weisbord.
14. In addition to works previously cited, most notably those by Bain and Parris, Ceaser, Davis, Hess, and Ladd, I have drawn heavily in describing developments after 1968 on Nelson W. Polsby and Aaron Wildavsky, *Presidential Elections: Strategies of American Electoral Politics* (5th ed., New York, 1980). Also useful were James D. Barber, ed., *Choosing the President* (Englewood Cliffs, N.J., 1978); Judith Best, *The Case Against Direct Election of the President: A Defense of the Electoral College* (Ithaca, 1975); Alexander M. Bickel, *Reform and Continuity: The Electoral College, the Convention, and the Party System* (New York, 1971); Norman H. Nie *et al.*, *The Changing American Voter* (Cambridge, Mass., 1976); Neal R. Pierce, *The People's President: The Electoral College in American History and the Direct-Vote Alternative* (New York, 1968); and Austin Ranney, *Curing the Mischiefs of Faction* (Berkeley, 1975).

15. "New Rules and New Games in Presidential Nominations," *The Journal of Politics*, XLI (1979), 785.
16. The authoritative study is Herbert E. Alexander, *Financing Politics: Money, Elections and Political Reform* (2nd ed., Washington, 1980).
17. "The Decline of the Party in American Elections," *Political Science Quarterly*, XCII (1977), 23, 41. For an even more pessimistic appraisal, see Walter Dean Burnham, "The End of Party Politics," *Transaction*, VII (1969), 12–22.
18. Ladd, Jr., *Transformation*, 232.
19. *Presidential Elections*, vii, 265.
20. *Presidential Campaign*, 92.
21. Pierce, *People's President*, 297.
22. *Presidential Campaign*, 94.
23. See K. Kolson, "Party, Opposition, and Political Development," *The Review of Politics*, XL (1978), 163–82, for a clever assault on Richard Hofstadter's persuasive view of the origins of parties and a brief but telling critique of recent theoretical justifications of American parties. Representing the most extreme position in denouncing political parties as inimical to "strong democracy" is Benjamin R. Barber's, "The Undemocratic Party System: Citizenship in an Elite/Mass Society," in Robert A. Goldwin, ed., *Political Parties in the Eighties* (Washington, 1980). Other essays in this symposium reflect the wide diversity of views that currently exist regarding basic features of the American electoral system, as do the works, previously cited, of Barber, Burnham, Ceaser, Ladd, Polsby and Wildavsky, Sayre and Parris, and Ranney.

Index